THREE TWEETS TO MIDNI
Effects of the Global Information Ecosystem
on the Risk of Nuclear Conflict

"A gripping story of how social media can result in a nuclear catastrophe, either through a blunder or through the actions of a malignant provocateur. No issue could be timelier or more important, considering the profligate use of tweets today by the president and other government officials, and the need for deliberation in dealing with national security crises."

— **WILLIAM J. PERRY**, 19th US Secretary of Defense

"Highlights new and rising dangers that social media pose to managing any future great power crisis, and in the extreme to avoiding nuclear war. It is a must-read for policy makers, legislators, foreign policy experts, nuclear strategists, and indeed for any serious student of national security."

— **JAMES N. MILLER**, former US Under Secretary of Defense for Policy

"The next nuclear crisis will be tweeted. How decision makers cope with the increasing speed and volume of information during that crisis will weigh heavily on whether the world can avoid nuclear catastrophe. The authors in this volume brilliantly help us understand—and get ahead of—the challenges from today's information ecosystem."

— **KEITH PORTER**, President, the Stanley Center for Peace and Security

"We know that the new media environment has an impact on nuclear crises, but how and when does it matter? This pathbreaking volume assembles an impressive interdisciplinary lineup to explore these questions with new frameworks, new evidence, and new arguments. An important opening contribution to what is clearly a phenomenon that is here to stay."

— **VIPIN NARANG**, Associate Professor of Political Science at MIT and a member of MIT's Security Studies Program

Three Tweets to Midnight:

Effects *of the*
Global Information Ecosystem
on the Risk of Nuclear Conflict

The Hoover Institution gratefully acknowledges the following individuals and foundations for their significant support of this publication.

HANK J. HOLLAND
LYNDE AND HARRY BRADLEY FOUNDATION
THE DAVIES FAMILY
ROBERT AND MARION OSTER

The Stanley Center for Peace and Security, the Hoover Institution, and the Center for International Security and Cooperation at Stanford are pleased to collaborate in supporting this scholarship and bringing forward our collective understanding of its profound implications for the future of journalism, nuclear weapons policy, and international peace and security.

Three Tweets to Midnight

Effects *of the* Global Information Ecosystem *on the* Risk of Nuclear Conflict

EDITORS
Harold A. Trinkunas
Herbert S. Lin
Benjamin Loehrke

CONTRIBUTING AUTHORS
Kelly M. Greenhill
Danielle Jablanski
Jaclyn A. Kerr
Mark Kumleben
Jeffrey Lewis
Herbert S. Lin
Benjamin Loehrke
Rose McDermott
Ben O'Loughlin
Paul Slovic
Kate Starbird
Harold A. Trinkunas
Kristin Ven Bruusgaard
Samuel C. Woolley

HOOVER INSTITUTION PRESS
Stanford University | *Stanford, California*

With its eminent scholars and world-renowned library and archives, the Hoover Institution seeks to improve the human condition by advancing ideas that promote economic opportunity and prosperity, while securing and safeguarding peace for America and all mankind. The views expressed in its publications are entirely those of the authors and do not necessarily reflect the views of the staff, officers, or Board of Overseers of the Hoover Institution.

hoover.org

Hoover Institution Press Publication No. 707

Hoover Institution at Leland Stanford Junior University,
Stanford, California, 94305-6003

Copyright © 2020 by the Board of Trustees of the
Leland Stanford Junior University

First printing 2020
28 27 26 25 24 23 22 21 20   8 7 6 5 4 3 2

Manufactured in the United States of America

The paper used in this publication meets the minimum requirements of the American National Standard for Information Sciences—Permanence of Paper for Printed Library Materials, ANSI/NISO z39.48-1992. ∞

Cataloging-in-Publication Data is available from the Library of Congress.
ISBN 978-0-8179-2335-8 (paperback)
ISBN 978-0-8179-2336-5 (ePub)
ISBN 978-0-8179-2337-2 (Mobipocket)
ISBN 978-0-8179-2338-9 (PDF)

Contents

List of Figures and Tables

Acknowledgments

This project began offline. Domestic and global political events in 2016 and 2017 shook loose much complacency about social media and their role in reshaping how the world interacts. While platforms such as Facebook and Twitter were once hailed as liberation technologies, scholars increasingly began to worry about how the rapid changes wrought by social media might also affect international security. An early example of the kinds of interactions made possible by the emerging global information ecosystem was the unprecedented and combative use of social media by the US president to directly talk about North Korea and its nuclear and missile programs. This raised the immediate question of how such communications would be interpreted in Pyongyang and whether direct, instantaneous, globally broadcast, and potentially escalatory rhetoric could make the outbreak of a catastrophic war with North Korea more likely.

Over an informal conversation in mid-2017 at Stanford University's Center for International Security and Cooperation (CISAC), the organizers of this project began to ask if nuclear crises, like the one brewing with the United States and North Korea, might be particularly susceptible to destabilizing effects from information driven through social media. Decisions on the use of nuclear weapons would be made under extreme stress, with imperfect information, potentially in just minutes, by a small group of advisers or a single decision maker. No decision would be more fraught, with millions of lives in the balance. Yet the psychology of it would be prone to leading decision makers to engage in heuristic thinking, leaving them vulnerable to emotional responses and misinterpretation.

How would 280-character missives be read during a nuclear crisis? How might the new information ecosystem, as reshaped by social media, affect leaders and publics before and during crises? And how might digital misinformation and disinformation affect the likelihood of international conflict?

This volume, and the two multidisciplinary workshops that informed it, were the product of a partnership between the Stanley Center for Peace and Security, the Hoover Institution at Stanford University, and CISAC.

The Stanley Center for Peace and Security hosted an exploratory workshop at its Strategy for Peace Conference in October 2017, the observations from which were then summarized in a briefing paper titled "Three Tweets to Midnight: Nuclear Crisis Stability and the Information Ecosystem."[1] For more in-depth study of the arguments surfaced at that workshop, the organizers commissioned a set of working papers and hosted a second workshop at the Hoover Institution in September 2018. This volume is the culmination of the two events and features the contributions of authors for the 2018 workshop.

Participants in those workshops provided invaluable insights that shaped the trajectory of this project. For their contributions and thoughtful arguments, the editors thank James Acton, Jeffrey Berejikian, Malfrid Braut-Hegghammer, Paul Edwards, Jennifer Erickson, Henry Farrell, Anya Fink, Matt Fuhrmann, Tom Glaisyer, Deborah Gordon, Robert Gorwa, Andy Grotto, Rosanna Guadagno, Brian Hanson, Peter Hayes, Colin Kahl, Jennifer Kavanagh, Rupal Mehta, Anna Péczeli, Steve Pifer, Keith Porter, Philip Reiner, Scott Sagan, John Scott-Railton, Lior Tabansky, Phil Taubman, Devon Terrill, Ben Valentino, Heather Williams, and Amy Zegart.

The editors give special thanks to Amy Zegart for her early thought contributions and support throughout this project. As a professor of political science, codirector of CISAC, and Davies Family Senior Fellow at the Hoover Institution, Zegart was uniquely well positioned to recognize an opportunity to invest in and contribute to an innovative research project that aimed to address highly important policy questions that were of immediate relevance. Throughout the writing of this volume, the editors benefited from her questions, insights, and participation. In addition, we are grateful for the support of the Hoover Institution and, in particular, the Robert and Marion Oster National Security Affairs Fellows Program and the Lakeside Foundation in making this work possible by providing critical funding and meeting space. We also thank CISAC for providing the staff support that kept this whole enterprise moving. Herb Lin's work at CISAC on this project was also supported in part by the Carnegie Corporation of New York grant G-17-55292 (International Program), "For research, teaching, international engagement, and outreach in international security."

In addition to contributing as an author, Danielle Jablanski was an essential partner in every aspect of this project from ideation to implementation, both while she was at the Stanley Center for Peace and Security and as part of CISAC. The editors also thank Patty Papke, Cayte Connell, and Caitlin Lutsch at the Stanley Center for Peace and Security, Matt Ellison at the Hoover Institution, and Alida Haworth at CISAC for their work that made this project possible.

We would also like to acknowledge the work of the *Bulletin of the Atomic Scientists*, whose iconic Doomsday Clock provided an inspiration for the front cover of our book. The clock was conceived in 1947 by the *Bulletin* as a means of conveying to humanity the organization's collective expert assessment of the risks posed by nuclear weapons. Each year, the Science and Security Board of the *Bulletin* (of which one of the editors, Herb Lin, is a member) updates the Doomsday Clock. As of the time of writing in 2019, the clock stands at two minutes to midnight, the closest it has been since 1953. We share the concern of the experts and staff of the *Bulletin* over the growing risk of nuclear conflict, which was a major motivation for the writing of this volume. That its title is *Three Tweets to Midnight* reflects creative license rather than any disagreement by the editors with the assessment of the Science and Security Board of the *Bulletin of the Atomic Scientists*.

Finally, we would like to be clear that the views expressed in this book are those of the editors and authors, and any remaining errors are ours alone.

HAROLD A. TRINKUNAS

HERBERT S. LIN

BENJAMIN LOEHRKE

Notes

1. Stanley Center for Peace and Security, "Three Tweets to Midnight: Nuclear Crisis Stability and the Information Ecosystem," 58th Strategy for Peace Conference, January 2018, https://www.stanleyfoundation.org/resources.cfm?id=1646&title=Three-Tweets-to-Midnight:-Nuclear-Crisis-Stability-and-the-Information-Ecosystem.

Chapter 1

Retweets to Midnight:

Assessing the Effects of the Information Ecosystem on Crisis Decision Making between Nuclear Weapons States

Danielle Jablanski, Herbert S. Lin, and Harold A. Trinkunas

What if the Cuban Missile Crisis had taken place in today's global information environment, characterized by the emergence of social media as a major force amplifying the effects of information on both leaders and citizens? President Kennedy might not have had days to deliberate with the Executive Committee of the National Security Council before delivering a measured speech announcing to the world the discovery of Soviet medium- and intermediate-range nuclear-armed missiles in Cuba.[1]

Nongovernmental open source intelligence organizations like Bellingcat could have used commercially available satellite imagery to detect the presence of these missiles and publicize them to the world on October 12, 1962, four days earlier than the president did. Imagine pictures of the missile sites going viral on social media, alarming millions around the world. Imagine that these real-time images were accompanied by deliberate information operations from adversaries seeking to cast doubt on the facts to sow confusion and cause paralysis among domestic populations and between NATO leaders, as well as by internet trolls promoting misinformation and reposting and propagating tailored information leaks.

The shooting down of a U-2 spy plane over Cuba might have been news within the hour, becoming the subject of numerous tweets and relentless commentary on Facebook and other platforms. When the Joint Chiefs of Staff's recommendation to invade Cuba was overruled

Figure 1.1. Hypothetical tweet by President John F. Kennedy during Cuban Missile Crisis.

Source: Scott Sagan, "The Cuban Missile Crisis in the Age of Twitter," lecture at Stanford's Center for International Security and Cooperation, April 3, 2018.

by President Kennedy, "alt" social media accounts that served as fronts for disgruntled Pentagon officials might have leaked the proposed invasion plan to induce the administration to reverse course on the chosen alternative—a blockade. Pressured by public opinion and the Joint Chiefs of Staff, President Kennedy might not have had the luxury of picking which of Premier Khrushchev's letters to respond to, which the historical record shows helped to de-escalate the crisis. In this situation, which former secretary of defense William J. Perry has characterized as the closest the world has come to nuclear catastrophe, the current global information ecosystem could have magnified the risk of the conflict's escalating into all-out nuclear war.[2]

What's New? Characteristics of the Modern Information Ecosystem

Social media and the resulting dynamics for interpersonal interconnectivity have increased the volume and velocity of communication by orders of magnitude in the past decade. More information reaches more people in more places than ever before. Algorithms and business models based on advertising principles utilize troves of user data to draw aggregate inferences, which allow for microsegmentation of audiences and direct targeting of disinformation or misinformation. Mainstream-media outlets no longer serve their traditional role as gatekeepers with near-universal credibility.[3] In this ecosystem, propaganda can rapidly spread far and wide, while efforts to correct false information are more expensive, often fall short, and frequently fail altogether.

Nor are all of the voices on social media authentic. Some inauthentic voices are those of paid human trolls, for example from the Internet Research Agency, revealed to have created and spread false information on behalf of the Russian government prior to the 2016 US presidential election.[4] Others are Macedonian entrepreneurs who at one point discovered ways to monetize an affinity among some voters for fake news critical of Hillary Clinton.[5] Some voices are not even human, as demonstrated by the introduction of "bots"—automated social media accounts designed to mimic human behavior online that further complicate our ability to discern fact from fiction within the ecosystem.

Rapid transmission of content and curated affinity networks polarize citizens around divisive issues and create waves of public opinion that can pressure leaders.[6] So many different narratives emerge around complex events that polities splinter into their disparate informational universes, unable to agree on an underlying reality. Does this unprecedented availability of information and connectivity amplify the ability of actors to sow discord in the minds of the domestic publics and even the leadership of adversaries? Could these dynamics affect leaders and citizens to the degree that miscalculation or misperception can produce crisis instability ultimately leading to a nuclear exchange? Can governance mechanisms be designed and implemented that are capable of countering and combating the manipulation of information in this ecosystem?

This volume argues that the present information ecosystem increasingly poses risks for crisis stability. Manipulated information, either artificially constructed or adopted by a strong grassroots base, can be used by interested actors to generate pressure from various constituencies on leaders to act. At the same time, these leaders themselves face information overload and their ability to distinguish between true and false information may be impaired, especially if they are receiving information simultaneously from their own sources and other sources from within their constituencies. Such confusion can ultimately lead to inaction or bad decisions. Or, this environment might produce an accelerated reaction based on slanted or unanalyzed information. Most worrisome is the possibility that the rapid spread of disinformation or misinformation via social media may in the end distort the decision-making calculus of leaders during a crisis and thereby contribute to crisis instability in future conflicts, the effects of which could be most severe for nuclear weapons states.

The Psychology of Complex Decision Making and Nuclear Crisis

Many theories of deterrence rely on the rationality assumption, namely that a rational actor can be convinced that the cost-benefit ratio associated with initiating an attack is unfavorable due to a credible threat of retaliation by the adversary. The risk of a nuclear exchange during the Cold War led theorists to focus on how leaders might approach crises and what could be done to avert deterrence failure. This prompted debates about a range of putatively rational actions that nuclear states might engage in to build a reliable framework for deterrence: reassurances to allies by extending the nuclear umbrella, force postures designed to ensure a survivable retaliatory capability, credible signaling to convince adversaries that any attack would meet with massive retaliation, etc.[7]

But human decision makers are just that—human—and a great deal of psychological research in the past few decades has demonstrated the limits of rational thinking and decision making. Paul Slovic has written extensively about the human brain, decision making, and limits for comprehending the weight of decisions that could imperil large numbers of human lives. Various psychological processes come into play when considering a cognitive calculation on the value of lives lost in large numbers, including psychic numbing, tribalism, the prominence effect, imperative thinking, and victim blaming. As Slovic and Herbert Lin argue in chapter 3, this implies that leaders facing the task of making a decision on whether to order the use of nuclear weapons find it difficult to operate "rationally."

Psychology also tells us that—more often than not—fast, intuitive judgements take precedence over slower, more analytical thinking. Fast thinking (also identified as System 1 thinking by the originator of the concept, Daniel Kahneman) is intuitive and heuristic, generating rapid, reflexive responses to various situations and—more often than not—useful in daily life. Slow thinking (also known by cognitive psychologists as System 2 thinking) is more conceptual and deliberative.[8] Although both are useful in their appropriate roles, their operation in today's information ecosystem can be problematic. "Fast thinking is problematic when when we are trying to understand how to respond to large-scale human crises, with catastrophic consequences," Slovic and Lin write. "Slow thinking, too, can be incoherent in the sense that subtle influences—such as unstated, unconscious, or implicitly held attitudes—can lead to considered decisions that violate one's strongly held values." The prevalence of heuristic and "imperative thinking" among humans suggests that an overarching important goal, such as national defense in the face of a nuclear crisis, would likely eclipse consideration of second-order effects and consequences, such as the likelihood of massive loss of life on all sides or catastrophic effects on the global environment, to the extent that such discussion is actively, if not subconsciously, avoided.[9]

Observers have always anticipated that leaders would be under severe time pressures when deciding whether or not to use nuclear weapons, the most important of which is "launch on warning," the pressure to launch fixed land-based ICBMs before they can be destroyed on the ground by incoming enemy warheads. Fast, reflexive thinking (i.e., System 1 thinking) is more likely to be used under the kind of pressure this scenario highlights. Against a ticking clock, combined with the difficulty of comprehending the consequences of nuclear conflict, the argument that rational and deliberate decision making and deterrence will likely prevail, particularly under the added weight of the misinformation and disinformation that might propagate through the global information ecosystem during a crisis, is a highly debatable proposition.

The possibility that decision makers may rely on incorrect perceptions of potential adversaries has long been an important critique of rational deterrence theory. International relations theorists such as Robert Jervis have argued that the failure of deterrence can frequently be attributed to misperception among leaders: of intentions, of capabilities, of the consequences of conflict, etc. This misperception can have its roots in leaders' psychology, in lack of information, and in leaders' assumptions about what information the other side has or how they in turn perceive the situation.[10]

In the 1980s, Jervis had already argued that misperception was a quite common cause for deterrence failure. In today's global information ecosystem, there are more data available than ever before. But rather than reducing the likelihood of misperception through the greater availability of information about potential adversaries, the present information environment provides unprecedented opportunities for manipulation of leaders' and publics' perceptions about intentions, capabilities, and consequences of conflicts—cheaply, rapidly, and at scale.

Tools and Tactics in the Modern Information Ecosystem

Social media have emerged as a modern vehicle for changing narratives. Social media are arguably optimized to try to keep users in a "fast" pattern of thinking, promoting impulsive and intuitive responses to engage users emotionally and maximize both advertising revenue and user experience.[11] This characteristic of social media platforms may also provide avenues by which these same users can be manipulated more effectively for political aims. Although the ability for propaganda to be both insidious and anonymous is not a new phenomenon, automation, algorithms, and big data are being employed by various actors to selectively amplify or suppress information viewed by hundreds of millions of people via social media and online networks.[12] There is evidence of targeted influence campaigns in at least forty-eight countries to date.[13] Facebook, YouTube, WhatsApp, Instagram, and Reddit have also been platforms for a variety of divisive information operations.

As Mark Kumleben and Samuel C. Woolley note in chapter 4, campaigns have often made use of networks made of "bots"—partially or wholly automated—to introduce and circulate false or malign information, craft and control the narrative at the outset of a real event, and depict a manufactured consensus base around an issue. For example, an estimated 15 percent of Twitter's approximately 335 million users (as of 2018) are bots. Bots are employed as a tool to promote a mix of authentic and inauthentic content, automate the amplification of specific sources, disrupt and overwhelm channels and conversations with irrelevant noise, and harass individuals or groups online to silence or intimidate them.

Information operations have more than commercial or political/electoral implications. We are also witnessing an increase in states using such strategies to shape potential battlefields. Using the example of information operations against NATO, Kate Starbird employs a mixed-method analysis in chapter 5 of this volume to understand online communities and their communication patterns. In this case study, Starbird used a data set that included 1,353,620 tweets (75 percent retweets) from 513,285 sources. She mapped accounts into five clusters based on narrative and user characteristics and looked at the interactions between them. One cluster, associated with NATO and other verified accounts, carried positive information about anniversaries and anecdotes that promoted support for NATO. Another cluster, which she named the "international left, anti-NATO," involved content related to past negative NATO actions and events. Pro-Russian and official Russian accounts deliberately penetrated, amplified, and mingled with this cluster and a third cluster that she characterized as pro-Trump and alt-right. Starbird's team also observed interactions between the mainstream-media cluster and the official NATO clusters, both highly critical of Russia. Her findings illustrate structured narratives being shaped, infiltrated, and leveraged by different actors and audiences online in real time.

Starbird's chapter is a case study in how networks and communities can converge and diverge on the same topic, with various actors rescoping and redirecting traffic and conversation to achieve political effects. These dynamics may be an important factor in shaping support for NATO among the general public, which may ultimately have important security implications. A broader lesson is that analysis of information operations often focuses on election meddling while ignoring potentially broader campaigns with the longer-term goal of undermining partnerships, alliances, and international stability. Such operations may, for example, be used by adversaries to propagate social media statements by American leaders in combination with "fake news" and disinformation in an effort to affect the perceptions of traditional US allies—NATO member countries, South Korea, or Japan—of the reliability of US treaty commitments or extended nuclear deterrence.

Most people would like to believe that they are hard to fool, but it is often difficult to distinguish between authentic and fake content. Research shows that deliberately false information is often deeply embedded in otherwise factual content. Text and image repetition plays to the "illusory truth" bias (i.e., information seen more frequently is perceived as being more likely to be true). Discernment of bad information can depend on individual levels of education and skepticism. Repetition of a concept, even by attempting to dispel a false narrative, can serve to reinforce original beliefs. Compatibility with worldview, coherence of argument, credibility of source, consensus of others, and supporting evidence offer a scaffolding framework that supports what individuals come to believe. With decreased trust in media, conflicting expert opinions around every topic, and selective and simplistic sorting of complex information, social media platforms provide a growing medium for manipulation of individuals, groups, and larger institutions.

The current information ecosystem may very well be experiencing a "post-truth" moment. Despite traditional Western enlightenment thinking that it was only possible to discern truth based on evidence and science, mass susceptibility to media environments where facts are less appealing than emotion and opinion dates back centuries. Rose McDermott writes in chapter 2, "Many people rely on their emotions as the most readily accessible, accurate, and immediate source of truth." They prefer fast, emotional processing because "analysis of abstract knowledge requires so much additional effort." Appealing to this cognitive trait eases information overload and allows us to fall back on biases—biases that "make us prone to systematic error or susceptible to systematic manipulation by others." McDermott also highlights the tendency for individuals to more readily accept information that aligns with previously held convictions.

Extrapolating from the psychological findings described above to a systematic impact on public opinion from social media is suggestive, but not dispositive. Rather than social media altering public opinion, it may be that social media reveal more clearly the full spectrum of opinion. Exposure to propaganda may not result in conversion or persuasion to new and different points of view, though it may crystallize or harden existing prejudices and political inclinations. Indeed, it is a fact that polarization and tribalism predate social media, as do interdependent narratives formed about systems, identities, and issues. Ben O'Loughlin argues in chapter 9 that certain narratives or worldviews have a stronger role in shaping issue-specific narratives, such as views on nuclear weapons and war. He also argues that "through identity narratives, communication is used to shape behavior." In his view, it would be difficult for disinformation and misinformation to penetrate long-standing social networks, although it could be a very powerful tool for mobilization.

Crisis Stability and Escalation Risks

Although the underlying causal mechanisms need additional study, the present information environment—where misinformation and disinformation can be used to potentially alter, polarize, or harden leaders' and publics' perceptions of intentions, capabilities, risks, and consequences during international disputes—raises the specter that stability during crises can be deliberately manipulated, at greater speed, on a larger scale, and at a lower cost, than at any previous time in history.

In chapter 7, Kristin Ven Bruusgaard and Jaclyn Kerr argue that "if there were ever to be perfect crisis stability—and thus a perfect absence of risk of a crisis resulting in nuclear use—then nuclear weapons would serve no useful purpose as a deterrent and, in the absence of other forms of deterrence, aggressive states would have no reason to fear undertaking aggressive subnuclear military action." But there is no perfect crisis stability, and today's global information ecosystem makes the problem worse rather than better. Crisis stability is influenced by a battle of perceptions in which each actor determines whether it is in its interest to strike first or to take actions which knowingly could be perceived as escalatory. Bad information, public disorder, and panic can all lead to miscalculations or misperceptions that can prompt a state to strike first or escalate.

Kelly Greenhill argues in chapter 6 that the current information ecosystem contributes to political escalation through the "nonmilitary shifts in scope and intensity whereby states or actors adopt more aggressive rhetoric, articulate more expansive war aims, or announce decisions to relax or otherwise shift the prevailing rules of engagement." In this ecosystem, rumors, conspiracy theories, myths, propaganda, and fake news—what might be called "extra-factual information"—can inadvertently catalyze resolve that did not previously exist in leaders, the public, and adversaries, or can tie leaders' hands once escalatory rhetoric is broadcast publicly.

Effective signaling "requires reducing risks of misperception and tailoring messages accordingly," according to King's College London's Heather Williams.[14] But the use of social media by senior political leaders can increase the risk of misperception. For example, official and personal social media have been used by the US president both to diminish and to woo partners and adversaries and to announce presidential policy intentions. Military leaders have used social media to announce new capabilities. Adversaries, whether government or military officials, in both their individual and official capacities, monitor social media messaging of leaders and their subordinates. This means that leaders and the bureaucratic institutions that support them are vulnerable to information operations because they monitor social media to understand, at least partially, leaders' intentions.

Moreover, it is entirely possible that actors peddling falsified information about an adversary can come to believe their own propaganda. In chapter 8, Jeffrey Lewis outlines examples of how various false stories propagated by Russian official sources related to US missile defense systems in Europe affected arms control negotiations: "The [Russian] disinformation campaign was part of a continuing effort to paint US missile defense systems to be deployed in Poland and Romania as systems that could be converted to house offensive missiles, armed with nuclear weapons, and used to decapitate the Russian leadership." While completely untrue, Russian arms control negotiators came to believe this to be a reality, insisting that these false stories were evidence of American breaches of existing arms control agreements.

In addition, deliberate interference using information operations during a time of crisis could accompany a physical attack. Ven Bruusgaard and Kerr identify three overarching effects related to manipulating information and narratives on nuclear weapons: to enhance deterrence by confusing adversaries' understanding of your capabilities or their own capabilities; confusing their understanding of your goals and intentions; and instigating conflict by a third-party proxy with manipulated or false information sparking political, military, or public crises. And as Kumleben and Woolley point out in chapter 4, even before an attack, long-term information operations and manipulation of false alarms could lead to desensitization, false evacuations, and countermanding of real warnings. The very rapid dynamic of information flows on social media affects the two main principles for crisis stability articulated by historian Lawrence Freedman: the need for government leaders to outline clear objectives *before* a crisis and the desire for *increased* time for processing information during a crisis.[15] The dynamics of the global information ecosystem and their real-time effects on crises can no longer be ignored.

Conclusions

Against a backdrop of multiplatform communication suffused with a mix of information—true and false, official and unofficial, from friend and from foe, emotionally charged and serenely rational—the dynamics of the modern information ecosystem suggest unprecedented pressures on government decision makers during crisis. The timelines for decision making will be far more constrained, a fact likely to lead to a greater reliance on fast thinking by decision makers just at a time—during a crisis—when slow, deliberate, analytical thinking is most important.

As Ven Bruusgaard and Kerr write in chapter 7, information plays a critical role in assessing the actions, motives, and likely responses of other states, and thus informs available options for decision-making, reinforces or undermines biases, confuses or clarifies analysis, and dampens or amplifies pressures through public feedback or panic.[16] During the Cuban Missile Crisis, analog systems, government monopoly on both secret and public information, and the relatively lengthy decision time available to leaders helped to avoid disaster. Kennedy and Khrushchev had many days to deliberate and shape their proposed responses before they were revealed to the public.[17]

Leaders temperamentally reliant on fast thinking may well neglect or undervalue important considerations that should be taken into account. Indeed, if today's media environment existed during the Cuban Missile Crisis, American and possibly Soviet leaders would have been awash in a sea of unverified or unverifiable, emotionally laden, and politically fraught information on their adversary's intentions, force postures, and public opinion. Decision makers predisposed to impulsive thinking and whose personal information environments will include raw social media feeds as well as vetted information from their support agencies may well be more likely to act on those impulses.

The emergence of a crisis will also affect the modern information environment for the average person. Data show that publics strongly disapprove of inaction in response to provocation.[18] The simplistic, expedient, and repetitive nature of modern social media communication is likely to reinforce this sentiment, driving more citizens into a greater reliance on fast, reflexive thinking of their own. The result could well be increased public pressure on leaders to act more quickly than would be wise.

As for the future, it is reasonable to expect that social media platforms will continue to grow and evolve in this "new normal" ecosystem and provide ever greater ease for like-minded individuals to connect and share information, both innocent and malign. New tools—including video and audio deep fakes, explicit coordination between information operations and real-world events, and microtargeting of individuals with customized messaging—will enable further pollution of the information ecosystem. Dissecting the effects and impacts of information operations on publics and adversaries prior to a crisis, on publics and leaders during a crisis, and ultimately on decision making will be increasingly difficult in this rapidly evolving environment. Introducing, framing, and controlling narratives has become a new type of warfare being fought online each day—often in 280 characters or fewer.

Notes

1. Len Scott and Steve Smith, "Lessons of October: Historians, Political Scientists, Policy-Makers and the Cuban Missile Crisis," *International Affairs* 70, no. 4 (October 1994): 659–84, https://doi.org/10.2307/2624552.

2. Former secretary Perry has said the odds of nuclear war were worse than those estimated by President Kennedy, which was "somewhere between one out of three and even," because Kennedy did not know at the time that the Soviets already had tactical nuclear weapons on Cuba and authorization to use them in the event of a US invasion (which was the unanimous recommendation of the

Joint Chiefs of Staff at the time). William J. Perry, *My Journey at the Nuclear Brink* (Stanford, CA: Stanford University Press, 2015).

3. Philip M. Napoli, "Social Media and the Public Interest: Governance of News Platforms in the Realm of Individual and Algorithmic Gatekeepers," *Telecommunications Policy* 39, no. 9 (October 2015): 751–60, https://doi .org/10.1016/j.telpol.2014.12.003; Michael Latzer, Katharina Hollnbuchner, Natascha Just, and Florian Saurwein, "The Economics of Algorithmic Selection on the Internet," in *Handbook on the Economics of the Internet*, ed. Johannes M. Bauer and Michael Latzer (Cheltenham, UK: Edward Elgar, 2016), 395.

4. Neil MacFarquhar, "Inside the Russian Troll Factory: Zombies and a Breakneck Pace," *New York Times*, February 18, 2018, https://www.nytimes.com /2018/02/18/world/europe/russia-troll-factory.html.

5. Samanth Subramanian, "Inside the Macedonian Fake-News Complex," *Wired*, February 15, 2017, https://www.wired.com/2017/02/veles-macedonia -fake-news.

6. Jürgen Pfeffer, Thomas Zorbach, and Kathleen M. Carley, "Understanding Online Firestorms: Negative Word-of-Mouth Dynamics in Social Media Networks," *Journal of Marketing Communications* 20, no. 1–2 (March 4, 2014): 117–28, https://doi.org/10.1080/13527266.2013.797778.

7. Patrick M. Morgan, "Deterrence and Rationality," *Deterrence Now* (Cambridge, UK: Cambridge University Press, 2003), 42–79.

8. Daniel Kahneman, *Thinking, Fast and Slow* (New York: Farrar, Straus and Giroux, 2011).

9. Michael J. Mazarr, *Rethinking Risk in National Security: Lessons of the Financial Crisis for Risk Management* (Basingstoke, UK: Palgrave Macmillan, 2016).

10. Robert Jervis, "War and Misperception," *Journal of Interdisciplinary History* 18, no. 4 (Spring 1988): 675–700.

11. Sonya Song and Steven Wildman, "Using Online Media Audience Data to Develop and Refine Media Strategy," in *Media Business Models: Connecting Media to their Markets*, ed. C. Scholz and S. S. Wildman (Lisbon, Portugal: Media XXI, in press).

12. See, for example, Herbert Lin and Jaclyn Kerr, "On Cyber-Enabled Information Warfare and Information Operations," in *Oxford Handbook of Cybersecurity* (New York: Oxford University Press, forthcoming).

13. Samuel C. Woolley and Philip N. Howard, "Computational Propaganda Worldwide: Executive Summary," Computational Propaganda Research Project, Oxford Internet Institute, Oxford University, June 2017.

14. Heather Williams, "'Blind Moles' with Smartphones: Social Media and Nuclear Crisis Escalation," paper presented at Effects of the Global Information Ecosystem on the Risk of Nuclear Conflict conference sponsored by the Stanley Center for Peace and Security, the Center for International Security and Cooperation, and the Hoover Institution, Stanford University, September 7, 2018.

15. Lawrence Freedman, "Escalators and Quagmires: Expectations and the Use of Force," *International Affairs* 67, no. 1 (January 1991): 15–31.

16. See chapter 7, this volume.

17. US State Department, "The Cuban Missile Crisis, October 1962," Office of the Historian, https://history.state.gov/milestones/1961-1968/cuban-missile-crisis.

18. Jessica Chen Weiss and Allan Dafoe, "Authoritarian Audiences, Rhetoric, and Propaganda in International Crises: Evidence from China," *International Studies Quarterly* 63, no. 4 (December 2019): 963–73.

Chapter 2

Psychological Underpinnings of Post-truth in Political Beliefs

Rose McDermott

Although both the idea and the reality of so-called fake news or disinformation campaigns long precede the debate promoted by the 2016 electoral process in the United States, the frequency and intensity of the discussion around their prevalence and influence have increased significantly since President Trump took office. For example, the report on the investigation into foreign interference in the 2016 US election by Special Counsel Robert S. Mueller III explicitly cites the activities of specific Russian individuals, but the implicit indictment for manipulating the election was placed at the door of Facebook, Twitter, and other forms of social media that facilitated these campaigns.[1]

In an era when technological innovations support increasingly cheap and easy ways to produce media that look official, the ability to separate real from artificial has become increasingly difficult. The challenge for the public becomes much more complicated when leaders and others strive for conscious manipulation of public opinion, presenting false information or discounting true information as "fake." The relative success of these strategies depends on many factors, including the education and skepticism of recipients. But they are increasingly facilitated by search engine algorithms that optimize information to be presented in order of interest, as opposed to importance or authenticity. Such algorithms may appear to operate without intent but in fact directly reflect the intent of their creators, who typically desire the most views in order to maximize profits. And yet most people believe that what a Google search returns, or what a Facebook feed presents, reflects a reasonably representative sample of "reality," when in fact that may be far from the truth.[2]

However, the public is not the only audience susceptible to such manipulation. Leaders can be influenced by false beliefs as well, falling prey to the universal human psychological biases that can affect all people. Lack of proper information, as well as the inability to distinguish real from false information, can exert a decisive influence on decision making in general, with especially dangerous implications for crises that occur under time pressure.

As much as the public discussion has focused on so-called fake news, the underlying political and social challenge involved in separating truth from fiction and in correcting misinformation results from natural psychological biases. The following discussion examines the psychological foundations that render individuals susceptible to a post-truth media environment and that allow this environment to emerge, escalate, and persist. After clarifying some definitional terms, the sources of susceptibility follow. A discussion of exacerbating factors precedes the conclusion.

Definitional Issues

"Post-truth" as a term was first used by Steve Tesich in *The Nation* to refer to earlier political scandals, including Watergate, the Iran-Contra affair, and the First Gulf War.[3] Ralph Keyes took up the term more explicitly in *The Post-Truth Era*.[4] Post-truth can be defined as "relating to or denoting circumstances in which objective facts are less influential in shaping public opinion than appeals to emotion and personal belief."[5] Thus, post-truth is distinct from the concept of fake news, which involves the deliberate portrayal and spread of false information, whether through traditional broadcast or print media, or via the internet or other forms of social media such as Twitter. To qualify as fake, the story has to be generated with the conscious intent to deceive or mislead the reader in order to achieve some financial or political goal.

As a term, "post-truth" originated long before the current administration, even before Donald Trump emerged as a presidential candidate, and it will likely endure long after he leaves office. Indeed, the reality of post-truth politics constitutes a much older practice, pre-dating even the advent of modern media. Political pamphlets from the seventeenth and eighteenth centuries were rife with emotional claims and triggers. The US government even established an institution designed to create just such a post-truth environment leading up to the First World War, in an effort to garner support for a fight that was opposed by the vast majority of Americans.[6] George Creel, who led the Committee for Public Information in this era, was a master at manipulating the public to support a war that most Americans originally opposed. Indeed, post-truth communication encompasses an enduring and endemic aspect of politics and, as such, deserves to be examined independently of the current administration. Given its increasing prevalence, the post-truth world will likely endure long after Trump leaves office.

But post-truth represents a much broader phenomenon than fake news, which only comprises one element of the larger reality. The foundation for post-truth is laid when people consider opinions to be as legitimate as objective facts or when people weigh emotional factors as heavily as statistical evidence. When such tendencies hold sway among even a significant minority of the public, they can exert a strong influence on public policy debates, as well as on behavioral outcomes such as voting.

"Post-truth" was the Oxford Dictionary 2016 International Word of the Year, which is given to the word that the editors believe most defines "the ethos, mood, or preoccupation of that particular year and to have lasting potential as a word of cultural significance." According to the *Oxford Dictionary*, there was a 2,000 percent increase in its usage over the course of one year, in 2016.[7] In Britain, it was most evident in the debate surrounding the Brexit vote, so clearly this phenomenon is not restricted to American political discourse. Indeed, it has emerged as an international political pandemic. In the United States, it has become most closely related to the style of communication characterized by Trump. As David Frum wrote in 2016, Trump and his campaign were "qualitatively different than anything before seen from a major-party nominee."[8] Chris Cillizza argued, "There is no doubt that even in the quadrennial truth-stretching that happens in presidential campaigns, Trump has set records for fabrication."[9] Yet despite what elites were writing and warning, voters saw Trump as more honest than Clinton by an 8 point margin in the November 2, 2016, ABC-Post poll. This despite an analysis by PolitiFact that showed that 129 of 169 statements made by Trump that week were false, whereas 59 of Clinton's 212 statements were false.[10] In other words, what voters believed ran exactly opposite to the facts.

Note that post-truth is distinct from two other related concepts with which it is often conflated. Post-truth is not identical to the 2006 Merriam-Webster word of the year: truthiness. This word, introduced by Stephen Colbert on the opening night of his popular satirical show *The Colbert Report* on *Comedy Central* in 2005, refers to "believing something that feels true even if it isn't supported by facts," such as beliefs held by anti-vaccination campaigners.[11] This is part of post-truth—but post-truth encompasses a much broader phenomenon because it also includes beliefs that run contrary to facts. It includes the way individuals use feelings and beliefs to inform and advocate for policies completely divorced from those emotions and thoughts without any seeming awareness of the contradiction.

Post-truth is also distinct from the concept of fake news, which involves the deliberate portrayal and spread of false information, whether through traditional broadcast or print media or via the internet or other forms of social media such as Twitter. To qualify as fake, the story has to be generated with the conscious intent to deceive or mislead the reader in order to achieve some financial or political goal. In the wake of the 2016 election, there was much discussion of how the monetization strategies of social media encouraged some content authors, including a notorious Macedonian village manufacturing anti-Clinton propaganda, to engage in false journalism because it generated revenue. In this case, the decision to target presidential candidate Hillary Clinton was driven by the greater returns that such a partisan focus generated.[12]

Note that fake news is distinct from the existence of a satirical news show such as the aforementioned *The Colbert Report* or any of its successors. Indeed, these shows are explicitly satirical and instead use real facts in ironic contexts to make political points. In these cases, the audience is supposed to be in on the joke and realize that the presentation is intentionally designed to evoke humor as well as awareness. Real "fake news," as opposed to satirical fake news shows, consists of stories that have no basis in fact but are presented as being objective or factually accurate. Accusations of news being fake, despite being real, constitute an essential part of the post-truth world. What distinguishes the processing of real as opposed to fake news lies in the depth of information processing involved. The more engaged the recipient is and the more that person treats incoming information with appropriate interrogation, as opposed to accepting it wholesale, the less likely he is to become trapped in post-truth reality.

Several features characterize this concept of post-truth. First, it relies heavily on appeals to emotion, such as fear and anger, which may be instigated in response to one incident but later brought to bear against another wholly unrelated incident, simply because both events are united by the identity of the opponent or the emotion of the perceiver. Much of the time, this hostility revolves around political ideology. For example, Democrats may characterize Republicans as racist and then easily transfer that anger onto other aspects of Republican ideology as well. But there are myriad divisions around which it is possible for individuals to coalesce outrage, including race, gender, religion, and sexual orientation, among many other possibilities.

Second, post-truth arguments separate fact from the specific details of a policy. So, feelings about one issue, such as abortion, are used to inform debates about other issues, such as tax policy, in ways that are unrelated to any substantive connections between the topics. In other words, when material and ideological interests around values conflict, values tend to triumph. For example, if people who are adamantly opposed to abortion attach to the Republican Party for that reason, they may simply adhere to the Republican line on taxes, even if that position runs against their material interests. This is particularly likely when it comes to evaluating topics that are abstract, remote, pallid in nature, or difficult to understand.[13] Because partisans come to trust a party around an emotionally based issue they care about, it becomes easy to transfer that trust onto other issues where their actual interest may not, in fact, be accurately reflected or represented. Third, in a post-truth world, repetition reigns. Talking points, irrespective of any given question, come to serve as a substitute for more nuanced debate or discussion. Finally, in post-truth discussions, rebuttals to one's position are ignored or dismissed, thus refusing the benefits of repetition to the opposition. In addition, the opposition itself may serve only to enhance the commitment to the original idea, in a process known as belief polarization, as a result of biased assimilation of incoming information.[14] In all these ways, facts no longer weigh as heavily as the emotional triggers that politicians can elicit. Through these mechanisms, partisans can choose to believe the world is only as they see it, on both sides.

Alternative Sources of Belief

The susceptibility that people have to accepting feelings as facts does not constitute a new phenomenon, nor is it just restricted to news items or objective issues. But before mentioning some of the structural factors that tend to exacerbate underlying psychological dynamics, it is worth noting the foundational psychological and cognitive sources of belief, which are not simply restricted to scientific facts.[15] To be clear, the current discussion does not go into depth on the first two of these foundational sources of belief mentioned below—religion and precedent—because they are not primarily psychological phenomena, although they still merit mention. The final foundational reason, stressing the importance of emotion in informing belief, offers the basis for the remainder of this examination.

For the majority of academics and other elites, scientific truth constitutes the gold standard upon which belief is supposed to be formulated. If beliefs do not derive from this source, the burden of proof lies with the person who disputes them to prove why another standard might be substituted. However, for many people in the world, and most non-elites in the United States, facts are not assumed to provide the default standard by which beliefs are established. For most people, other sources of belief are understood to hold equal legitimacy to scientific facts. First, and most common, religion and faith provide the guiding principles by which people live their lives. From this perspective, for many people, just because they cannot see and measure God does not mean that God does not exist. Indeed, faith in the absence of facts is taken as a demonstrable sign of piety and status in many religions. This means that believing things they cannot see or prove is not alien to many people and applying such habits to the political realm would not feel unusual.

Second, history matters. Our own legal system relies on precedent or custom in making decisions about guilt and responsibility, even when modern neuroscience may cast serious doubt on such issues as free will.[16] Finally, and most critically for our purposes, many people rely on their emotions as the most readily accessible, accurate, and immediate source of truth. This argument has a long and distinguished history in psychology, with William McDougall arguing against William James's more pragmatic approach that belief itself was a form of emotion.[17] Modern empirical demonstrations of this theoretical argument use those with affective disorders to demonstrate how emotions operate on decision making in general.[18] This works precisely because affect and emotion provide sources of information about one's present hedonic state, with implications for future feelings as well, which other forms of input do not offer.[19] Emotion regulation is a difficult, complex task which the vast majority of people have a hard time mastering.[20] As a result, people seek ways to make themselves feel better, or at least less bad, and this can easily take precedence over attempting to keep sophisticated thoughts and cognitions grounded in empirics that may be hard to assess. This privileging of fast, easy, automatic emotional processing over complex intellectual assessment is exacerbated precisely because analysis of abstract knowledge requires so much additional effort.[21]

The natural, common tendency for most people is to rely on these other factors instead of, or in addition to, facts in order to negotiate their daily lives, especially in areas that really matter to them like religious faith and family. This means that most people are used to evaluating important experiences independent of objective scientific facts and methods. As a result, approaching news and political issues from a similar perspective would seem easy and normal. Indeed, it is most effortless for people to rely on basic and universal psychological biases which serve to reduce cognitive load. Everyone has to process way too much information every day, so easy, familiar, natural processes quickly become default strategies, regardless of whether the task is political in nature or not.[22] In an effort to negotiate the tasks we all need to accomplish every day, we rely on those intuitive psychological shortcuts which prove effective and efficient most of the time. But that means we may not notice the ways that these biases make us prone to systematic error or susceptible to systematic manipulation by others.

A few of these basic biases are worth noting. By now, many people are aware of the various well-documented judgmental approaches, including prospect theory.[23] But there are others that also produce systematic biases in information processing, although they may not have been as meticulously and rigorously documented. These include well-known phenomena such as biased assimilation, whereby people subject information to different levels of scrutiny based on whether or not they are predisposed to believe it. Material that is commensurate with pre-existing beliefs is simply accepted, whereas information which diverges from a person's prior beliefs is subjected to all kinds of interrogation, meaning that people are much more accepting of information they already agree with.[24] In addition, confirmation bias can also serve to exacerbate these deficiencies in information processing by encouraging people to seek or interpret information in ways that are consistent with their beliefs and to ignore information which presents challenges, raises questions, or refutes those inferences.[25]

Why Are People Susceptible to Such Biases?

Contrary to popular scientific opinion, and bemoaned by many policy makers, people do not naturally gravitate toward scientific truth. In fact, on average, people try to avoid it. Humans show a proclivity to accept whatever information they are exposed to wholesale, in a surprisingly gullible manner. In short, the natural human default is to accept what others tell them as true. Moreover, if claims do not contain specific aspects, it makes it less likely that people will seek to test their accuracy, while specific claims induce skepticism, making them much more likely to generate close critique.[26] In general, individuals have to work very hard to resist believing lies. This means it takes a lot of extra effort for most people to resist, rather than believe, a lie. Believing simple lies is a lot easier than evaluating complex facts.[27]

Why would this be the case? The enormous energy required by basic brain processing explains most of it. In order to discern whether something is a lie, the brain must first treat it as true. Only once we assume something is true can we try to compare a statement against all other existing knowledge, information, and feelings to determine whether it is a lie.[28] This takes an enormous amount of extra time and energy that most people do not want to spend on every statement.

This also means that several strategies can easily defeat the brain's lie-detection system, primary among them the power of repetition, which generates a sense of illusory truth.[29] Repetition simply overwhelms our cognitive resources. Moreover, when information is retracted, it exerts the opposite of the intended effect.[30] Rather than making people realize the earlier information was false, retraction instead serves to simply reinforce the earlier information through repetition. This can produce the frequent blowback or sleeper effects, whereby people remember the idea but not the source, and thus give more credibility to the idea than it deserves, serving to simply reinforce the previous falsehood through repetition.

In addition, basic information-processing strategies such as biased assimilation and belief perseverance mean that we integrate new information into our preexisting theories and models of the world.[31] We accept supporting information without question, subject information that reinforces our beliefs to much less rigorous scrutiny than evidence that seemingly refutes it, and treat neutral information as supportive. This means that everyone tends to cherry-pick data that support their views and denigrate their opponents' positions. This is where emotion inserts a decisive influence: outrage at the supposed misrepresentation of the other side exacerbates disagreement and misunderstanding. Memory effects can exaggerate these dynamics as well. We tend to remember things more easily contingent on mood, place, and state.[32]

So how do people decide whether something "feels" true? Norbert Schwarz and colleagues have put forward a powerful and persuasive model of the factors that influence such truth-validation decisions.[33] When people seek to judge the truth, they assess five basic factors: compatibility, coherence, credibility, consensus, and support. Compatibility assesses whether the information fits with what the person already knows and feels, and also whether it is consistent with his worldview. Compatibility thus illustrates one of the ways in which social identity can influence evaluations of the truth of a message by shaping whose evaluation counts and which messages matter. In this way, compatibility helps provide an explanation for how emotion serves as a source for evaluation of the truth—people are more likely to believe things that fit with their preexisting feelings and beliefs, in a process often referred to as biased assimilation.[34] Coherence refers to whether or not the story is internally coherent and plausible. Does it make sense? Simple stories have an inherent advantage on this dimension, because stories which are easy to process are interpreted as more coherent.[35] Credibility evaluates the source of information. Consensus asks whether other people share the view under consideration. If many people believe it, it is assumed to be more likely to be true. This mechanism shows how social media can quickly enforce and magnify false information, particularly when individuals restrict themselves to echo-chamber enclaves. And support reflects whether the claim has much evidence in its favor, although which evidence is available or considered credible can be influenced by the other forces.

According to the Schwarz et al. model, people can evaluate information in one of two ways: they can rely on relevant facts and details, which takes a lot of effort, or they can rely on how easy, or "fluent," it is to process the information.[36] Note that these two models align with the System 1 versus System 2 information-processing model put forth by Daniel Kahneman in *Thinking, Fast and Slow*.[37] Because it requires so much less effort, people find it much easier to believe things that only require easy, or System 1, processing. For example, if a person were to evaluate the dimension of consensus from an analytic standpoint, she would have to figure out, and track, who believes what and why. This would require a great deal of effort, especially if such efforts had to be repeated for every piece of information she encountered. Or she could instead rely on an intuitive assessment of whether lots of other people believe it. Indeed, Leon Festinger pointed this out in his seminal work on social comparison in noting that people assume that if most people believe something, there must be some element of truth in it in a "where there is smoke, there must be fire" kind of way.[38] Politicians who often use terms such as "lots of people are saying this" or "everyone knows that" are implicitly relying on this natural psychological tendency for humans to accept consensually agreed-upon information more readily than more contentious information. One of the benefits of presenting claims of false equivalency, as often occurs in the climate change debate, for example, results from making people more skeptical of information that appears to have achieved less consensus than might be the case in reality.

Fluency, or ease of processing, can be influenced by many factors unrelated to objective facts. Repetition, for example, can make things more familiar and thus easier to process. In this way, President Trump's constant repetition of claims of "no collusion" in reference to Russian interference in the 2016 elections not only serves to drive home this message but also distracts from other convincing evidence, such as that which would support obstruction of justice charges.[39] Repetition of visual presentation, including things as simple as font or emoji, can similarly serve to bypass systems that might otherwise demand more interrogation. In this way, highly fluent stories can thus circumvent even the need for repetition. But the flip side means that when things are not fluent, and thus harder to process, they will inspire greater scrutiny, explaining why complex arguments may instigate greater skepticism, or System 2 processing, than easy-to-process simplistic claims. Importantly, the Schwarz et al. model illustrates why attempts to correct misinformation often backfire.[40] Because of memory effects, the repetition of the false information will only strengthen its mental association, as the source of the information is quickly forgotten but the content remains active and reinforced. People remain quite sensitive to their feelings, while relatively ignorant or insensitive to their source, especially if it lies in subtle or background areas like color, rhyme, or smell.[41]

These are, of course, not the only factors that can influence an individual's evaluation of truth claims. The ones mentioned above fall under an area often referred to as unmotivated biases, proceeding from the assumption that if people knew they were doing them, they would see their errors and want to change. But more motivated factors can influence the assessment of truth and credibility as well. Cognitive dissonance has forcefully demonstrated that people often change their beliefs to align with behavior that may be shaped by entirely irrelevant forces, particularly under conditions of high perceived choice and low objective justification.[42] Indeed, other forms of motivated reasoning can encourage individuals to espouse beliefs for various reasons, including self-interest they may be unwilling to openly acknowledge.[43]

These psychological tendencies are not by any means restricted to the less educated. Rather, they represent universal aspects of human information processing. We all share basic biases in information gathering and we all suffer from biased reasoning and biased recollection. These dynamics evolve for good reason; cooperation and social support constitute an essential advantage for humans and indeed are much more important than knowing the objective truth. And if we believe something, it is easier to convince others and enlarge our coalition, because confidence conveys authority and conviction.[44]

Exacerbating Factors

If these underlying psychological dynamics were not enough, a couple aspects of the modern political environment make individuals even more susceptible to treating opinion and feeling as fact in a post-truth world. First, there is an overall loss of trust in institutions, including the media.[45] The public also does not trust experts, at least partly because they so often contradict each other on all kinds of issues (such as nutrition), making people likely to dismiss all experts rather than try to sort through arguments on their own.[46] In addition, denigration of experts provides an easy way for coalitions to organize against opponents, just as increasing self-selection in media diets reduces the likelihood that people will encounter information with which they disagree. In striving for balance, the mainstream news media sometimes bestow false credibility on one side of a debate that actually lacks strong scientific support, such as with climate change. For observers confused by complex contradictory arguments or turned off by negativity, it is simply easier to retreat to tribal loyalties.[47] Indeed, recent polls show that conservatives with the highest education levels are the ones who are most likely to disbelieve the existence of climate change.[48] Source identification saying information is provided by "Exxon" or "the National Science Foundation" makes little difference in perceived credibility.[49]

In addition, there is no question that there have been massive changes this century in the way we obtain information. The rise of social media in particular means that, for good or bad, there are no longer any central gatekeepers that vet the information that reaches the mass public. User-generated information, as well as the democratization of information facilitated by the emergence of the internet as a global commons, has supported the emergence of echo chambers. The vastness of the internet encourages selective sorting, meaning people use ideas, concepts, and keywords they are already aware of in order to seek out new information. This increases the prospects that they will only encounter positions they already agree with, in an online version of self-selecting into environments, groups, or relationships based on what makes people feel comfortable. But in an online world, this also makes it less likely that people will encounter new or discordant ideas or opinions. In addition to solidifying views, this also encourages people to have an unrealistic sense of how popular their opinions are, since they increasingly encounter only consonant ideas and opinions. When news is curated by friends and personalized, it immediately and directly increases interest and relevance and also attention.[50] It also increases a sense of false consensus, since fewer people are exposed to information they disagree with. Search algorithms clearly exacerbate this tendency as well, since they are built to show a viewer what they predict the viewer wants to see based on past viewing and searching behavior, drastically reducing the incidence of oppositional messages by design.[51] As the Cambridge Analytica scandal that recently indicted Facebook clearly illustrates, social media platforms allow strategies developed by professional advertising agencies to be applied to political campaigns through processes of micro-targeting, where partisans only have to preach to the converted.[52] This allows for the introduction of election manipulation on a massive, individualized scale that has never been possible before. This does not only relate to the Russian manipulation of the American election in 2016, it also allows all kinds of corporations and other groups seeking an electoral advantage to target large numbers of individuals with divisive messaging. This alone has served to further divide an already polarized public. These processes can become even more destructive as the targeting becomes more sophisticated and individualized.

Implications for Leaders

Although most of this discussion has focused on how the mass public may be susceptible to a post-truth environment, there is no reason to believe that leaders and other elites, who share the same fundamental psychological structures as other humans, would not fall prey to systematic tendencies on the part of others, particularly foreign leaders desiring to mislead. Clearly, leaders and other elites seek to manipulate the mass public by spreading false, misleading, and biased information, depending on followers to spread such misinformation campaigns on their own through the destructive facilitative platforms provided by social media. However, leaders themselves should be attentive to information that comes from other countries as well, since much of the most important information remains largely secret, making it more difficult to verify. Indeed, it may be impossible to secure independent corroboration for much of it. National leaders clearly do not have the time or training to properly vet or analyze information appearing on social media platforms from other countries—this falls within the purview of the intelligence community. And yet credible social media information may prove critically important not only in formulating long-term policies but also in responding to urgent short-term crises.

Of course, all information is filtered through preexisting beliefs, as noted in the literature on biased assimilation. This means that any given leader will prove more inclined to believe some information over other information if it more closely conforms to that leader's worldview. Work in so-called motivated biases shows the ways that wishful thinking can influence leaders' beliefs about the world in all kinds of ways.[53] Politicians tend to be more focused on broader political considerations, including public-opinion polls and fund-raising considerations, making them more likely to pay attention to information that serves, but may also harm, their longer-term electoral or reputational interests. Even when they might not believe something, if they know that such information will play well with their constituency, they may pretend to believe it. Religion and monogamy provide great examples of this kind of faked authenticity. Not every leader is as religious or as faithful as he pretends, but he knows that such performance is expected by a constituency whose support he needs in order to get elected and stay in power. It is easier for a politician to pretend to be what he is not in order to gain the support of his followers than to live a life of truth that may get him kicked out of office. But, again, people's willingness to toss someone out of office may depend, in part, on the recursive ability of that leader to manipulate his followers into believing him over what they see themselves.

When foreign leaders present information to each other, the stakes may be even higher, particularly in a crisis situation. Leaders may be deliberately exposed to misinformation campaigns from foreign governments, or even domestic opponents, about, say, the existence of weapons of mass destruction, for years before any formal decision must be made or any overt crisis develops. In addition, it can prove exquisitely difficult to discern another leader's motives in offering information that may or may not be true, or concessions they may or may not have any intention of implementing. And, of course, the danger here can work in both directions, encompassing both System 1 and System 2 inference errors. For example, President George W. Bush launched a war against Iraqi leader Saddam Hussein on the ostensible basis of incorrect beliefs regarding the existence of weapons of mass destruction in Iraq. That war drew the United States into a destructive, costly, and ongoing conflict in the Middle East. Here again, the elusive nature of truth is thrown into bas-relief, since many believed that Bush launched the war for other purposes and was simply seeking a justification that would convince others of the importance of his cause.

The influence of the new global information environment on leader perception and behavior is at least twofold. First, and primarily, the facilitative and largely unregulated platforms provided by social media offer a rich foundation upon which to manipulate the public by spreading rumors, inciting outrage, and perpetuating misinformation. The sheer volume of such efforts will make it increasingly difficult for people to separate truth from lies. Second, leaders themselves may prove susceptible to disinformation campaigns perpetuated by adversaries, either because they assimilate incoming information in light of pre-existing beliefs they may want to be true or because they themselves do not possess an adequate framework for evaluating the accuracy of information they encounter. While this may be the purpose of the intelligence community, it is likely easier for leaders to believe they can properly interpret information on social media since they are more likely to be familiar with it from their personal lives than it is for these leaders to assume they can properly interpret complex statistical data. And yet they may be wrong about this. Familiarity does not necessarily engender accuracy in perception. Either way, leaders may end up relying on inaccurate information in making decisions that have global consequences.

Conclusion

Humans possess universal psychological strategies that make it hard to detect lies for a reason. Storytelling is one of the most ancient forms of communication and entertainment. It allowed for the transfer of massive amounts of information across generations in preliterate cultures for millennia. Storytelling produces strong social bonds in a community and provides cohesive explanations and expectations. Storytelling provides shared knowledge and history and a sense of collective future within a community. That is why stories can become such powerful tools of deception. In a contest between propositional logic and narrative that is rich with emotion, there is no contest in power or persuasion.[54] Narrative wins every time. Emotion provides the foundation for myth, history, ritual, and social relationships. Narrative flow makes us receptive both emotionally and behaviorally to the information contained therein. This is why it constitutes such a powerful recruiting tool for all sorts of extremism. Visceral emotional states induce intense attentional focus because the information in stories proved crucial for generations. If someone told a story about a person in a community who died as a result of eating a particular food or fighting with a specific neighbor, those people who paid attention to those stories and avoided that food and stayed away from those neighbors would have been much more likely to survive than those who did not.

Falsifiability may provide the cornerstone of the scientific method but believability constitutes the hallmark of a good narrative.[55] When a fact is plausible, scientists still need to test it—that is the purpose of hypothesis generation and testing. But when a story is plausible, the vast majority of people will believe it is true.[56] This process of believing stories potentiates cooperation among those who might not have anything else in common except their belief.[57] The benefits offered by such cooperation far exceed the costs associated with believing lies.[58]

Inoculating against such tendencies is exceedingly challenging. Retractions and corrections may work in the short run but fail over time as memory retains content and forgets the source, strengthening the false belief. Confronting falsehoods with facts only strengthens the lie by exposing more people to it and by making it more fluent and believable through repetition and familiarity. We can certainly increase suspicion through warning prior to exposure, but instilling widespread distrust can easily backfire in other ways. The most obvious solution involves implementing more stringent regulation of social media. This could happen in a variety of ways. For example, Congress could break up Facebook or require a different business model, such as a pay-for-use model. Or, more significantly, Facebook, Twitter, and other forms of social media could be released from indemnity against libel charges. However, another strategy likely to be effective lies in striving to make the truth as fluent, simple, and easy to understand as a lie. Couching the truth in compelling, simple, emotional stories about history or family or competition could do this. Describing the Russians as an opposing sports team whom no one would want to give a list of plays to, or talking about Facebook as a mean girl in middle school, might go far in helping people understand the endemic, nefarious nature of the internal and external enemies we confront.

Notes

An earlier version of this chapter was first published as "Psychological Underpinnings of Post-Truth in Political Beliefs," in *Political Science and Politics* 52 (2): 1–5, January 2019 (American Political Science Association/Cambridge University Press). That article has been revised and greatly expanded for publication in this volume.

1. Robert S. Mueller III, "Report on the Investigation into Russian Interference in the 2016 Presidential Election" (Washington, DC: Department of Justice, March 2019).

2. Jaron Lanier, *Ten Arguments for Deleting Your Social Media Accounts Right Now* (New York: Henry Holt, 2018).

3. Steve Tesich, "A Government of Lies," *The Nation* 254, no. 1 (January 1992): 12–14.

4. Ralph Keyes, *The Post-Truth Era: Dishonesty and Deception in Contemporary Life* (New York: St. Martin's Press, 2004).

5. Oxford Dictionaries, Word of the Year, 2016, en.oxforddictionaries.com /word-of-the-year/word-of-the-year-2016.

6. Richard Vaughn, "How Advertising Works: A Planning Model," *Journal of Advertising Research* 20, no. 5 (1980): 27–33.

7. Oxford Dictionaries, Word of the Year, 2016.

8. David Frum, "The Seven Broken Guard Rails of Democracy," *The Atlantic*, May 31, 2016.

9. Chris Cillizza, "How the Heck Can Voters Think Donald Trump Is More Honest Than Hillary Clinton?" *Washington Post*, November 2, 2016.

10. Scott Clement and Emily Guskin, "Post-ABC Tracking Poll Finds Race Tied, as Trump Opens Up an 8-Point Edge on Honesty," *Washington Post*, November 2, 2016.

11. "Stephen Colbert Resurrects His Colbert Report 'The Word' Segment to Define 'Trumpiness,'" *The Week*, July 19, 2016, https://theweek.com/speedreads /636881/stephen-colbert-resurrects-colbert-report-word-segment-define -trumpiness.

12. Samanth Subramanian, "Inside the Macedonian Fake-News Complex," *Wired*, February 15, 2017, https://www.wired.com/2017/02/veles-macedonia -fake-news.

13. Eugene Borgida and Richard E. Nisbett, "The Differential Impact of Abstract vs. Concrete Information on Decisions," *Journal of Applied Social Psychology* 7, no. 3 (September 1977): 258–71.

14. Charles G. Lord, Lee Ross, and Mark R. Lepper, "Biased Assimilation and Attitude Polarization: The Effects of Prior Theories on Subsequently Considered Evidence," *Journal of Personality and Social Psychology* 37, no. 11 (1979): 2098–2109.

15. Arthur Lupia, "Communicating Science in Politicized Environments," *Proceedings of the National Academy of Sciences* 110, no. S3 (August 20, 2013): 14048–54.

16. William M. Landes and Richard A. Posner, "Legal Precedent: A Theoretical and Empirical Analysis," *Journal of Law and Economics* 19, no. 2 (1976): 249–307.

17. William McDougall, "Belief as a Derived Emotion," *Psychological Review* 28, no. 5 (September 1921): 315–27.

18. Martin P. Paulus and Angela J. Yu, "Emotion and Decision-Making: Affect-Driven Belief Systems in Anxiety and Depression," *Trends in Cognitive Sciences* 16, no. 9 (September 2012): 476–83.

19. Gerald L. Clore, Karen Gasper, and Erika Garvin, "Affect as Information," in *Handbook of Affect and Social Cognition*, ed. Joseph P. Forgas (Mahwah, NJ: Lawrence Erlbaum Associates, 2001), 121–44.

20. James J. Gross and Hooria Jazaieri, "Emotion, Emotion Regulation, and Psychopathology: An Affective Science Perspective," *Clinical Psychological Science* 2, no. 4 (2014): 387–401.

21. Michael D. Robinson and Gerald L. Clore, "Belief and Feeling: Evidence for an Accessibility Model of Emotional Self-Report," *Psychological Bulletin* 128, no. 6 (2002): 934–60; Norbert Schwarz, Eryn Newman, and William Leach, "Making the Truth Stick & the Myths Fade: Lessons from Cognitive Psychology," *Behavioral Science & Policy* 2, no. 1 (2016): 85–95.

22. Daniel Kahneman, *Thinking, Fast and Slow* (New York: Farrar, Straus and Giroux, 2011).

23. Daniel Kahneman and Amos Tversky, "On the Interpretation of Intuitive Probability: A Reply to Jonathan Cohen," *Cognition* 7, no. 4 (1979): 409–11.

24. Lord, Ross, and Lepper, "Biased Assimilation and Attitude Polarization."

25. Raymond S. Nickerson, "Confirmation Bias: A Ubiquitous Phenomenon in Many Guises," *Review of General Psychology* 2, no. 2 (1998): 175–220.

26. Schwarz, Newman, and Leach, "Making the Truth Stick & the Myths Fade."

27. Dan Ariely, *The Upside of Irrationality: The Unexpected Benefits of Defying Logic* (New York: HarperCollins, 2010).

28. Daniel T. Gilbert, "How Mental Systems Believe," *American Psychologist* 46, no. 2 (1991): 107.

29. Lynn Hasher, David Goldstein, and Thomas Toppino, "Frequency and the Conference of Referential Validity," *Journal of Verbal Learning and Verbal Behavior* 16, no. 1 (February 1977): 107–12.

30. Colleen M. Seifert, "The Continued Influence of Misinformation in Memory: What Makes a Correction Effective?" *Psychology of Learning and Motivation* 41 (2002): 265–92.

31. Lord, Ross, and Lepper, "Biased Assimilation and Attitude Polarization."

32. Gordon H. Bower, "Mood and Memory," *American Psychologist* 36, no. 2 (February 1981): 129.

33. Schwarz, Newman, and Leach, "Making the Truth Stick & the Myths Fade"; Stephan Lewandowsky, Ullrich K. H. Ecker, Colleen M. Seifert, Norbert Schwarz, and John Cook, "Misinformation and Its Correction: Continued Influence and Successful Debiasing," *Psychological Science in the Public Interest* 13, no. 3 (2012): 106–31.

34. Lord, Ross, and Lepper, "Biased Assimilation and Attitude Polarization."

35. Philip N. Johnson-Laird, "Inference with Mental Models," in *The Oxford Handbook of Thinking and Reasoning*, ed. Keith J. Holyoak and Robert G. Morrison (Oxford, UK: Oxford University Press, 2012), 134–45.

36. Schwarz, Newman, and Leach, "Making the Truth Stick & the Myths Fade"; Lewandowsky et al., "Misinformation and Its Correction."

37. Kahneman, *Thinking, Fast and Slow*.

38. Leon Festinger, "A Theory of Social Comparison Processes," *Human Relations* 7, no. 2 (1954): 117–40.

39. Barry H. Berke, Noah Bookbinder, and Norman L. Eisen, "Presidential Obstruction of Justice: The Case of Donald J. Trump," Brookings Institution, August 22, 2018.

40. Schwarz, Newman, and Leach, "Making the Truth Stick & the Myths Fade."

41. Kimberlee Weaver, Stephen M. Garcia, Norbert Schwarz, and Dale T. Miller, "Inferring the Popularity of an Opinion from Its Familiarity: A Repetitive Voice Can Sound Like a Chorus," *Journal of Personality and Social Psychology* 92, no. 5 (May 2007): 821–33.

42. Leon Festinger, *A Theory of Cognitive Dissonance* (Stanford, CA: Stanford University Press, 1962).

43. Charles S. Taber and Milton Lodge, "Motivated Skepticism in the Evaluation of Political Beliefs," *American Journal of Political Science* 50, no. 3 (July 2006): 755–69.

44. Robert Trivers, "The Elements of a Scientific Theory of Self-Deception," *Annals of the New York Academy of Sciences* 907, no. 1 (April 2000): 114–31.

45. Clare Malone, "Americans Don't Trust Their Institutions Anymore," FiveThirtyEight, November 16, 2016.

46. Rebekah H. Nagler, "Adverse Outcomes Associated with Media Exposure to Contradictory Nutrition Messages," *Journal of Health Communication* 19, no. 1 (2014): 24–40.

47. Marc J. Hetherington, "Putting Polarization in Perspective," *British Journal of Political Science* 39, no. 2 (April 2009): 413–48.

48. "Global Warming and Environmental Regulation, Personal Environmentalism," Pew Research Center, October 5, 2017, https://www .people-press.org/2017/10/05/7-global-warming-and-environmental-regulation -personal-environmentalism.

49. Soojung Kim, "Questioners' Credibility Judgments of Answers in a Social Question and Answer Site," *Information Research* 15, no. 1 (March 2010).

50. Iryna Pentina and Monideepa Tarafdar, "From 'Information' to 'Knowing': Exploring the Role of Social Media in Contemporary News Consumption," *Computers in Human Behavior* 35 (June 2014): 211–23; Anne Oeldorf-Hirsch and S. Shyam Sundar, "Posting, Commenting, and Tagging: Effects of Sharing News Stories on Facebook," *Computers in Human Behavior* 44 (March 2015): 240–49.

51. James G. Webster, "User Information Regimes: How Social Media Shape Patterns of Consumption," *Northwestern University Law Review* 104, no. 2 (December 2010): 593–612.

52. Fritz Plasser and Gunda Plasser, *Global Political Campaigning: A Worldwide Analysis of Campaign Professionals and Their Practices* (Westport, CT: Greenwood Publishing Group, 2002).

53. Irving L. Janis and Leon Mann, *Decision Making: A Psychological Analysis of Conflict, Choice, and Commitment* (New York: Free Press, 1977); Robert Jervis, *Perception and Misperception in International Politics*, new ed. (Princeton, NJ: Princeton University Press, 2017).

54. Jerome Bruner, "The Narrative Construction of Reality," *Critical Inquiry* 18, no. 1 (Autumn 1991): 1–21.

55. Karl Popper, *The Logic of Scientific Discovery* (London: Routledge, 2005).

56. Kurt Braddock and James Price Dillard, "Meta-Analytic Evidence for the Persuasive Effect of Narratives on Beliefs, Attitudes, Intentions, and Behaviors," *Communication Monographs* 83, no. 4 (2016): 446–67.

57. Steven R. Corman, "Understanding the Role of Narrative in Extremist Strategic Communication," in *Countering Violent Extremism: Scientific Methods and Strategies*, ed. Laurie Fenstermacher (Dayton, OH: Air Force Research Laboratory, 2011), 36.

58. Ernst Fehr and Simon Gächter, "Altruistic Punishment in Humans," *Nature* 415, no. 6868 (January 10, 2002): 137.

Chapter 3

The Caveman and the Bomb in the Digital Age

Paul Slovic and Herbert S. Lin

The unleashed power of the atom has changed everything save our modes of thinking, and we thus drift toward unparalleled catastrophe.

—*Albert Einstein*

I am deeply moved if I see one man suffering and would risk my life for him. Then I talk impersonally about the possible pulverization of our big cities, with a hundred million dead. I am unable to multiply one man's suffering by a hundred million.

—*Albert Szent-Györgyi*

"No human decision is more fraught than one involving the use of nuclear weapons—a decision on which may ride the lives of millions of people and potentially the fate of civilization."[1] Albert Einstein and his colleagues recognized this fundamental truth in 1946 when they formed the Emergency Committee of Atomic Scientists to "promote new types of essential thinking . . . to harness the atom for the benefit of mankind and not for humanity's destruction."[2]

Nevertheless, in the following years, hydrogen bombs—with vastly more destructive power than the bombs dropped on Hiroshima and Nagasaki—emerged from the efforts of the scientific community as the focus of national security turned toward the Soviet Union and the Cold War got under way in earnest. Some seventy years after Einstein's words, there is little evidence that we have changed our modes of thinking, but psychological studies of risk perception and decision making have taught us that he was correct. Although our minds are capable of rational deliberation, our thinking is dominated by the fast, intuitive reactions that helped us survive in the cave and remain useful in the modern world except when the stakes are high.[3]

Decisions about the use of nuclear weapons have the highest stakes possible, and fast, intuitive reactions may be the worst way to make such decisions. Yet today the advent of social media increases the likelihood of such reactions. A social media environment that increases the velocity and reach of information, creates potent vectors for disinformation, eliminates journalistic fact-checking, and changes how political leaders interact with other leaders and constituencies poses enormous challenges for responsible decision making during crises between nuclear-armed states.

Applying what we now know about the limitations of the human mind can help to reduce the risks from nuclear weapons that we have accepted for decades. This chapter aims to honor Einstein's insight by documenting what we have learned about human thinking and its implications for decisions regarding the use of nuclear weapons.

From the inception of the atomic age, decisions regarding nuclear weapons have been recognized as extraordinarily challenging.[4] Some of the designers and builders of the first A-bombs thought that the weapons program was unconscionably immoral and should be stopped. In the midst of World War II and facing the prospect of Adolf Hitler with an atomic bomb (a plausible threat given German intellectual preeminence in physics at the time), they relented and continued their work, even after the tide of the war had turned decisively against Hitler's armies. A number of them argued that the bomb did not need to be used against Japan, at least not without first demonstrating its power to the Japanese, but they were overruled as they lost the debate over the necessity and morality of dropping the bomb.[5]

The postwar trajectory of the nuclear weapons story and the arms race is well known, starting with a few fission bombs and progressing by 1986 to more than 60,000 in the stockpiles of the United States and Soviet Union (later Russia) alone, some of these almost a thousand times more powerful than the original Hiroshima device. Nine nations currently possess these weapons.[6]

Some Psychological Considerations

Shortly after the dawn of the nuclear era, psychologists and other behavioral scientists began the empirical study of the cognitive and social factors influencing human decision making in the face of risk. The findings are worrisome, identifying numerous cognitive limitations documenting a form of bounded rationality that falls far short of the optimistic assumptions that characterized earlier theorizing by economists and other proponents of rational choice explanations for human behavior. Here we shall briefly describe a few selected findings that challenge the ability of our leaders to make rational decisions about using nuclear weapons. In addition, we shall also discuss ways that today's social media likely exacerbate these already daunting challenges.

Thinking: Fast and Slow

Much recent study regarding the psychology of decision making acknowledges a distinction between two modes of thinking: fast and slow.[7] Fast thinking relies on intuition, quick impressions, reflexive judgments, and gut feelings. Slow thinking relies on careful analysis and deliberation, often with numbers and calculations. We rely on fast thinking most of the time as our default mode of thought because it is easier, feels right, and works pretty well to guide us in our daily lives. In this sense, it is often helpful to rely on gut feelings, honed by direct experience, as this behavior has proven effective enough to enable our species to survive a long and dangerous journey from the cave to the modern world.

Slow thinking is more recent in origin. Our brains evolved the capacity to think symbolically and apply logic and reason to guide our decision making. Slow thinking enables us to imagine and critically evaluate consequences beyond those right in front of our eyes. Indeed, it has accomplished technological and other miracles. When the potential consequences of our decisions are extreme and outside the realm of our direct experience, it is important for decision makers to recognize the need to think more carefully and to make the effort to do so.

Both of these valuable modes of thought, fast and slow, have serious downsides. Fast thinking is problematic when we are trying to understand how to respond to large-scale human crises, with catastrophic consequences. Our fast, intuitive feelings do not obey the rules of arithmetic or logic. They do not add properly and they do not multiply, as the introductory quotation by Nobel laureate Albert Szent-Györgyi recognizes. This leads to an absence of feeling that has been characterized as "the more who die, the less we care."[8] Slow thinking, too, can be incoherent in the sense that subtle influences—such as unstated, unconscious, or implicitly held attitudes—may lead to considered decisions that violate one's strongly held values. The failings of both fast and slow thinking pose problems for decisions about nuclear weapons.

Psychic Numbing and the Fading of Compassion

Military planners and decision makers (who for this chapter include the civilian leadership of the military) presumably accept the proposition that during conflict the taking of noncombatant deaths should be avoided. Not at all costs, however. The laws of war (law of armed conflict, international humanitarian law) are based on ethical principles stating that (1) under some circumstances, it is morally justifiable to engage in armed conflict; and (2) that once engaged in armed conflict, care must be taken to avoid excessive collateral damage in any attack, defined as a degree of death and destruction of noncombatants and nonmilitary property that would be excessive in relation to the direct military advantage anticipated in that attack. Adherence to these principles (and international law) requires that planners place a value on inadvertent damage that a military operation may cause so that such damage can be weighed against the value of the military objectives.

Toward that end, think for a moment about two questions. First, how *should* we value the protection of human lives? And second, how *do* we value the protection of human lives?

Here are two answers to the first question, based on slow thinking combined with a value set that posits the importance of all noncombatant human lives regardless of nationality or ideological affiliation.

If we believe that every noncombatant life has equal value, then the value of protecting those lives should increase in a straight line as the number of lives at risk increases, as shown in figure 3.1a. This is a simple process of addition.

When additional losses of life threaten the extinction of a people, as in the case of genocide, the very next life at risk is even more valuable to protect than the life before it, causing the value line to curve upward as in figure 3.1b.

Figure 3.2 illustrates what research tells us about how most people (including entirely well-meaning military planners and decision

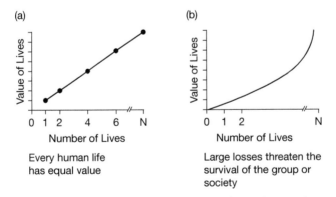

Figure 3.1. Two normative models for valuing noncombatant lives as the number at risk increases. Source: Paul Slovic, "'If I Look at the Mass, I Will Never Act': Psychic Numbing and Genocide," *Judgment and Decision Making* 2, no. 2 (April 2007): 79–95.

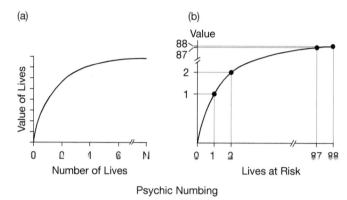

Psychic Numbing

Figure 3.2. Psychic numbing. A descriptive model where the value of a life depends on how many lives are at risk. Source: Slovic, "'If I Look at the Mass, I Will Never Act.'"

makers) actually tend to feel about the value of protecting noncombatant lives as the number of lives at risk increases. The outcomes depicted in figure 3.2 are driven by the fact that intuitive judgments and feelings—based on fast thinking—often override our more thoughtful judgments.

Figures 3.2a and 3.2b show that the biggest change in value occurs with the first life, going from zero to one. On an emotional level, we care greatly about protecting single lives, something known to researchers as "the singularity effect."[9] But as the numbers increase, "psychic numbing" begins to desensitize us.

Figure 3.2b is an elaboration of figure 3.2a. It shows that two lives do not feel twice as valuable to protect as one. In fact, as the number of lives at risk increases, the additional lives seem to add less and less value as the curve flattens. This means you probably will not feel much different about a threat to eighty-eight lives than you feel about a threat to eighty-seven lives. This curve also shows that a life that is so valuable to protect if it is the first or only life at risk seems to lose its value against the backdrop of a larger tragedy, with many lives endangered.

But it gets even worse than this.

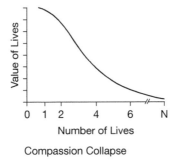

Compassion Collapse

Figure 3.3. Compassion Collapse: Value sometimes decreases when many lives are at risk. Source: Slovic, "If I Look at the Mass, I Will Never Act."

Figure 3.3 is supported by research and observations indicating that, as the number of lives in danger increases, we sometimes lose feeling and value the sum total of those lives even less.[10]

Psychic numbing and compassion collapse may have important effects on how planners and decision makers consider nuclear conflict. Ethical planners and decision makers are expected to weigh the value of accomplishing their military objectives relative to the value of the likely collateral damage. Evaluating the prospect of millions of expected non-combatant deaths in accordance with figure 3.1 would make it difficult to proceed with that option. But human beings' feelings actually follow the patterns depicted in figures 3.2 or 3.3. In other words, psychic numbing and the fading away of compassion reduce the perceived value of protecting large numbers of lives. Such a reduction, if large enough, enables the planner and decision maker to proceed to kill millions in a manner they believe to be consistent with the laws of war.

Numbing in War

Unfortunately, psychic numbing and compassion deficits and their grim implications are not mere figments of laboratory experiments. They appear to occur frequently in the annals of warfare. In World War II, even prior to nuclear weapons, commanders did not refrain from using conventional firebombs to attack cities and civilians (e.g., in Dresden and Tokyo) with dead human beings becoming mere statistics, "human beings with the tears dried off," as Paul Brodeur once said.[11]

Tokyo was one of more than sixty Japanese cities partially or totally destroyed by firebombing, which was orchestrated by General Curtis LeMay. Hundreds of thousands of Japanese civilians died in those attacks. LeMay was congratulated by General Hap Arnold after his "success" with Tokyo. Questioned after the war about the morality of the bombings, LeMay replied: "Killing Japanese didn't bother me. . . . It was getting the war over that bothered me. So, I wasn't particularly worried about how many people we killed."[12]

In 1954, LeMay, by then commander of the US Strategic Air Command, which operated US strategic forces, entertained a preemptive nuclear attack on the Soviet Union to prevent it from challenging American military and political superiority. It was estimated that the 750 atomic bombs he envisioned using would leave sixty million dead. By 1962, his associate General Thomas Power was prepared to deliver almost three thousand nuclear bombs, many of them thermonuclear, killing at least one hundred million people in order to decapitate Soviet leaders. LeMay was similarly aggressive in urging President Kennedy to bomb Cuba and take out the Soviet missile sites there, a move that would have put the world on the brink of nuclear war.[13]

Military analyst Daniel Ellsberg reports other sobering examples of numbness to consequences from the same era. Technological advances allowed substitution of H-bombs for A-bombs in planning for a possible war against the Soviet bloc, thus raising the expected death toll from executing the US nuclear war plan from about fifteen million in 1955 to more than two hundred million in 1961. He writes, "There was no new judgment of the necessity for the dramatic change in the planned-for effects of our attack. The war planners were simply assuming, correctly, that [Strategic Air Command] meant to replace their atomic weapons of the first decade of the nuclear era with the newly available H-bombs, thermonuclear warheads, against essentially the same ever-expanding target system."[14] Ellsberg notes that "the risk the presidents and Joint Chiefs were consciously accepting, however small they saw the probability of carrying out the [US nuclear war plan], involved the possible ending of organized society—the very existence of cities—in the northern hemisphere, along with the deaths of nearly all its human inhabitants."[15]

Reporting on a briefing on the US nuclear war plan given to President Kennedy in September 1961, political scientist Scott Sagan notes a key passage in the briefing's text: "While personnel casualties would be somewhat reduced if urban-industrial installations were not directly attacked, nevertheless, because of fallout from attack of military targets and co-location of many military targets with urban-industrial targets, the casualties would be many millions in number. Thus, limiting attacks to military targets has little practical meaning as a humanitarian measure."[16]

In 2017, President Trump, speaking before the United Nations, threatened to "totally destroy North Korea" if that "depraved" regime did not halt its provocative missile testing.[17] The president gave no indication that he had seriously attempted to appreciate the consequences of killing twenty-five million people. Moreover, his bellicose threat dramatically calls attention to the possibility that we have created weapons whose vast destructive power may be beyond our comprehension.

The American public appears similarly numb to the consequences of nuclear conflict. A recent survey suggests that Americans, like their leaders, are willing to abandon the principle of noncombatant immunity under the pressures of war. When considering the use of nuclear weapons in a hypothetical scenario about war with Iran, almost 60 percent of Americans prioritized protecting US troops and achieving American war aims, even when doing so would result in the deliberate killing of millions of foreign noncombatants. These findings suggest that public opinion is unlikely to be a serious constraint on any president contemplating the use of nuclear weapons in wartime.[18]

The incongruity between the singular importance of protecting individual lives and the acceptability of mass killing is brought home in the 1981 proposal by negotiations expert Roger Fisher that the secret code the president needs to initiate a nuclear attack be implanted near the heart of a person whose life the president would have to take to begin the process of killing millions.[19] Reactions to this proposal have ranged from "My god, that would be the taking of an innocent life!" to "If the president had to do that, he might never respond!" and "That would distort the president's judgment!"

Tribalism and Dehumanization

Much of mass killing in warfare is accompanied not by the absence of feeling but rather by intense emotions such as anger and hatred. Such emotions thrive in an "us versus them" environment, a phenomenon often referred to as tribalism. Because the US government viewed Japan as a threat during World War II, all Japanese people were considered to be a threat, even US citizens of Japanese descent, who were thus forcibly relocated to isolated camps. The American government created propaganda featuring crude images of Hirohito and Axis leaders as animals and murderers.[20] Dehumanizing images and phrases may explain why, in August 1945, 85 percent of US citizens approved of the bombings of Hiroshima and Nagasaki.[21] One poster showed Uncle Sam holding in one hand a caricatured Japanese male that strongly resembles Hirohito by the nape of his coat, and a giant mosquito tagged with the name *malaria* in the other hand. The caption read: "ENEMIES BOTH! IT'S YOUR JOB TO HELP ELIMINATE THEM."

It is well known that making enemies distinctively different and then dehumanizing them is a critical factor in turning normal people into mass murderers.[22] Jews were first distinguished as "the other" by being forced to wear yellow stars on their clothing. Later they were stripped of their names by Nazi captors, who tattooed numbers on their forearms. They were called vermin and rats, thus in need of extermination. Similarly, Tutsis in Rwanda were called cockroaches during the massacres.

In practice, it is often that little distinction is made between an enemy's military forces and the civilian compatriots of the enemy. It is true that compliance with the laws of war obligates military forces to

Figure 3.4. "Enemies Both! It's Your Job to Help Eliminate Them," 1942–1945. Office for Emergency Management, Office of War Information, Domestic Operations Branch. National Archives Catalog, 514207

refrain from explicitly targeting noncombatants. But, acknowledging the inevitability of noncombatant casualties, the laws of war forbid only attacks that cause such casualties that are "excessive" compared to the military advantages gained by the attack. The word "excessive" does not have a precise definition and is inherently subjective, i.e., dependent on human judgments.

But if it is human judgment that determines the meaning of "excessive" in any given instance, it is inevitable that all of the psychological considerations described above will be a part of such determinations—and fast, intuitive, reflexive thinking in particular will tend to drive those determinations unless mechanisms are put into place to allow for more reflective deliberation. Additionally, the subjective nature of such determinations facilitates post hoc rationalization—a reflexive judgment can be followed by a justification that had nothing to do with the original judgment.

The historical record is clear that senior US officials knew that firebombing Tokyo or using the atomic bomb against Hiroshima and Nagasaki would cause massive civilian casualties.[23] But what were the mental processes that underlay their decisions to proceed? The most frequently offered rationale was that these actions were necessary to win the war against Japan—and Japanese civilians and civilian infra-structure were part of the Japanese war effort. For example, LeMay wrote in 1965 that in bombing Japan:

> We were going after military targets. No point in slaughtering civilians for the mere sake of slaughter. Of course there is a pretty thin veneer in Japan, but the veneer was there. It was their system of dispersal of indus-try. All you had to do was visit one of those targets after we'd roasted it, and see the ruins of a multitude of houses, with a drill press sticking up through the wreckage of every home. The entire population got into the act and worked to make those airplanes or munitions of war . . . men, women, children. We knew we were going to kill a lot of women and kids when we burned [a] town. Had to be done.[24]

At the same time, there is considerable evidence that senior military leaders in the United States saw the Japanese as subhuman. For exam-ple, Admiral William Halsey called Japanese pilots in the Pacific "lit-tle yellow monkeys."[25] Such evidence suggests the decisions to attack Japanese civilians were at least in part motivated (or enabled) by dehu-manization of the Japanese enemy. To the extent that this is true, the natural human abhorrence to killing other humans no longer inhibits such action, as attacks on nasty animals or insects do not implicate this abhorrence.

Tribalism and dehumanization also enable people to believe that victims deserve their fate.[26] Effects of this belief can be compounded by the "just world" hypothesis, which states that people need to believe that the world is just and that therefore people get what they deserve.[27] For example, German sociologist Gabriele Rosenthal's interviews with three generations of non-Jewish Germans reveal the ways in which perpetrators blamed Jews for their own destruction during the Holocaust.[28] Blaming the victims allows the perpetrator to act without guilt against victims seen as less than human, to believe that the victims are evil, and the killing that leaders have told him to do is morally *proper*.[29] Tribalism, dehumanization, and victim-blaming enable mass murder to proceed without challenge from normal feelings, i.e., feelings that would arise from human beings' being recognized as similar to one's self.

Avoiding Trade-offs and Devaluing Foreign Lives

Experimental and historical evidence demonstrates that decision makers find trade-offs between competing values difficult to make and thus tend to avoid them.[30] What common units can be used to compare the value of protecting national security versus protecting noncombatant enemy civilians? How can one justify sacrificing or compromising one basic value for another? Numerous studies have demonstrated that the heuristics used to resolve trade-off conflicts are often noncompensatory. That is, rather than finding a common currency with which to evaluate trade-offs, a decision maker will prioritize his or her different goals and focus on achieving those of highest priority. As Kenneth Hammond and Jeryl Mumpower observed, "When our values conflict, we retreat to singular emphasis on our favorite value" (see also Robert Jervis).[31] This simplistic strategy has more recently been described as a "prominence effect" that leads decisions to favor security objectives over lifesaving objectives because the former are more defensible.[32]

Psychologist Abraham Maslow in 1943 proposed a hierarchy of needs, a prime characteristic of which is that a person will seek to satisfy a given need (e.g., food) only after he or she has satisfied higher-priority needs (e.g., air).[33] Paul Slovic invoked Maslow's hierarchy of needs to argue that leaders will attend to fundamental needs for safety and security before they will respond to lower-priority needs such as the moral obligation to protect others. Slovic proposed the prominence of political and national security objectives, obviously highly defensible, over humanitarian lifesaving (less defensible) as an explanation for the reluctance of the US government to intervene to prevent genocides and mass atrocities.[34] For example, early in the Syrian war, while acknowledging "very real and legitimate" humanitarian interests in Syria—eighty thousand people had already been killed and millions had lost their homes—President Obama said his "bottom line" has to be "what's in the best interest of America's security."[35]

The prominence effect can be thought of as an attentional spotlight on the most inherently defensible attributes of a decision, driving those attributes to assume greater, and sometimes extreme, priority and importance in a decision maker's thinking. For decisions pertaining to the development and use of nuclear weapons (and indeed to most decisions involving the use of military force), the historical record described earlier suggests that the spotlight will be on the perceived contributions to national security interests, as in the decisions to bomb Hiroshima and Nagasaki to protect our military personnel in the waning days of World War II, despite the likely loss of many Japanese lives. The same security prominence can be seen in LeMay's desire to launch preemptive nuclear strikes against the Soviet Union.[36]

The devaluation of lives may also be inadvertent. The prominence effect suggests that high-priority objectives, in particular those seen as offering enhanced security, will draw attention away from less prominent and lower-priority goals. All eyes are on options that protect the homeland, and decision makers fixated on security are likely to be inattentive to other important factors, such as the number of noncombatants who will die. Under such circumstances, many noncombatant lives may be placed at risk. But this devaluation of human lives may not be deliberate—this would be abhorrent to leaders with conscience who truly do value those lives. Rather, with the attentional spotlight on security objectives, leaders will have only peripheral awareness at best—and no awareness at worst—of other considerations. It is not that an objective such as minimizing the number of deaths is seriously considered in light of the security benefits and rejected—it is that little or no conscious thought is expended at all in such consideration.

Similarly, psychic numbing, compassion fade, tribalism, and dehumanization are psychological processes that often operate without conscious awareness, especially under the pressure of stressful circumstances (an example of which is clearly the contemplation of a real nuclear war). These processes create a deficient understanding of death and damage projections that does more than confound rational balancing of costs and benefits—it may encourage shallow assessments that give short shrift to consequences altogether.

For example, these processes may contribute to what political scientist Michael Mazarr has named "imperative driven decision making."[37] Imperatives are forceful calls to action that feel so obviously correct that deeper analysis seems unnecessary, e.g., "We have to stop the spread of communism in Southeast Asia," prior to escalating US commitments in Vietnam, or "We can't allow these beautiful little babies to be murdered by chemical weapons," prior to sending a volley of missiles at a Syrian air base.

Mazarr asserts that "decision makers under the influence of an imperative are scratching an immediate itch, not thinking about the possible outcomes of their actions."[38] He describes this shallow thinking as arising from pressures and constraints that leave decision makers with inadequate time for deliberate thinking and "classic outcome-oriented utility calculations."[39] He argues that:

- imperative-driven thinking is likely to obstruct careful analysis of utilities or objectives;
- imperatives are likely to generate subjective and shifting utilities rather than constant and objective ones;
- decision makers responding to imperatives will not engage in a legitimate comparison of alternatives;
- decision makers under the influence of an imperative will be blinded to many potential consequences and risks outside the scope of the imperative; and

- discussion of potential risks and second-order effects is likely to be downplayed and even actively discouraged.

Thus, an imperative such as "We must keep Muslim terrorists out of our country" that few would disagree with may lead to a blanket ban on travel and immigration that is not justified by evidence and fails to consider the harm done to thousands of innocent people or to the economy.[40]

Social Media

Social media are ubiquitous in American society. A recent survey indicates that 80 percent of all social media usage occurs on mobile devices.[41] A large fraction of US military personnel routinely carries mobile devices, and thus access to social media by such personnel should be assumed to be the default condition.

This point is particularly significant in light of the admonition of Russell Dougherty, former commander in chief of the Strategic Air Command:

> The nation has never experienced anything comparable to an agonizing debate regarding the use of nuclear options. Should this be the background of any such execution decision, *national cohesion may depend critically on keeping the fact of such debate from the public and from those in the nuclear commands who must respond.*[42]

In other words, if those charged with actually executing the war plan learn about debate regarding the wisdom and desirability of using nuclear weapons, they may not carry out their responsibilities as they are expected to do, despite their involvement in the Personnel Reliability Program intended to ensure that only the most trustworthy personnel are in the nuclear chain of command.[43] In a world of ubiquitous social media on ever-present mobile devices, it is hard to imagine keeping knowledge of such debate away from military personnel for very long.

How exposure to social media during crisis or conflict might affect the decisions of those in the nuclear command-and-control chain is unclear. Dougherty died in 2007, so it is impossible to ask him to elaborate on what he meant by "national cohesion," but in context it must refer to something like national will or unity. Conversely, a disruption of national unity might well mean discordance and a cacophony of different views that would increase the likelihood that some of those in the nuclear command-and-control chain would not carry out their missions. Hoping for such an outcome would increase an adversary's incentives to directly inject uncertainty and doubt into the US nuclear command-and-control system. Such an outcome would tend to weaken deterrence, which depends on certainty of response.

What is known about the affordances of social media and their impact on the information ecosystem is not particularly comforting. For example, if one wanted a media technology optimized for effectively broadcasting simplistic imperatives for action, one could hardly do better than 280-character Twitter messages—and while short Twitter messages are arguably the most simplistic of the communications that appear on social media, the messages of most social media platforms are simplistic compared to those that are available from traditional media such as books or even newspapers. Social media tend to be rich in video content and imagery rather than text. Because people are connected to social media for many hours a day, they receive social media communications frequently—and they are neurochemically rewarded for engaging with social media.[44] These characteristics of social media and the patterns of behavior that they introduce suggest strongly that the content of social media messages is more likely to be processed with fast, intuitive thought rather than with reflective, deliberate thought.

This tendency toward fast, intuitive thought would be bad enough among the populace at large. But senior decision makers, including certain heads of state, are known to be active social media users, and they are just as likely to be pushed by their social media usage into fast, intuitive thought. In other words, exposure to social media at higher levels of command—those with the authority to order the use of nuclear weapons—may increase the likelihood of taking rash action and of premature use. Note as well that although it is widely believed that only the president has the authority to order the use of nuclear weapons, the president's ability to delegate his or her authority to other parties remains—and the details of who may or may not have pre-delegated authority to order the use of nuclear weapons are withheld from public knowledge as a highly protected secret.

Where Next? Slow Down the Decision-Making Process for Using Nuclear Weapons

The psychological and communication issues described above show the need to ensure that the vast lethal potential of nuclear weapons is not unleashed because psychic numbing, compassion fade, tribalism, and dehumanization have distorted the decision-making calculus. The risk of distorting the decision-making calculus can be reduced in many ways. For example, analytic procedures for decision making, facilitated by skilled guides, can help deepen understanding of options, objectives, and the trade-offs that need to be made consistent with the considered values associated with the objectives and the likely outcomes of the various possible actions. Knowledge of outcome probabilities and uncertainties must also factor into the decision-making calculus.

Exercising these decision-aiding procedures is a necessity as well, and it is particularly valuable to involve principals (i.e., the people who would actually be making decisions amid a crisis, rather than stand-ins, no matter how respectable or smart). As an example of such an exercise, consider the Proud Prophet exercise, played out over a couple of weeks in June 1983. This exercise included the use of actual war plans and the personal involvement of the chairman of the Joint Chiefs of Staff and the secretary of defense. It is noteworthy that after this simulation, which ultimately terminated in a global thermonuclear exchange, the nuclear rhetoric of the administration in office at the time changed, becoming significantly less bellicose.[45] Finally, the operational dimensions of such exercises deserve significant attention, so as to ensure that informed decisions regarding nuclear weapons will be translated into commands that will be faithfully and precisely executed.[46]

But the biggest distortion of all on rational decision making is the pressure of time. Adequate time is needed for deliberation in nuclear decision making and for assessment of trade-offs and options—and it is also needed if the president and his or her advisers need to wait for more information.[47] In turn, the time available for decision making is primarily limited by the possibility that a president might want to exercise a launch-on-warning option for US land-based ICBMs. If it were known in advance that a president would never want to do so, or if the nuclear forces were configured in such a way that launch-on-warning was not a requirement for force survivability, significant additional time would be available to engage in nuclear decision making.

Fisher's proposal to require the president to kill an innocent individual (presumably a volunteer!) before he or she could order a nuclear attack was intended to confront the president with the reality and consequences of that decision. But less extreme measures can be and have been taken under similar circumstances. For example, during the Cuban Missile Crisis, President Kennedy asked his brother, Robert, to serve as a devil's advocate to reduce the likelihood of groupthink and a falsely arrived-at consensus. One could imagine a senior adviser to the president with the specific role (perhaps among other roles) of forcibly introducing into deliberations evidence of the likely human consequences of a decision. Another more intrusive possibility is that the nuclear chain of command be arranged so that the concurrence of two or more decision makers (e.g., the president *and* the secretary of defense) would be required to launch nuclear weapons.[48] Looping in a second party would be harder to do if the launch decision window was not extended, but with a reconfigured nuclear arsenal, the launch decision window could be extended significantly.

Yet decisions about nuclear weapons will always be impossibly difficult to make even by the most sober and clear-thinking of leaders. The historical record shows that it is dangerously naïve to believe that national leaders will not resort to the use of nuclear weapons when security is threatened. The psychology described here documents perceptions and reasoning that increase the likelihood of future use and may be difficult to eradicate. And, to our knowledge, no president has been adequately briefed or trained to make knowledgeable trade-offs and wise choices in this most difficult of all decisions.[49] A seasoned commander with nuclear weapons responsibilities described the struggle to prepare his mind "to be able to make the tough decisions," humbled by the recognition that "there are no 'experts' in waging nuclear conflict."[50]

This outlook is pessimistic even before taking into consideration the changing nature of today's digital media environment, which blurs the line between truth and strategic misinformation and disinformation, and which transmits falsehoods at unprecedented speed to a global audience. As we have seen, media such as Twitter also can be used by leaders to communicate, one on one, bypassing advisers, congressional scrutiny, and diplomatic channels. The skillful and malicious destruction of truthfulness in information not only shatters the confidence in facts crucial to decision making, it also weakens the bonds of trust between the president and commanders. As Dougherty points out, "There is no room for deception or make believe within the nuclear commands; their weapons are real."[51]

Conclusion

In this chapter, we have reviewed numerous psychological processes, conscious and nonconscious, active and passive, that help explain how our government and we citizens can allow nuclear war to occur. Essential to this tolerance for mass killing are cognitive and social mechanisms such as psychic numbing, compassion collapse, tribalism, dehumanization of others, blaming of victims, attentional failures, and faulty decision-making processes, all of which work to destroy feelings and understanding that would normally stop us from planning, executing, and tolerating such inhumane acts. What reason is there to believe that we are now in a new age of enlightenment where we will no longer behave in this way? How can we prevent the lethal potential of nuclear weapons from being unleashed because these psychological processes, some of which have guided humans since we left our caves, have inhibited rational decision making?

In a *Wall Street Journal* op-ed written in January 2007, George P. Shultz, William J. Perry, Henry A. Kissinger, and Sam Nunn—respected public servants from both major US political parties—endorsed the goal of a world free of nuclear weapons and encouraged working energetically on a variety of actions needed to achieve that goal.[52] We endorse that sentiment, believing that it is too dangerous to continue on a course that presumes the rationality of national leaders under the most emotionally stressful circumstances possible, including untrustworthy social media and extreme time pressures. Absent the global elimination of nuclear weapons (unlikely for the foreseeable future), perhaps the most practical approach for now is to develop ways to improve the circumstances under which nuclear decision making takes place. The most important first step is to find ways to increase the time available to deliberate and to require the participation of multiple decision makers, all of whom have been carefully trained for the most difficult decision any human beings will have to make.

Notes

1. This quote is taken from the Stanley Center for Peace and Security policy brief "Three Tweets to Midnight," which summarized the proceedings of the conference that led to this chapter.

2. Albert Einstein, "Atomic Education Urged by Einstein," *New York Times*, May 25, 1946.

3. Daniel Kahneman, *Thinking, Fast and Slow* (New York: Farrar, Straus and Giroux, 2011).

4. Richard Rhodes, *The Making of the Atomic Bomb* (New York: Simon and Schuster, 2012); Richard Rhodes, *Dark Sun: The Making of the Hydrogen Bomb* (New York: Simon and Schuster, 1995).

5. Rhodes, *The Making of the Atomic Bomb*.

6. Hans M. Kristensen and Robert S. Norris, "Global Nuclear Weapons Inventories, 1945–2013," *Bulletin of the Atomic Scientists* 69, no. 5 (September 2013): 75–81, https://doi.org/10.1177/0096340213501363.

7. Kahneman, *Thinking, Fast and Slow*.

8. Daniel Västfjäll and Paul Slovic, "The More Who Die, the Less We Care: Psychic Numbing and Genocide," in *Imagining Human Rights*, ed. Susanne Kaul and David Kim (Berlin: De Gruyter, 2015), 55–68.

9. Johanna Wiss, David Andersson, Paul Slovic, Daniel Västfjäll, and Gustav Tinghog, "The Influence of Identifiability and Singularity in Moral Decision Making," *Judgment and Decision Making* 10, no. 5 (January 1, 2015).

10. Daniel Västfjäll, Paul Slovic, Marcus Mayorga, and Ellen Peters, "Compassion Fade: Affect and Charity Are Greatest for a Single Child in Need," *PloS One* 9, no. 6 (2014): e100115.

11. Paul Brodeur, *Outrageous Misconduct: The Asbestos Industry on Trial* (New York: Pantheon Books, 1985).

12. Rhodes, *Dark Sun*, 21.

13. Rhodes. *Dark Sun*, 575–76.

14. Daniel Ellsberg, *The Doomsday Machine: Confessions of a Nuclear War Planner* (London: Bloomsbury Publishing, 2017), 270.

15. Ellsberg, *Doomsday Machine*, 272.

16. Scott D. Sagan, "SIOP-62: The Nuclear War Plan Briefing to President Kennedy," *International Security* 12, no. 1 (Summer 1987): 51.

17. Donald Trump, "Remarks by President Trump to the 72nd Session of the United Nations General Assembly" (New York, September 19, 2017), https://www.whitehouse.gov/briefings-statements/remarks-president-trump-72nd-session-united-nations-general-assembly.

18. Scott D. Sagan and Benjamin A. Valentino, "Revisiting Hiroshima in Iran: What Americans Really Think about Using Nuclear Weapons and Killing Noncombatants," *International Security* 42, no. 1 (Summer 2017): 41–79.

19. Philip M. Boffey, "Social Scientists Believe Leaders Lack a Sense of War's Reality," *New York Times*, September 7, 1982, https://www.nytimes.com/1982/09/07/science/social-scientists-believe-leaders-lack-a-sense-of-war-s-reality.html.

20. John Dower, *War without Mercy: Race and Power in the Pacific War* (New York: Pantheon, 2012).

21. David W. Moore, "Majority Supports Use of Atomic Bomb on Japan in WWII," Gallup, August 5, 2005, https://news.gallup.com/poll/17677/Majority-Supports-Use-Atomic-Bomb-Japan-WWII.aspx.

22. James E. Waller, *Becoming Evil: How Ordinary People Commit Genocide and Mass Killing* (New York: Oxford University Press, 2007); Philip Zimbardo,

The Lucifer Effect: Understanding How Good People Turn Evil (New York: Random House, 2008).

23. Rhodes, *The Making of the Atomic Bomb*; Rhodes, *Dark Sun*; Thomas R. Searle, "'It Made a Lot of Sense to Kill Skilled Workers': The Firebombing of Tokyo in March 1945," *Journal of Military History* 66, no. 1 (2002): 103–33.

24. Curtis E. LeMay and MacKinlay Kantor, *Mission with LeMay: My Story* (Garden City, NY: Doubleday, 1965).

25. "Halsey Home," *Life Magazine* 16, no. 4 (January 24, 1944).

26. Waller, *Becoming Evil*, 212–19.

27. Melvin J. Lerner, *The Belief in a Just World: A Fundamental Delusion* (New York: Plenum Press, 1980).

28. Gabriele Rosenthal, ed., *The Holocaust in Three Generations: Families of Victims and Perpetrators of the Nazi Regime* (Leverkusen, Germany: Barbara Budrich, 2010).

29. Dave Grossman, *On Killing: The Psychological Cost of Learning to Kill in War and Society* (New York: Open Road Media, 2014).

30. John W. Payne, James R. Bettman, and David A. Schkade, "Measuring Constructed Preferences: Towards a Building Code," *Journal of Risk and Uncertainty* 19, no. 1–3 (1999): 243–75; Phil Tetlock and C. B. McGuire, Jr., "Cognitive Perspectives on Foreign Policy," in *Psychology and the Prevention of Nuclear War: A Book of Readings*, ed. Ralph K. White (New York: New York University Press, 1986).

31. Kenneth R. Hammond and Jeryl Mumpower, "Formation of Social Policy: Risks and Safeguards," *Science Communication* 1, no. 2 (1979): 245–58; Robert Jervis, *Perception and Misperception in International Politics* (new edition) (Princeton, NJ: Princeton University Press, 2017).

32. Paul Slovic, "When (In)Action Speaks Louder Than Words: Confronting the Collapse of Humanitarian Values in Foreign Policy Decisions," *University of Illinois Law Review* 2015, no. 1: 8.

33. Abraham H. Maslow, "A Theory of Human Motivation," *Psychological Review* 50, no. 4 (1943): 370–96.

34. Slovic, "When (In)Action Speaks Louder than Words."

35. Office of the Press Secretary, "Remarks by President Obama and President Park of South Korea in a Joint Press Conference," Washington, DC, May 7, 2013, https://obamawhitehouse.archives.gov/the-press-office/2013/05/07/remarks-president-obama-and-president-park-south-korea-joint-press-confe.

36. Rhodes, *The Making of the Atomic Bomb*; Rhodes, *Dark Sun*.

37. Michael J. Mazarr, *Rethinking Risk in National Security: Lessons of the Financial Crisis for Risk Management* (Basingstoke, UK: Palgrave Macmillan, 2016).

38. Ibid., 81.

39. Ibid., 83.

40. Leaf Van Boven and Paul Slovic, "The Psychological Trick Behind Trump's Misleading Terror Statistics," *Politico*, January 28, 2018, http://politi.co/2nhtyvr.

41. Greg Sterling, "Nearly 80 Percent of Social Media Time Now Spent on Mobile Devices," Marketing Land, April 4, 2016, https://marketingland.com /facebook-usage-accounts-1-5-minutes-spent-mobile-171561.

42. Russell E. Dougherty, "The Psychological Climate of Nuclear Command," in *Managing Nuclear Operations* (Washington DC: Brookings Institution Press, 1987), 420, emphasis added.

43. Department of Defense, "ADA290994: Nuclear Weapon Personnel Reliability Program (PRP). Change 1. DODD-5210.42-CHANGE-1," May 25, 1993, https://fas.org/nuke/guide/usa/doctrine/dod/dodd-5210_42.htm.

44. Dar Meshi, Diana I. Tamir, and Hauke R. Heekeren, "The Emerging Neuroscience of Social Media," *Trends in Cognitive Sciences* 19, no. 12 (December 2015): 771–82, https://doi.org/10.1016/j.tics.2015.09.004.

45. Paul Bracken, *The Second Nuclear Age: Strategy, Danger, and the New Power Politics* (New York: Macmillan, 2012).

46. Russell E. Dougherty, "The Psychological Climate of Nuclear Command," in *Managing Nuclear Operations,* eds. Ashton B. Carter, John D. Steinbruner, and Charles A. Zraket, (Washington, DC: Brookings Institution Press, 1987).

47. "Authority to Order the Use of Nuclear Weapons," Pub. L. No. S. Hrg. 115-439, § Foreign Relations (November 14, 2017), https://www.foreign.senate .gov/hearings/authority-to-order-the-use-of-nuclear-weapons-111417.

48. Herbert S. Lin, "A Two-Person Rule for Ordering the Use of Nuclear Weapons, Even for POTUS?" *Lawfare* (blog), November 9, 2016, https://www .lawfareblog.com/two-person-rule-ordering-use-nuclear-weapons-even-potus.

49. Indeed, it has been said that it would be highly undesirable to have the president participate personally in the presidential decisions made in exercises and war games because it might tend to provide the adversary with insights into what he or she might actually do in a crisis. See Dougherty, "The Psychological Climate of Nuclear Command," 421–22.

50. Dougherty, "The Psychological Climate of Nuclear Command."

51. Ibid., 412–13.

52. George P. Shultz, William J. Perry, Henry A. Kissinger, and Sam Nunn, "A World Free of Nuclear Weapons," *Wall Street Journal*, January 4, 2007, https://www.wsj.com/articles/SB116787515251566636.

Chapter 4

Gaming Communication on the Global Stage:

Social Media Disinformation in Crisis Situations

Mark Kumleben and Samuel C. Woolley

In December 2016, then Pakistani defense minister Khawaja Asif tweeted a none-too-subtle threat: "Israeli def min threatens nuclear retaliation presuming pak role in Syria against Daesh. Israel forgets Pakistan is a Nuclear state too."[1] In this tweet, Asif was reacting to a completely fictitious threat allegedly made by Israel's defense minister, published by fake news website AWD News, related to a purported Pakistani role in supporting the Islamic State (also known as Daesh or ISIS). The Israeli Defense Ministry denied the statement, also through Twitter, and the diplomatic issue was settled with nothing worse than embarrassment for Asif. Future such incidents of nuclear misinformation, however, may end with more than bruised egos.

In a geopolitical environment where military action is often taken to advance a strategic narrative rather than to seize physical resources, social media can become a critical source of narrative change and a unique type of open-source intelligence.[2] Strategic narratives are purposeful communications employed to persuade or influence target audiences to undertake action. Targets can include allies and partners and, in conflict situations, adversaries when deployed alongside other forms of power.[3] Computational propaganda, which involves the deliberate and frequently automated manipulation and distribution of misleading information over social media, threatens the integrity of that information space, both compromising leaders' ability to use social media for legitimate purposes and contaminating any intelligence gleaned from these platforms.[4] In a crisis scenario, speed and accuracy of information flow are key to mitigating damage. Generally, this includes the ability of decision makers to communicate with the public and to be aware of large-scale patterns of civilian activity. Currently, social media are an effective and inexpensive way to do this, but computational propaganda may turn these websites from assets into liabilities.

In this chapter we address the ways in which various tools and tactics, from automated bots imitating real people to state-sponsored trolling targeting activists and journalists, are being used to interrupt and confuse information flows during crises.[5] These mechanisms for manipulating political communication, and the cybertroops often behind them, have played a role in major elections and security crises in more than thirty countries to date.[6] In particular, we focus on how digital propaganda affects leaders' perceptions of current events and unpack the role of social media platforms as crucial communication devices in these cases. First we define computational propaganda and political bots and explain the ways in which they are generally leveraged for control and coercion in political communication. Then we discuss the role of social media in crisis communication. Finally we explore two case studies—a false alarm in Hawaii and advertisements targeted at political figures in the United Kingdom—in which computational propaganda and social media have played a role in pivotal crises.

Computational Propaganda, Political Bots, and Crisis Communication

Computational propaganda is a phenomenon unique to political communication in the digital age. It is best defined as the use of automation, algorithms, and big data over social media in attempts to manipulate public opinion.[7] Propaganda, what author Philip Taylor calls "munitions of the mind," is an effort to use psychology to affect human perception and behavior in a conflict.[8] What separates the emergent form of computational propaganda from former iterations is that it is most usually automated and anonymous. Examples include Russian-backed online campaigns to influence elections in France and Germany in 2017 via misinformation and disinformation. Whereas efforts to propagate biased or misleading information prior to widespread use of the internet were dependent upon traditional one-to-many media (television, newspapers, pamphlets, radio, etc.), computational propaganda relies upon social media platforms such as Facebook and Twitter. These sites host content from billions of users, a many-to-many communication model that can be as useful for sowing confusion and misleading information as for promoting democratic conversation. Computational propaganda makes use of ever-increasing computational power and advancements in artificial intelligence to massively amplify certain ideas, people, or institutions while suppressing information on others.[9] In addition to influencing public opinion through social media, computational propaganda manipulates perceptions of public opinion, misleading media outlets and decision makers alike. In the complex ecosystem of social media, this manipulation not only affects public opinion directly—it also distorts opinion formers' and decision makers' understanding of public sentiment.

Political bots are a crucial tool for computational propaganda. These automated computer programs are built to look like real social media users and can communicate with human users in "AstroTurf" (fake grassroots) efforts to spread disinformation, boost interaction, or defame opposition.[10] They use automation to achieve what Woolley has termed "manufacturing consensus" to give the illusion of popularity or dissent over social media in order to create bandwagon support or derision for a politician or political idea.[11] Tens of thousands of political bots and botnets (groups of bots) imitate human users in order to spread political messages on websites such as Twitter and Facebook.[12] Currently, Twitter boasts 335 million users, of which as many as 15 percent are estimated to be bots.[13] Bots can post material much faster than humans can and require comparatively little investment for even the most sophisticated programs. Because social media bot networks are available for hire, even technologically unsophisticated actors can use them. Social media attacks are force multipliers for any attempt to create confusion and disorder, particularly in crisis situations. As social media become increasingly important in surveying public opinion and predicting public reactions to events, computational propaganda becomes a potential complication.

Political bots can be divided into several categories: sockpuppet bots, amplifier bots (which are linked to approval bots), spam bots, troll bots, and sleeper bots.[14]

Sockpuppet bots, also known as cyborgs, are accounts that are part human and part bot.[15] To create such an account, a human will register an account on Twitter and then will set up automated programs to post tweets, intermittently tweeting nonautomated tweets and interacting with friends, resulting in account behavior that mixes both manual and automated operations.[16] These bots are often used to start conversations online that are subsequently spread and legitimized by amplifier and approval bots.

Amplifier bots are fully automated accounts that are employed to spread information by "liking," sharing, retweeting, and republishing content.[17] This activity is often performed in conjunction with approval bots, which like, retweet, and comment on specific posts and profiles to validate their credibility.[18] Both amplifier and approval bots are implemented to manufacture consensus for fringe politicians and false normalcy for extremist ideas.[19]

Spam bots are used to disrupt streams of communication, often through the flooding of hashtags with irrelevant noise in order to redirect trending topics.[20]

Troll bots are deployed to harass and silence specific individuals and groups, such as female journalists and activists.[21] They often overwhelm profiles with threats or spread jeopardizing private information about their targets, among other intimidation tactics.

Sleeper bots are bots that can engage in all of the aforementioned behaviors but are distinguished in that they can lie dormant for long stretches of time. Consequently, if mobilized, thousands of sleeper bot accounts can emerge and spread massive amounts of disinformation at once. These bots are also harder to detect due to the fact that their profiles have established internet histories, making it easier for them to masquerade as authentic accounts.

Computational propaganda has been used by political actors across the world and in many different ways. It has been a major factor in interrupting the normal flow of information and political communications during elections and major events in democratic countries including France, Germany, the United States, and the United Kingdom.[22] In countries including Azerbaijan, Bahrain, Mexico, Russia, Turkey, and Ukraine, government-sanctioned actors have used massive networks of bots to deluge journalists and democratic activists with libel and threats.[23] The Islamic State and other terrorist groups have consistently used social media bots in order to exaggerate their online presence and promote radicalization.[24]

So far, computational propaganda has been particularly noticeable on Twitter. This is in part because of that company's historic openness to automation as well as its policies allowing public developers to deploy their own communication software on the platform. As a platform designed for spreading messages to the public, and one where journalists congregate in efforts to both spread and gather news, it is a natural target for political bots.[25] Furthermore, many politicians use the platform for self-promotion and public information sharing.[26] However, politicians do not control the discussion, even on political issues. Rather, research suggests that "non-elite actors, such as individual bloggers and concerned citizens" produce the majority of the most widely read tweets.[27] Twitter sorts posts on issues based on the tagged words they contain, such as #Syria or #NATOSummit. This is particularly tempting to bots, which can take over a popular hashtag's search results with their coordinated messaging. The Assad regime has made use of bot networks to take over hashtags that had been used to spread information about the Syrian conflict, posting irrelevant content to crowd out real news.[28]

The manipulation of public opinion online using bots and disinformation is not, however, solely relegated to Twitter—though its use there has been more widely studied because the company, unlike its competitors, has a more open policy for sharing data with academic researchers. Facebook, YouTube, WhatsApp, Instagram, Reddit, and a variety of other social media platforms around the globe have facilitated the flow of computational propaganda during major political events.[29] In this chapter, we focus on case studies that involve Twitter because—in these cases—political leaders, news entities, and propagandists used the site in efforts to control information flows during crisis situations. We argue, however, that the cases outlined here are representative of similar occurrences on Facebook, YouTube, and other social media platforms. These cases are meant to be not exhaustive but rather illustrative of a broader trend.

Social Media and Crisis Communication

In a crisis situation, governments must avoid public disorder if they are to properly coordinate a response. In the context of a nuclear attack where limited information is available, public panic would amplify the chaos, causing trillions of dollars in indirect damage.[30] Social media, including Twitter, are considered useful tools for informing and organizing the public in disaster scenarios, though they are far from perfect.[31] Although great numbers of affected people used Twitter during Hurricane Sandy, tweets became less and less informative as the crisis worsened and citizens were in greater need of information.[32] After the 2013 Boston Marathon bombings, Americans took to social media to discuss the hunt for the bombers, but misinformation spread far more quickly than attempts to correct it.[33] Such online rumor mills can result in a compounding cycle of disinformation, where prominent figures repeat or discuss disinformation that is then reported on by media outlets, sowing confusion even in the attempt to provide clarity.[34] Journalists often find information on social media and news articles from traditional media outlets are commonly shared by social media users.

It is hopeless to try to stop citizens from using social media to find information, since it is many people's primary mode of access to news and communication, particularly in situations like natural disasters where phone networks may be jammed.[35] Social media are thus as essential a part of civil defense as any other warning system. In a nuclear context, civil defense is not simply damage mitigation, but also part of credible deterrence.[36] If adversaries know that they will be able to use computational propaganda to sow panic, they may be more willing to act, believing that the leaders of a panic-stricken country will be more vulnerable in high-stakes negotiations.

Different countries have different cultural perceptions of the escalatory nature of cyberattacks and information warfare. Russian cyberwarfare institutions are quite aware of divergences in NATO and Russian approaches to information warfare—where NATO defines information warfare as tactical and limited, Russia sees it as a continuation of peacetime politics by other means.[37] Government communications, information operations, computational propaganda, and cyberattacks all exist on a spectrum of political internet activity. Varying understandings of that spectrum may cause unintended or unexpected escalation—although propaganda attacks will not take us over the brink of open hostilities, they may bring us unnecessarily closer to it. Propaganda itself may not be an act of war, but it can often be seen as a way to "prepare the ground" for direct or indirect action, to make the population in a target country more vulnerable to other forms of power deployed to attempt to persuade the government to change its policies.[38] Furthermore, public disorder may act as an escalatory force in itself, as civilian officeholders will feel pressure to react to foreign propaganda campaigns, particularly when these campaigns are conducted through means which are seen as illegitimate or deceitful.

Case Studies

Social media disinformation affects the flow of information in a crisis situation in two major, symmetric, ways. It attacks the transmission of information from the government to the public and from the public to decision makers. As such, we will present one case study of each type, highlighting how disinformation may interfere with timely and accurate communication.

Hawaii and North Korea: Government-to-Public Communication

On January 13, 2018, the Hawaii Emergency Management Agency sent out a cell phone alert warning residents of a ballistic missile threat heading for the state. In the half hour before an official notification of the false alarm was issued, public figures in Hawaii took to Twitter to inform the public that the warning was sent in error. Although Representative Tulsi Gabbard responded quickly, it took Governor David Ige fifteen minutes to access his Twitter account.[39] The alert was not fully countermanded for thirty-eight minutes. The United States has not prioritized civil defense against nuclear threats since the Cold War, although civil defense could reduce the casualties from a terrorist or rogue state attack.[40] This lack of public awareness means that nuclear false alarms may result in confusion and disorder rather than orderly safety preparations. This provides an opportunity for hostile actors to use information networks to replicate incidents like the Hawaii panic.

Information warfare may be a secondary consideration for targeted governments in many crisis scenarios where other, more direct forms of the use of force—particularly military—are at play, but it retains relevance in any case where decision makers must communicate with the public. Deployed as part of a hybrid cyberattack strategy, including attacks on infrastructure and penetration of government networks, computational propaganda could seriously damage the political will required to maintain standoffs with foreign powers. For instance, North Korean hackers could trigger a similar false alarm to the Hawaii scenario, but follow that up with a deluge of alarmist misinformation to extend the panic and compound the damage from other cyberattacks. According to cybersecurity experts, many American public alert and emergency management systems—even 911 calls—are highly vulnerable to hacking which could either jam these systems or falsely activate them.[41] The public response to such an event would be difficult to predict, but the political fallout could easily affect the decision making of civilian leadership.

Perhaps worse than merely causing alarm, such events undermine existing civil defense preparedness. In 2005, a false alarm was erroneously issued mandating the evacuation of Connecticut. Because the alarm did not seem credible, almost nobody followed its instructions.[42] A disinformation campaign which sought to undermine public confidence in such alerts could reduce preparedness in vulnerable populations. This would be a powerful tool for states seeking asymmetric advantages against a more powerful adversary. US forces in Korea have reportedly received false messages via SMS and Facebook ordering evacuations.[43] This is a seriously worrying sign that North Korea understands the potential of social media to wage information warfare. Although the US military is a comparatively hard target, North Korea could amplify the effect of its limited nuclear capacity by desensitizing civilians (including military families or contractors) to nuclear alerts, issuing false evacuation orders from shelters, or countermanding real warnings. This tactic would be available to most actors—state or non-state—whose strategies would benefit from mass confusion.

Jeremy Corbyn: Public-to-Government Influence

Jeremy Corbyn, the far-left leader of Britain's Labour Party, is unlikely ever to engage in nuclear brinkmanship. In fact, Corbyn has refused to say whether or not he would ever fire nuclear weapons, even in retaliation.[44] However, as part of a tide of antiestablishment politics, Corbyn provides a worrying example of how outsider politicians may be dangerously vulnerable to misinformation.

During the 2017 election campaign, Labour campaign chiefs who disagreed with Corbyn's strategy devised targeted ads to be seen by Corbyn and his close aides, deceiving Corbyn into thinking that the campaign staff were following his instructions.[45] These ads would have contained left-wing messages favored by Corbyn, but which campaign

HQ considered ineffective. Tom Baldwin, a former Labour director of communications, claims that party officials spent around £5,000 on these targeted ads in order to save money for other initiatives. This is a worryingly small cost for the ear of a powerful figure, and it has only come to light because of the peculiar internal circumstances of the Labour Party. We have no idea who else is targeting ads at Corbyn, or at decision makers in other countries who use their own social media accounts rather than delegating them to staff. Advertisements on social media can be displayed to extremely narrow demographic groups and lists of targets, in practice ensuring that they are seen by a single person.[46] TV ads run during *Fox and Friends* have been both explicitly and implicitly targeted at President Trump.[47] But the UK campaign is the first solid evidence we have that social media ads are being targeted to influence decision makers.

Corbyn's supporters in the Labour Party are known for their use of social media, both as a campaign tool and as a means of information gathering. Corbyn follows thousands of journalists, campaigners, and Labour Party members and may see information or arguments posted by any of these people. Corbyn is also seriously distrusted by the military and intelligence services in the United Kingdom and would likely reciprocate that suspicion in turn.[48] If a leader such as Corbyn—with antiestablishment tendencies and easily influenced by social media— were to come to power in a nuclear-armed country, targeted social media misinformation could be a powerful method of influence.

Though Corbyn himself is clearly a pacifist, such a scenario could easily arise in a more dangerous situation. In Pakistan, for instance, Prime Minister Imran Khan's successful campaign made heavy use of social media to encourage voting.[49] These trends will only increase in countries without reliable election infrastructure. As the case of disinformation at the beginning of this chapter shows, Pakistan's former defense minister evidently uses Twitter on his own, without checks on what he may be reading or repeating.[50] If such deception attacks can be carried out by campaign staffers, they would be trivial for a state actor to implement—convincing a foreign leader that he is hearing the real concerns of the people, not the intelligence briefings he mistrusts. When public opinion on dangerous issues is running high, as it often does over questions like Kashmir or the South China Sea, a populist leader could potentially be manipulated by his social media exposure. Online nationalism runs so high in China over territorial disputes that the government has had to censor social media users calling for war with the Philippines, a US ally.[51] While China has extensive control of its social media ecosystem, countries which use US-based social media platforms like Facebook would have great difficulty tamping down warlike popular sentiment, whether from real users or propaganda campaigns. A leader who sees social media as the voice of the people may follow that voice regardless of its true origin.

Conclusion

Social media have become near-ubiquitous tools for spreading information, and their use will only continue to expand in this capacity. Moreover, social media use is increasing in many developing countries, some of which, such as India and Pakistan, are longtime adversaries and offer potential for generating nuclear crises. In future crisis scenarios, governments will need to use social media to supplement traditional alert systems, but as we have seen in this chapter, they may be vulnerable to being attacked through disinformation campaigns or direct cyberwarfare. Decision makers will also use social media more as information-gathering tools, both through open-source intelligence and via their own personal accounts. This creates a vulnerability that cuts two ways: antiestablishment candidates who distrust their intelligence services may be misled by social media disinformation while decision makers with insufficient institutional support (such as Khawaja Asif) may be tricked by fake news.

In short, social media are an ever-growing part of the information environment that underlies decision making. Computational propaganda contaminates that environment, bringing information warfare straight into our pockets. The danger is that computational propaganda interferes with information flow between leaders and civilians—both the transmission of decisions to the public and decision makers' understanding of public sentiment.

Notes

1. Emma Graham-Harrison, "Fake News Story Prompts Pakistan to Issue Nuclear Warning to Israel," *The Guardian*, December 25, 2016, https://www.theguardian.com/world/2016/dec/26/fake-news-story-prompts-pakistan-to-issue-nuclear-warning-to-israel.

2. Karsten Friis and Jens Ringsmose, eds., *Conflict in Cyber Space: Theoretical, Strategic and Legal Perspectives* (New York: Routledge, 2016).

3. Laura Roselle, Alister Miskimmon, and Ben O'Loughlin, "Strategic Narrative: A New Means to Understand Soft Power," *Media, War & Conflict* 7, no. 1 (April 2014): 70–84, https://doi.org/10.1177/1750635213516696.

4. Samuel C. Woolley and Philip N. Howard, "Political Communication, Computational Propaganda, and Autonomous Agents—Introduction," *International Journal of Communication* 10 (2016): 4482–90.

5. Nick Monaco and Carly Nyss, "State-Sponsored Trolling: How Governments Are Deploying Fake News as Part of Broader Harassment Campaigns," Institute for the Future working research papers, February 2018.

6. Samantha Bradshaw and Philip Howard, "Troops, Trolls and Troublemakers: A Global Inventory of Organized Social Media Manipulation," Computational Propaganda Project Working Paper Series (Oxford, UK: Oxford University, June 2017), http://comprop.oii.ox.ac.uk/2017/07/17/troops-trolls-and-trouble-makers-a-global-inventory-of-organized-social-media-manipulation.

7. Woolley and Howard, "Political Communication, Computational Propaganda, and Autonomous Agents—Introduction."

8. Philip M. Taylor, "Munitions of the Mind: A History of Propaganda from the Ancient World to the Present Day" (Manchester, UK: Manchester University Press, 2003).

9. Bradshaw and Howard, "Troops, Trolls and Troublemakers."

10. Samuel C. Woolley and Philip N. Howard, "Computational Propaganda Worldwide: Executive Summary," Working Paper 2017.11, Project on Computational Propaganda, Oxford University, June 2017.

11. Samuel C. Woolley and Douglas Guilbeault, "Computational Propaganda in the United States of America: Manufacturing Consensus Online," Work-

ing Paper 2017.5, Project on Computational Propaganda, Oxford University, June 2017.

12. Emilio Ferrara, Onur Varol, Clayton Davis, Filippo Menczer, and Alessandro Flammini, "The Rise of Social Bots," *Communications of the ACM* 59, no. 7 (July 2016): 96–104, https://doi.org/10.1145/2818717.

13. Alessandro Bessi and Emilio Ferrara, "Social Bots Distort the 2016 U.S. Presidential Election Online Discussion," *First Monday* 21, no. 11 (November 7, 2016), https://doi.org/10.5210/fm.v21i11.7090.

14. Woolley and Howard, "Computational Propaganda Worldwide: Executive Summary."

15. Renee DiResta, John Little, Jonathon Morgan, Lisa-Maria Neudert, and Ben Nimmo, "The Bots That Are Changing Politics," Vice, *Motherboard* (blog), November 2, 2017, https://motherboard.vice.com/en_us/article/mb37k4 /twitter-facebook-google-bots-misinformation-changing-politics.

16. Zi Chu, Steven Gianvecchio, Haining Wang, and Sushil Jajodia, "Detecting Automation of Twitter Accounts: Are You a Human, Bot, or Cyborg?" *IEEE Transactions on Dependable and Secure Computing* 9, no. 6 (November/December 2012): 811–24, https://doi.org/10.1109/TDSC.2012.75.

17. DiResta et al., "The Bots That Are Changing Politics."

18. Ibid.

19. Woolley and Guilbeault, "Computational Propaganda in the United States."

20. Katina Michael, "Bots Trending Now: Disinformation and Calculated Manipulation of the Masses," *IEEE Technology and Society* 36, no. 2 (June 2017): 6–11, https://doi.org/10.1109/MTS.2017.2697067.

21. Andalusia Knoll Soloff, "Mexico's Troll Bots Are Threatening the Lives of Activists," Vice, *Motherboard* (blog), March 9, 2017, https://motherboard .vice.com/en_us/article/mg4b38/mexicos-troll-bots-are-threatening-the -lives-of-activists.

22. Clementine Desiguad, Philip N. Howard, Samantha Bradshaw, Bence Kollanyi, and Gillian Bolsover, "Junk News and Bots during the French Presidential Election: What Are French Voters Sharing over Twitter in Round Two?" Comprop Data Memo 2017.4, May 4, 2017, http://comprop.oii.ox.ac .uk/wp-content/uploads/sites/89/2017/05/What-Are-French-Voters-Sharing -Over-Twitter-Between-the-Two-Rounds-v7.pdf; Douglas Guilbeault and Samuel Woolley, "How Twitter Bots Are Shaping the Election," *The Atlantic*, November 1, 2016, https://www.theatlantic.com/technology/archive/2016/11 /election-bots/506072; Philip N. Howard and Bence Kollanyi, "Bots, #StrongerIn, and #Brexit: Computational Propaganda during the UK-EU Referendum," ArXiv:1606.06356, June 20, 2016, http://arxiv.org/abs/1606.06356; Lisa-Maria Neudert, "Computational Propaganda in Germany: A Cautionary

Tale," Working Paper 2017.7, Project on Computational Propaganda, Oxford University, June 2017.

23. Monaco and Nyss, "State-Sponsored Trolling."

24. Leanna Garfield, "ISIS Has Created Thousands of Political Bots—and Hacktivists Want You to Destroy Them," *Business Insider*, December 14, 2015, http://uk.businessinsider.com/anonymous-battles-isis-political-bots-2015-12.

25. Paul Farhi, "The Twitter Explosion," *American Journalism Review* 31, no. 3 (June 1, 2009): 26–32; Anders Olof Larsson and Moe Hallvard, "Bots or Journalists? News Sharing on Twitter," *Communications: The European Journal of Communication Research* 40, no. 3 (2015): 361–370, https://doi.org/10.1515/commun-2015-0014.

26. Jennifer Golbeck, Justin M. Grimes, and Anthony Rogers, "Twitter Use by the U.S. Congress," *Journal of the American Society for Information Science and Technology* 61, no. 8 (August 2010): 1612–21, https://doi.org/10.1002/asi.21344.

27. Todd P. Newman, "Tracking the Release of IPCC AR5 on Twitter: Users, Comments, and Sources Following the Release of the Working Group I Summary for Policymakers," *Public Understanding of Science* 26, no. 7 (October 1, 2017): 815–25, https://doi.org/10.1177/0963662516628477.

28. Norah Abokhodair, Daisy Yoo, and David W. McDonald, "Dissecting a Social Botnet: Growth, Content and Influence in Twitter," in *Proceedings of the 18th ACM Conference on Computer Supported Cooperative Work & Social Computing*, New York, March 14–18, 2015: 839–851, https://doi.org/10.1145/2675133.2675208.

29. Samuel C. Woolley, "Automating Power: Social Bot Interference in Global Politics," *First Monday* 21, no. 4 (April 4, 2016), http://firstmonday.org/ojs/index.php/fm/article/view/6161.

30. Jonathan Medalia, "Nuclear Terrorism: A Brief Review of Threats and Responses," Congressional Research Service, February 10, 2005, http://www.dtic.mil/docs/citations/ADA437865.

31. Alexander Mills, Rui Chen, JinKyu Lee, and H. Raghav Rao, "Web 2.0 Emergency Applications: How Useful Can Twitter Be for Emergency Response?" *Journal of Information Privacy and Security* 5, no. 3 (July 1, 2009): 3–26, https://doi.org/10.1080/15536548.2009.10855867.

32. Patric R. Spence, Kenneth A. Lachlan, Xialing Lin, and Maria del Greco, "Variability in Twitter Content Across the Stages of a Natural Disaster: Implications for Crisis Communication," *Communication Quarterly* 63, no. 2 (March 15, 2015): 171–86.

33. Kate Starbird, Jim Maddock, Mania Orand, Peg Achterman, and Robert M. Mason, "Rumors, False Flags, and Digital Vigilantes: Misinformation on Twitter after the 2013 Boston Marathon Bombing," Illinois Digital Environment for Access to Learning and Scholarship, March 1, 2014, https://doi.org/10.9776/14308.

34. Woolley and Guilbeault, "Computational Propaganda in the United States."

35. Huiji Gao, Geoffrey Barbier, and Rebecca Goolsby, "Harnessing the Crowdsourcing Power of Social Media for Disaster Relief," *IEEE Intelligent Systems* 26, no. 3 (May/June 2011): 10–14, https://doi.org/10.1109/MIS.2011.52.

36. Todd S. Sechser and Matthew Fuhrmann, *Nuclear Weapons and Coercive Diplomacy* (Cambridge, UK: Cambridge University Press, 2017).

37. Keir Giles, "The Next Phase of Russian Information Warfare," NATO Strategic Communications Centre for Excellence, November 2017, 16.

38. Keir Giles, "Working Paper: Russia's Hybrid Warfare: A Success in Propaganda," Bundesakademie Für Sicherheitspolitik," February 18, 2015, https://www.baks.bund.de/de/aktuelles/working-paper-russias-hybrid-warfare -a-success-in-propaganda.

39. Michael Sheetz, "Hawaii's Governor Knew the Missile Alert Was Fake in Two Minutes—But He Didn't Know His Twitter Password," CNBC, January 23, 2018, https://www.cnbc.com/2018/01/23/hawaii-gov-ige-knew-missile-alert -fake-didnt-know-twitter-password.html.

40. Gordon Sander, "Americans Are Unprepared for a Nuclear Attack," *Politico*, June 11, 2018, https://politi.co/2touIgW.

41. Tim Starks, "Hawaii Missile Alert Highlights Hacking Threat to Emergency Systems," *Politico*, January 16, 2018, http://politi.co/2Dl5ktv.

42. Mark Pazniokas, "Connecticut Evacuation: False Alarm," *Hartford Courant*, February 2, 2005, http://articles.courant.com/2005-02-02/news /0502020861_1_evacuation-order-false-alarm-emergency-alert-system.

43. Kim Gamel, "US Forces Korea Warns of Fake Evacuation Messages," *Stars and Stripes*, September 21, 2017, https://www.stripes.com/news/pacific /us-forces-korea-warns-of-fake-evacuation-messages-1.488792#.WcUkpsZulLO.

44. Jim Pickard and Henry Mance, "Jeremy Corbyn Backs Away from Nuclear Question," *Financial Times*, May 12, 2017, https://www.ft.com/content /d2ca7f4c-36ef-11e7-99bd-13beb0903fa3.

45. Tim Shipman, "Labour HQ Used Facebook Ads to Deceive Jeremy Corbyn during Election Campaign," *The Times*, July 14, 2018, https://www .thetimes.co.uk/article/labour-hq-used-facebook-ads-to-deceive-jeremy-corbyn -during-election-campaign-grlx75c27.

46. Michael Harf, "Sniper Targeting on Facebook: How to Target ONE Specific Person with Super Targeted Ads," *Medium* (blog), December 5, 2017, https://medium.com/@MichaelH_3009/sniper-targeting-on-facebook-how-to -target-one-specific-person-with-super-targeted-ads-515ba6e068f6.

47. Simon Dumenco, "John Oliver Is Running Ads on Cable News to Educate Just One Viewer: Donald Trump," *Ad Age*, February 13, 2017, http://adage.com /article/the-media-guy/john-oliver-running-ads-cable-news-educate-trump /307963.

48. Claire Newell, Hayley Dixon, Luke Heighton, and Harry Yorke, "MI5 Opened File on Jeremy Corbyn amid Concerns over His IRA Links," *The Telegraph*, May 19, 2017, https://www.telegraph.co.uk/news/2017/05/19/exclusive -mi5-opened-file-jeremy-corbyn-amid-concerns-ira-links.

49. Falah Gulzar, "Imran Khan: Social Media's Prime Minister?" *Gulf News*, June 26, 2018, https://gulfnews.com/news/asia/pakistan/imran-khan-social -media-s-prime-minister-1.2242467.

50. Graham-Harrison, "Fake News Story."

51. Kenneth Tan, "Chinese Censors Harmonize Online Posts Calling for War Following South China Sea Ruling," *Shanghaiist* (blog), July 13, 2016, http://shanghaiist.com/2016/07/13/hague_ruling_censored.

Chapter 5

Information Operations and Online Activism within NATO Discourse

Kate Starbird

As social media platforms such as Facebook, Twitter, Reddit, and WhatsApp have been adopted by people all around the world, they have become primary sites for political discourse and political activism. Researchers have noted how these platforms have played varied roles in diverse movements, from the protests and demonstrations of the Arab Spring to Black Lives Matter activism and numerous political campaigns, including those of Barack Obama in 2008 and Donald Trump in 2016.[1]

Social media have also become sites for information operations, political propaganda, and disinformation online. In April 2017, Facebook released a report acknowledging that its platform had been used by foreign governments (Russia) and nonstate actors (Wikileaks) to interfere with the 2016 elections in the United States.[2] Around the same time, researchers in the emerging field of computational propaganda documented the use of algorithmically controlled accounts (bots) and other techniques to spread political messages targeting populations in Brazil, Taiwan, Russia, Ukraine, the United States, and other countries.[3] More recently, it has been announced that the US State Department hired SCL (the parent company to Cambridge Analytica) to leverage social media to counteract terrorist propaganda.[4]

These information operations, which are growing as ubiquitous as the tools they leverage, take diverse forms. One emerging vector for information operations is "organic" online activism—that which can be infiltrated, shaped, and, in some cases, weaponized by "bad actors" with their own political motives. In ongoing research on online information operations and disinformation, researchers in my lab have studied how information operations are integrated into online activist communities within two very different contexts.

In one study, we examined the activities of paid trolls from the Russian government–funded Internet Research Agency (RU-IRA) in St. Petersburg within online discourse about #BlackLivesMatter during 2016.[5] Using a list of RU-IRA accounts provided to the House Intelligence Community by Twitter and cross-referencing those against accounts active in #BlackLivesMatter tweets, we identified RU-IRA trolls on both sides of the highly polarized conversation.[6] On the left, the RU-IRA trolls enacted the personas of pro–Black Lives Matter activists and sent messages in support of the movement. On the right, the RU-IRA trolls enacted conservative and alt-right personas who were highly critical of the movement. Although they diverged in support of Black Lives Matter, they converged in criticism of "mainstream" media and in political messaging that supported the election of Donald Trump—through direct support on the right and through anti–Hillary Clinton messaging on the left.

In a second line of research examining online discourse around the White Helmets humanitarian organization in Syria, we have noted how Russian government–controlled media (RT, Sputnik) and other information operators are integrated into a community of online activists and "independent" journalists supporting the Syrian government and President Assad.[7] In this context, information operations take on multiple forms, including employing paid trolls and dedicated propaganda agents, sharing content across "independent" websites, and seeding and amplifying more "organic" voices that share preferred content.[8] These activities are in many ways blended into authentic online activism.

This chapter offers an in-depth look at these integrated and, in some ways, indistinguishable phenomena—online activism and information operations—within social media (Twitter) conversations about the North Atlantic Treaty Organization during spring 2018. NATO is a military alliance among twenty-nine member states in North America and Europe. Initially formed after World War II to provide collective defense against potential attacks by the Soviet Union, since the end of the Cold War NATO's mission has evolved and its membership has grown, in part through the addition of many former Warsaw Pact (Soviet Union–aligned) countries. Russia therefore sees NATO as a threat to its security and other geopolitical interests. In recent years, tensions between Russia and NATO have increased, punctuated by Russian military aggression in Ukraine and its illegal (in NATO's perspective) annexation of Crimea.[9] Additionally, Russia's efforts to use hybrid warfare techniques that leverage online platforms to manipulate social and political realities in other countries have been documented in multiple contexts (including domestic politics in the United States and the United Kingdom) and are perceived as aggression by NATO and its member states.

During our window of analysis, Russia and NATO were on different sides of conflicts in Ukraine and Syria. Russia was accused of implementing a nerve-agent poisoning attack within a NATO country (the United Kingdom) against one of its former intelligence agents. And US president Trump (who had been a beneficiary of Russia's information operations in the 2016 election) made several public statements seen by many as weakening the NATO alliance. Considering the salience of these acute events, the increasingly contested nature of NATO's standing and role, the now established role of online activity within political discourse, and the rising influence of information operations online, the online conversations around NATO during this time period likely included political messaging, propaganda, and other types of information operations from multiple parties. This chapter provides a detailed description of the structure and dynamics of that specific conversation and contributes broader insight into how specific communities of online accounts (and external websites) work to shape political discourse.

Methods

Online political organizing, information operations, and disinformation are typically multiplatform endeavors that integrate different social media platforms, online websites, private messaging channels, and other resources. In part due to the public availability of tweets, this study focuses specifically on Twitter activity—and then uses that activity to get some sense of the surrounding information space (using links within tweets). We recognize that this provides a limited view of the broader conversation, but it does provide some insight into the structure and dynamics of online political discourse.

For ongoing research, we have been collecting data in real time, using the Twitter streaming API to track specific keyword terms related to breaking news events. The study presented here focuses on tweets that included the term NATO in the text and were sent between February 25, 2018, and June 17, 2018 (a few days after the close of the 2018 NATO summit). We then filtered this dataset to include only English-language tweets, limiting the scope of the investigation to messages written by or for English-speaking audiences. This Spring 2018 NATO Dataset includes 1,353,620 tweets posted from 513,285 distinct accounts.

To understand these data, we used a grounded, interpretative, mixed-method approach, integrating qualitative, quantitative, and visual analyses to examine the data from multiple levels—from "10,000 feet" views to tweet-by-tweet analysis. These analyses include descriptive statistics, network graphs, algorithmic clustering, temporal graphs (appendix A), and content analysis of highly retweeted tweets. We also identified the most influential accounts in terms of retweets (appendix B), the most linked-to web domains (appendix C), and the most frequent terms in account profile descriptions (appendix D) and tweets (appendix E). The raw output of many of these analyses is included in the appendices at the end of this chapter.

Note on Anonymization: Although Twitter data are public, we recognize that some users may not understand that their tweets can be collected, analyzed, and presented as findings in studies like these. For users who might have had an expectation of privacy, we make an effort to anonymize their account names here to protect their identities. This is especially true of citizen activists who could be personally identified by this research in ways that would put them in physical or reputational danger now or in the future. However, we also recognize that it is important to understand *who* some of the pivotal actors are in these networks—to understand how different actors fit into the larger networks and to assess what their underlying intentions might be. We therefore choose not to anonymize accounts associated with organizations (media, government, and nongovernmental organizations, or NGOs) and personal accounts of public individuals, including journalists, political figures, celebrities, and other high-profile media personalities.

The Structure of NATO Discourse on Twitter

Of the 1.3 million tweets we collected, almost three-quarters (73.7 percent) were retweets (where an account simply reposts another account's tweet). Those retweets function to disseminate information, and we can use them to generate a network graph that reveals some of the structure (in terms of common information trajectories) of the NATO conversation. In this graph, nodes are accounts and directional edges are drawn when one account retweets another. These edges appear as thousands of thin lines in figure 5.2. Nodes are sized by the number of retweets that account received (within our data). Edges are sized by the number of times one account retweeted the other. Accounts are then distributed into a layout that pulls together accounts that share edges or have similar edges.[10] For example, the @NATO and @NATOpress accounts are very close together, in part because they retweet each other but also because many of the same accounts retweet both. Finally, we use an

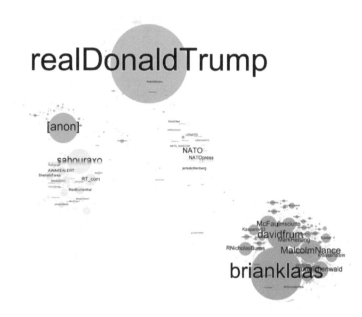

Figure 5.1. Retweet network graph of NATO (spring 2018) tweets (without edges). Source: This graph was created by the author using the Gephi software application. It is based on NATO tweets between February 25 and June 17, 2018. Nodes are accounts.

algorithm to detect "clusters" of accounts with similar edges and then use colors to distinguish between those clusters.[11] Above and following are two views of the graph that demonstrate the structure (figure 5.1, without edges) and dynamics (figure 5.2, with edges) based on retweet patterns. (For visual clarity, the graph in the figures has been trimmed to accounts that shared at least two tweets.)

The retweet network graph contains five distinct clusters. About two-thirds of all accounts in our data are grouped into one of those five clusters. (The remainder have been removed from the graph.) Comparing these clusters across multiple dimensions provides insight into the fragmented and contested nature of NATO-related discourse and some of the broader dynamics of political conversations—as well as political activism and information operations—on Twitter in 2018.

Figure 5.2. Retweet network graph of NATO (spring 2018) tweets (with edges). Source: This graph was created by the author using the Gephi software application. It is based on NATO tweets between February 25 and June 17, 2018. Nodes are accounts. Edges are retweets of one account by another.

Table 5.1 contains some basic statistics that help to describe the relative size and activity of each cluster. The appendices of this chapter include several other comparative views of the data across clusters. In the sections below, we synthesize those analyses to provide an in-depth description of each cluster—including the influential accounts, the communities that take shape around those accounts, and some of the content shared within each cluster.

Blue Cluster: US "mainstream" media and anti-Trump cluster

The Blue Cluster (lower right of the graph) is the largest cluster in terms of both number of accounts and number of tweets. The cluster consists of a core group of influencers surrounded by a large number of accounts that participate in the conversation solely through retweeting. Influential accounts in this cluster (see appendix B) include journalists, political commentators, government representatives and officials, and

Table 5.1 Descriptive Statistics for the Clusters of Accounts Shown in Figures 5.1 and 5.2.

Cluster	No. of Accounts	No. of Tweets	% Retweets	% w/ URL	Tweets per Account
Blue	118,269	427,609	90.0%	12.4%	3.62
Green	72,913	375,457	76.2%	27.8%	5.15
Red	72,216	224,531	82.0%	21.8%	3.11
Yellow	65,803	345,067	78.1%	33.1%	5.24
Pink	21,216	152,365	78.3%	14.1%	7.18

current or former US intelligence professionals. The temporal patterns (see appendix A)—i.e., very low troughs punctuated by very high peaks—underscore the media-driven nature of the NATO conversation within this cluster. In other words, the conversation consists of a large audience reacting to a relatively small set of influential voices.

Interestingly, Blue Cluster influencers include many self-identified conservatives and retired military officers. However, the rank-and-file members of this cluster are largely Democratic in their affiliations. Examining the terms they use in their account profile descriptions (see appendix D) reveals many retweeting accounts that identify with the anti-Trump "resist" movement: 15.3 percent (18,090) of users in this cluster have *resist* or *resistance* in their profiles. Other common profile terms (*liberal, democrat, progressive*) suggest US left-leaning political identities.

We next use the embedded links in the tweet data (where a tweet links to an external article) to identify the most-cited web domains (see appendix C). For tweets in the Blue Cluster, most external URLs link to Western "mainstream" media (e.g., *Washington Post*, CBS, ABC, CNN, Reuters, BBC).

In terms of the content, tweets in this cluster were predominantly critical of Trump's rhetoric and actions toward NATO—viewing them as weakening NATO and America's relationship to traditional (post–World War II) allies, and directly serving the interests of Russia and its leader, Vladimir Putin. The most frequent terms used across all unique tweets (excluding retweets, see appendix E) are *Trump, Putin, Russia, allies*, and *@realDonaldTrump* (in that order). The following tweet is the most retweeted in the Blue Cluster, receiving more than ten thousand retweets:

> @brianklaas (2018-05-31): For decades, Vladimir Putin's main foreign policy goal has been to weaken NATO by driving a wedge between the US & its closest allies. The G-7 summit is a very public display of Trump making Putin's dream come true.[12]

In terms of connection to other clusters, the Blue Cluster is situated most closely to the Yellow Cluster (official NATO accounts). Those two clusters have the most retweet edges between them (of any two clusters): 3.7 percent of retweets from Blue accounts are of Yellow accounts, and 7.8 percent of retweets from Yellow accounts are of Blue accounts (see appendix F), showing relatively significant overlap and information exchange between these two clusters.

Green Cluster: International Left, Anti-NATO Cluster

Green (in the lower left section) is the second-most-active cluster in terms of number of accounts and is quite different from the Blue Cluster with regard to structure and activity as well as political stance. This cluster is international and vocally political. Frequent profile terms (*world, truth, socialist, peace, anti-war, activist*) suggest a left-leaning orientation, but one that is markedly different from the mainstream American Democratic views held by the Blue Cluster.

Influential accounts include media explicitly associated with Russia's government (@RT_com, @SputnikInt), journalists who write for independent or alternative media (@MaxBlumenthal, @VanessaBeeley, @BenjaminNorton), political commentators (@Sahouraxo, @Partisan-Girl, @ShoebridgeC), and a number of highly engaged "information activists." Several of the political commentators (e.g., Sahouraxo) and information activists are at least partially anonymous—with no clear connection to a "real world" individual—making it difficult to assess their true affiliations and motivations.

Reflecting an interesting symmetry to the Blue Cluster in terms of divergent political orientations among the influencers, among the top twenty most-retweeted accounts in this ostensibly left-leaning cluster are @ClarkeMicah (British writer Peter Hitchens, a social conservative and critic of "left-wing" politics) and @NinaByzantina (the wife of Richard Spencer, a leader of the US alt-right movement). This intersection of seemingly far-left and alt-right is apparent within the Red Cluster as well and has been remarked upon as an emerging dynamic related to changing distinctions within and between political ideologies. The seam between the Red and Green clusters—i.e., the accounts that interact with accounts in both clusters—is likely to include targeted information operations from Russia and other foreign actors and is a particularly interesting area for future work.

Examining connections between tweets and external websites highlights how Russian government–funded media are integrated into the Green Cluster. More than a quarter (27.8 percent) of tweets from accounts in the Green Cluster contain a URL link, and the list of most tweeted domains features three websites explicitly affiliated with Russia's government (RT, SputnikNews, and TASS). In total, 14,810 tweets from the Green Cluster link to an article on RT.com. Other highly cited domains include several other websites from the "alternative media ecosystem"[13] that consistently echo the preferred narratives of Russia's media apparatus (e.g., GlobalResearch.ca, ZeroHedge, FortRuss, theDuran, 21stCenturyWire). And two of the prominent journalists (@MaxBlumenthal and @VanessaBeeley) have been repeatedly published on Russia's government-supported media (especially RT).

Considered as a whole, the Green Cluster can be characterized as a heterogeneous assemblage of political agents, government-supported media, "independent" news media, journalists, and online political activists. In many cases, it is difficult to differentiate between authentic grassroots political actors and accounts of political agents who are affiliated with governments (Russia, Syria) and other political organizations (e.g., Hezbollah). For example, the @sahouraxo account, by far the most influential (in terms of retweets) in the Green Cluster, has several markers suggesting a strong likelihood of being a political agent.[14]

In terms of activity, accounts in the Green Cluster are more engaged than other clusters in the NATO conversation, sending significantly more tweets per account. And a much higher percentage of these tweets are "originals" as opposed to retweets. The temporal pattern includes far fewer of the spikes we see in the Blue Cluster but is more sustained over time. When it does peak (for example around March 24, 2018, and April 14, 2018), those peaks are the culmination of several days of activity, although, interestingly, not always related to the same topic.

The content in this cluster is consistently critical of NATO but across a range of different topics, including criticizing past actions by NATO or NATO-affiliated governments in Libya and Yugoslavia/Kosovo and ongoing actions (or inaction) by NATO-affiliated forces in Syria, Yemen, and Afghanistan. For example:

> @sahouraxo (2018-03-20): Seven years ago today, Obama, Hillary and their NATO allies claimed they were invading Libya for "humanitarian" purposes—turning a country that had the highest standard of living in Africa into a war-torn failed state now ruled by slave-selling jihadists. <https://www.rt.com/op-ed/421711-libya-war-gaddafi-intervention/>[15]

> @mfa_russia (2018-03-24): Today is the 19th anniversary of #NATO bombing of #Yugoslavia. NATO targeted infrastructure & civilian areas, used depleted uranium, deployed "double-tap" strikes, returning to bomb targets after rescue & ambulance services had arrived. #WarCrimes #Serbia <image of burning buildings> <map of bombing sites>[16]

> @MaxBlumenthal (2018-04-09): The pattern's clear now: When the Syrian army advances or liberates cities from NATO/GCC backed insurgents, insurgents allege a chemical attack. Sources are invariably insurgent activists, NATO/GCC backed White Helmets, & SAMS. Independent confirmation is impossible. Bombs away![17]

@RT_com (2018-04-14): Lavrov:
- #Skripals poisoned with 3-Quinuclidinyl benzilate ("BZ")
- That's according to Swiss lab that worked with the samples that London handed over to the @OPCW
- Toxin never produced in Russia
- Was in service in the US, UK & other NATO states <https://www.rt.com/news/424149-skripal-poisoning-bz-lavrov/>[18]

Surges in activity (see appendix A) within the Green Cluster occur around each of these events—the anniversaries of the Libya invasion and the bombing in Yugoslavia, a chemical weapon attack in Syria, and the aftermath of the poisoning of former Russian military intelligence officer Sergei Viktorovich Skripal and his daughter. The "collective action" within this cluster leverages anniversaries of past NATO actions as opportunities to increase the visibility of their criticism of the organization. It consistently frames current events in war-torn Syria, Yemen, and Afghanistan through an anti-NATO lens and then amplifies those frames. And in cases like the poisoning of the Skripals, the cluster activates to signal, produce, and spread the preferred narratives of the Russian government (in this case, various denials of Russia's involvement and the suggested culpability, instead, of NATO countries).

The tweet activity in the Green Cluster can be characterized in some ways as "emergent" in the sense that there is no single force coordinating all of the articles and posts. A close look at the timelines reveals that many information cascades (where a tweet goes "viral" and creates a small spike) are "organic"—i.e., crafted and originally tweeted by a sincere activist. However, even those seemingly organic spikes are influenced in various ways—e.g., through intentional amplification by government-funded media and political operatives.

Our analyses (e.g., of the most influential web domains and accounts) show that Russian government–funded media are deeply integrated into this cluster. Although the online activity here is not fully orchestrated, it is cultivated through Russian government information operations in a number of ways—for example, through the production of news articles and the use of paid troll accounts that impersonate activists and generate viral content, consistently supporting the visibility of politically aligned journalists (and shaping those alignments) and purposefully amplifying "organic" content that aligns with their strategic narratives and goals.

In terms of connections to other clusters, the Green Cluster has some similarities to the Pink Cluster in terms of being strongly critical of NATO, a similarity we discuss below. Accounts in the Green Cluster also occasionally retweet accounts in the Yellow Cluster, but additional analysis is needed to fully understand what appear to be diverse dynamics within those intersections.

Red Cluster: Pro-Trump and Alt-Right Cluster

The Red Cluster, at the top and center of the graph, is predominantly a pro-Trump cluster of accounts that come together (in terms of network structure) as they amplify the US president's tweets. The most influential account in this cluster is, by far, @realDonaldTrump. The president's personal account is retweeted 53,090 times for two tweets criticizing Germany and other EU countries for not contributing enough funding to NATO. Other influential accounts in this cluster include members of the Trump administration (@VP, @PressSec, @StateDept), conservative media and political commentators (@FoxNews, @WiredSources, @SharylAttkisson), conservative activists (@VeteransBritain, @charliekirk11), and a prominent online voice of the alt-right (@JackPosobiec). Interestingly, @sahouraxo, a leading account in the Green Cluster and a likely political agent representing a group hostile to US and NATO interests, is also highly retweeted by accounts in the Red Cluster. In total, 750 accounts (mostly within the Red and Green clusters) retweet at least one of @realDonaldTrump's tweets and one of @sahouraxo's tweets, showing an overlap in the active audience (amplifiers) of these two accounts.

The broader audience within this cluster is decisively pro-Trump: 24.47 percent (17,670) of users in this cluster have *MAGA* or *Trump* in their profiles. Other frequent profile terms indicate explicit support of Trump (*trump2020, trumptrain*) and phrases echoing some of his rhetoric (*deplorable, americafirst, draintheswamp, buildthewall*). Beyond Trump-specific keywords, profiles also include identity terms commonly associated with the US conservative brand (*conservative, god, proud, christian, american, military, veteran*), and specific mention of conservative causes such as gun rights (*NRA, 2A*). A total of 831 accounts in this cluster reference the pro-Trump conspiracy theory *qanon* in their profile descriptions.[19]

A significant portion (more than 25 percent) of tweets from this cluster are retweets of Trump's two tweets criticizing NATO countries for not spending enough on defense.

@realDonaldTrump (2018-06-11 01:29): And add to that the fact that the U.S. pays close to the entire cost of NATO—protecting many of these same countries that rip us off on Trade (they pay only a fraction of the cost—and laugh!). The European Union had a $151 Billion Surplus—should pay much more for Military![20]

@realDonaldTrump (2018-06-11 01:42): Germany pays 1% (slowly) of GDP towards NATO, while we pay 4% of a MUCH larger GDP. Does anybody believe that makes sense? We protect Europe (which is good) at great financial loss, and then get unfairly clobbered on Trade. Change is coming!

These tweets constitute the "spike" at the far right of the graph in appendix A (during the NATO summit on June 11). The rest of the activity within the Red Cluster is consistently low volume, with a few much smaller spikes that correspond to White House announcements of Trump's "achievements" regarding diplomacy and trade and media reports supporting his actions. For example, some highly retweeted content credits Trump for pressuring and receiving commitments from NATO countries to increase spending.

The top most-cited domain in this cluster (dailybrian.com) was linked to in a series of spamlike tweets and consistently amplified by a small set of now-suspended accounts. This activity was likely automated—and these accounts therefore bots. We found other evidence of small networks of bots within our dataset (within other clusters as well) but did not determine these to be a dominant aspect of the dynamics we observed. In other words, there are bots—and bots do play a role at certain times, within certain conversations, and in promotion of certain accounts and websites—but bots are only one of many forces at work within this information space.

Other highly tweeted domains include conservative, far-right, and alt-right media outlets. Interestingly, the sixth-most-tweeted domain in the Red Cluster is RT.com (Russia Today), and the top twenty most-tweeted domains also contain two other websites (ZeroHedge and Russia-Insider) that consistently promote pro-Russian stances and narratives. This suggests that media affiliated with the Russian government media apparatus are influential in this pro-Trump, alt-right cluster (although not as influential as they are in the Green Cluster).

Yellow Cluster: NATO and Other Official Accounts Cluster

This cluster comes together around the intentional messaging of official NATO accounts. Influential voices include NATO-affiliated accounts, the accounts of NATO officials, and accounts associated with government officials and military branches within its member states, as well as journalists and news media. The most-highly-tweeted domains include the official NATO website, the US State Department, and the RAND Corporation (which frequently performs research funded by the US government), as well as social media platforms, "mainstream" news media, and websites specifically dedicated to news about defense in the United States. Frequent profile terms across the cluster suggest a largely European audience—including accounts from the United Kingdom and elsewhere in Europe—and converging interests in *politics*, *security*, and *defence*.

The content produced within and amplified across this cluster is consistently supportive of NATO, including messages intended to garner solidarity from citizens in its member states and around the world. Similar to some of the timing of content in the Green Cluster, thematic content is also used to align with anniversaries of salient historical events. For example:

> @NATO (2018-04-04): On this day in 1949, #NATO was founded. Do you remember when your country joined the Alliance? <Embedded video about NATO>[21]

During the early part of our data window (March 2018), tweet activity within this cluster was explicitly critical of Russia for the nerve-agent poisoning attack (inside the United Kingdom) on the Skripals:

> @guyverhofstadt (2018-03-13): We stand shoulder to shoulder with the British people. It must be made clear that an attack against one EU & NATO country is an attack on all of us. <https://www.washington post.com/world/theresa-may-says-highly-likely-russia-is-responsible -for-spys-poisoning/2018/03/12>[22]

Later, during the buildup of attention surrounding the NATO summit in June, a large portion of the content in this cluster leveled criticism at both Putin and Trump for various actions and perceived intentions:

> @ZcohenCNN (2018-06-15): Sec. Mattis: Putin seeks to shatter NATO. He aims to diminish the appeal of the western democratic model and attempts to undermine America's moral authority, his actions are designed not to challenge our arms at this point but to undercut and compromise our belief in our ideals[23]

@<anonymized> (2018-06-01): Anyone thinking that the UK can rely on special favours from Trump needs to look at how he has turned on Canada. (Remind you that Canada is a NATO ally, Commonwealth country and US's neighbour)[24]

Within the network graph, the Yellow Cluster functions as somewhat of a bridging cluster, which results in its central positioning within the graph. Accounts in Yellow are relatively highly retweeted by accounts in the other clusters, indicating that this cluster does perform a shaping role within the larger conversation. Information sharing goes the other direction as well, with accounts in Yellow occasionally retweeting content from the Blue, Red, and Green clusters.

The strongest relationship between any two clusters is between the Yellow and Blue clusters (see appendix F). More than 8 percent of retweets from the Yellow Cluster are of accounts within the Blue Cluster, suggesting that the audiences of these two clusters overlap. Some of the most influential accounts between these two clusters retweet each other as well, which facilitates the spread of information from one cluster to another. Similarly, but to a lesser extent, some of the Yellow Cluster influencers are also retweeted by accounts in the Blue Cluster. These effects demonstrate some synergy and mutual shaping between the official messaging of NATO, the Western mainstream media, and liberal democratic audiences.

Pink Cluster: Pro-Kurd and Anti-Erdoğan Activist Cluster

The Pink Cluster is narrowly focused, politically, on support of the Syrian Kurdish people and criticism of Turkish leader Recep Tayyip Erdoğan and the government of Turkey. It is much smaller than the other clusters but (similar to the Green Cluster) has a group of highly active accounts who tweet dozens and even hundreds of times. Common profile terms reveal a large number of accounts associating with and tweeting in support of Kurds, Kurdistan, and the Kurdish cause. Many profiles include non-English terms (primarily Turkish but other languages as well). The most highly retweeted account, by far, is an anonymous information activist account that tweets specifically for Afrin (also spelled Efrin), a city in northern Syria that was a site of ongoing violent conflict related to the Syrian civil war.[25]

Most of the NATO-related activity from this cluster is concentrated within one short period of time (on March 3, 2018) and is the result of a coordinated tweeting campaign in support of the Kurds in Afrin as that city was being captured by Turkish and Turkish-aligned forces. Those tweets call out Turkey for its military actions against Kurdish fighters and Kurdish people and for supporting the Free Syrian Army—which the Pink Cluster accounts liken to "terrorists" and "jihadis." This criticism is then extended to NATO, of which Turkey is a member state.

> @<anonymized> (2018-03-18 16:15): Shame on you NATO, US, UN, ANTI-ISIS COALITION! You watch silently as Turkey and its jihadis attack YPG, loyal anti-ISIS allies in #Afrin, bomb their towns, loot and destroy their homes and force them to flee in panic #TwitterKurds <link>[26]

> @KurdsCampaign (2018-03-18 19:01): We need to expose what is happening now in Afrin. These are the people who are gaining ground with support from Turkey, NATO, EU, UK, USA. The "moderate headchoppers" of the FSA & ISIS #BreakSilenceOnAfrin <link>[27]

Some of the content from this cluster appeals to NATO and NATO-allied countries to reconsider Turkey's status as a NATO partner.

> 2018-03-23 @<anonymized> Turkey placed 4,000 ISIS militants in Afrin. Turkey is now planning the same plan for manbij and sinjar. The US and the EU should stop Erdogan and Turkey now. Turkey makes ethnic cleansing against Kurds #NATO #USarmy #Syria #Daesh #USNavy @CENTCOM <embedded video of fighters marching through streets>[28]

> 2018-03-31 @<anonymized>: How can US support Turkey just because NATO member? #Erdogan uses excuse #PKK is terrorist to justify killing innocent civilians. Erdogan is terrorist & will continue his quest to

kill all #Kurds unless he's stopped. Silence implies agreement with Turkey's #genocide against Kurds

Other content uses the connection between NATO and Turkey to attack NATO more generally. For example, there are tweets that utilize the "associative property of disinformation" to connect Turkish forces with ISIS "terrorists," Turkey with NATO, and therefore ISIS with NATO:

@<anonymized> (2018-03-18): Congrats to #Nato and your army of #ISIS thugs who the #TurkishArmy led in looting and terrorizing #Afrin ##BreakSilenceOnAfrin <images of fighters holding guns in the air>[29]

A close look at the temporal graphs, timelines, and active accounts within this cluster provides numerous signals of authentic online activism in support of the Syrian Kurds. A few dedicated accounts use @mention campaigns, tagging tweets with the handles of celebrities, journalists, politicians, and other highly followed accounts to encourage them to amplify their messages and advocating for a "Twitter storm" to bring attention to their cause. However, this activism does become entangled with other efforts to inflict political damage on the standing of NATO, as other political actors recognize this situation as an opportunity to score political points. Reflecting this entanglement, there is a small but significant overlap in audience between the Pink and Green clusters, which factors into their proximity within the network graph.

Online Political Activism and Strategic Information Operations

This analysis of Twitter conversations related to NATO during spring 2018 demonstrates how online political discourse is structured—in this case, taking place within a small number of distinct communities, with limited (though interesting) communication between and across those communities. It also demonstrates how this discourse is shaped by mainstream media, alternative media, and grassroots activism, as well as by information operations that seek to leverage all of these. In one section of the network graph representing information trajectories within this conversation, mainstream media (influencers in Blue) and NATO official accounts (influencers in Yellow) function to spread—among liberal American Democrats in Blue and more diverse, international audiences in Yellow—messages of support for NATO against perceived aggression from Russia and Putin and against perceived efforts by Trump to undermine the alliance. For those critical of mainstream media, this confirms (to some extent) a view of mainstream media supporting the military defense–related interests of North American and Western European countries.

In another section of the graph, we can see the Russian government media apparatus integrated into the alternative media ecosystem and the online activism taking shape in both the international left (Green Cluster) and US alt-right (Red Cluster) online communities, using that integration to shape conversations toward its interests. These activities align with findings from previous work. In one study, we uncovered evidence of Russian information operations explicitly microtargeting similar US left-leaning and alt-right activist communities within Black Lives Matter discourse.[30] In another, we examined information operations related to a campaign criticizing and discrediting the White Helmets in Syria as members of the humanitarian response group were explicitly targeted for military attacks by the Syrian government and its allies.[31]

Interestingly, within the Green Cluster in this study, we see configurations of accounts and media very similar to those active in the campaign to discredit the White Helmets. This supports a view of this cluster as representing a more sustained online community that participates in many seemingly distinct political conversations and activist causes. As we saw in this study, the content of this cluster moves across topics but is persistent in its criticism of NATO, the United States, the United Kingdom, and other Western "intervention" in various conflicts around the world, both current and historical. Often, the messages echoing across this cluster attempt to bridge anger from one event to broader criticisms of NATO and the West, drawing from and connecting to longer-standing "anti-war" communities and "anti-imperialism" arguments. Not surprisingly, the messages also converge around Russia's geopolitical interests—e.g., by supporting Russia's intervention in Syria, defending against accusations of Russia's involvement in the poisoning of the Skripals, and dismissing criticism toward Russia and Putin.

In the Pink Cluster, we see an example of what is likely more emergent activism and what may be a current or future target of information operations. The Pink Cluster took its shape here around online activism in support of Kurdish people in Syria. Its content was loudly critical of a specific action by a NATO member state (Turkey targeting Kurdish forces in Afrin, Syria). While some content within the cluster attempted more nuanced criticism that distinguished between NATO and Turkey and sought to push NATO to take action against Turkey, other content attempted to bridge the criticisms of the community to broader criticisms of NATO and its other member states. Although its interactions with the Green Cluster were not significantly different (in terms of volume) from interactions between other clusters, there appear to be some natural affinities between the Green and Pink clusters. It could be valuable to examine the activities within this cluster and its interactions with accounts in the Green Cluster over time, to see if and how the two interact. A significant portion of the Green Cluster initially came together in support of the Palestinian cause before shifting focus to Syria and then moving on to other criticisms of NATO. It is possible that some part of the Pink Cluster could be intentionally brought into the Green Cluster through ongoing efforts (both by activists and information operators) to bridge the two. Future work will be needed to explore the dynamics between these two clusters over time to determine if their interactions do indeed expose intentional information operations designed to infiltrate, shape, and leverage this case of "emergent" online activism.

Conclusion

The analysis above demonstrates the persistent and evolving nature of some information operations whereby loose online communities of activists can be guided to move into new conversations and to focus on new causes. These operations use a variety of tactics, including generating online articles and spreading them across diverse alternative news media, amplifying (republishing articles of) friendly journalists, and employing online trolls who infiltrate communities and enact the part of activists. They also take advantage of authentic activists who at times end up spreading political propaganda, in some cases intentional disinformation. Unfortunately, it can be difficult in these contexts to differentiate between authentic activists and political agents and to disentangle organic activism from information operations.

While this work has focused on the online activities related to the political interests of Russia, NATO, the United States, and, to some extent, Syria, there are other entities at work in this conversation and many different state, nonstate, and even corporate actors in these and in other conversations around the globe. Although the social media companies have begun to make some changes to their platforms to address this phenomenon, we can assume that information operations will continue to be active in political discourse online and that they will continue to evolve as the systems and their users become more savvy.

Notes

This research was supported by the Office of Naval Research (grants N000141712980 and N000141812012) as well as the National Science Foundation (grants 1749815 and 1715078). I also wish to thank the University of Washington Social Media Lab for providing infrastructure support.

1. Philip N. Howard, "How Digital Media Enabled the Protests in Tunisia and Egypt," Reuters, January 29, 2011; Mathieu Jacomy, Tommaso Venturini, Sebastien Heymann, and Mathieu Bastian, "ForceAtlas2, a Continuous Graph Layout Algorithm for Handy Network Visualization Designed for the Gephi

Software," *PloS One* 9, no. 6 (June 10, 2014): e98679; Nikita Carney, "All Lives Matter, But So Does Race: Black Lives Matter and the Evolving Role of Social Media," *Humanity & Society* 40, no. 2 (April 13, 2016): 180–99; Derrick L. Cogburn and Fatima K. Espinoza-Vasquez, "From Networked Nominee to Networked Nation: Examining the Impact of Web 2.0 and Social Media on Political Participation and Civic Engagement in the 2008 Obama Campaign," *Journal of Political Marketing* 10, no. 1–2 (2011): 189–213; Chris Wells, Dhavan V. Shah, Jon C. Pevehouse, JungHwan Yang, Ayellet Pelled, Frederick Boehm, Josephine Lukito, Shreenita Ghosh, and Jessica L. Schmidt, "How Trump Drove Coverage to the Nomination: Hybrid Media Campaigning," *Political Communication* 33, no. 4 (2016): 669–76.

2. Alex Stamos, "An Update on Information Operations on Facebook," Facebook Newsroom, September 6, 2017, https://newsroom.fb.com/news /2017/09/information-operations-update.

3. Samuel C. Woolley and Philip N. Howard, "Computational Propaganda Worldwide: Executive Summary," Working Paper 2017.11, Project on Computational Propaganda, Oxford University, June 2017.

4. Pratheek Rebala, "The State Department Hired Cambridge Analytica's Parent Company to Target Terrorist Propaganda," *Time*, August 21, 2018, https://time.com/5372923/cambridge-analytica-state-department-terrorist -propaganda.

5. Leo Graiden Stewart, Ahmer Arif, and Kate Starbird, "Drawing the Lines of Contention: Networked Frame Contests Within #BlackLivesMatter Discourse," *Proceedings of the ACM on Human-Computer Interaction* 1, CSCW, article no. 96 (November 2017); Leo G. Stewart, Ahmer Arif, and Kate Starbird, "Examining Trolls and Polarization with a Retweet Network," in *Proceedings of the Eleventh ACM International Conference on Web Search and Data Mining*, Workshop on Misinformation and Misbehavior Mining on the Web, 2018; Ahmer Arif, Leo Graiden Stewart, and Kate Starbird, "Acting the Part: Examining Information Operations within #BlackLivesMatter Discourse," *Proceedings of the ACM on Human-Computer Interaction* 2, CSCW, article no. 20 (November 2018).

6. US House of Representatives Permanent Select Committee on Intelligence, Exhibit B, November 2017, https://democrats-intelligence.house .gov/uploadedfiles/exhibit_b.pdf.

7. The White Helmets (formally known as the Syria Civil Defense) are a humanitarian response organization that provides rescue and medical assistance in rebel-held areas of Syria. The official website of the organization is https:// www.whitehelmets.org/en; Tom Wilson, Kaitlyn Zhou, and Kate Starbird, "Assembling Strategic Narratives: Information Operations as Collaborative Work within an Online Community," *Proceedings of the ACM on Human-Computer Interaction* 2, CSCW, article no. 183 (November 2018).

8. Kate Starbird, Ahmer Arif, Tom Wilson, Katherine Van Koevering, Katya Yefimova, and Daniel Scarnecchia, "Ecosystem or Echo-System? Exploring

Content Sharing across Alternative Media Domains," Twelfth International AAAI Conference on Web and Social Media, Stanford, CA, June 25–28, 2018.

9. Andrew Monaghan, "The Ukraine Crisis and NATO-Russia Relations," *NATO Review* 1 (2014).

10. Jacomy et al., "ForceAtlas2."

11. Vincent D. Blondel, Jean-Loup Guillaume, Renaud Lambiotte, and Etienne Lefebvre, "Fast Unfolding of Communities in Large Networks," *Journal of Statistical Mechanics: Theory and Experiment* 2008, no. 10 (October 2008): P10008.

12. This tweet, sent from the account of political scientist Brian Klaas on May 31, 2018, provides political commentary about Putin's anti-NATO goals and how Trump's actions at the G-7 are aligned with Putin's goals.

13. Kate Starbird et al., "Ecosystem or Echo-System?"

14. The account history, highly political tweet patterns, and profile features (images, description) all suggest that this account is being operated as part of a political influence effort. This connection has been investigated by others, including the BBC: Sarah Abdallah, "Syria War: The Online Activists Pushing Conspiracy Theories," BBC News, April 19, 2018, https://www.bbc.com/news /blogs-trending-43745629.

15. This tweet, by an influential account that claims to be a geopolitical analyst from Lebanon, uses the anniversary of the invasion of Libya to catalyze criticism of NATO. It links to an article on RT, one of the flagship media outlets of the Russian government.

16. This tweet, by the official account of the Ministry of Foreign Affairs of Russia, leverages the anniversary of NATO action in Yugoslavia to resurface criticism of NATO. It contains embedded images from that conflict.

17. This tweet, by an American-born journalist who has become a prominent commentator on RT and Sputnik, questions the validity of claims about the use of chemical weapons by government forces in Syria.

18. This tweet, by the official account of RT (Russia Today), attempts to foster doubt about the nature of the poison—and the role of the Russian government—in the poisoning of Sergei and Yulia Skripal. It links to an article on RT.

19. QAnon is a community of online conspiracy theorists who follow an anonymous online personality, Q. Q shares cryptic messages, which the community members translate into their theories, which focus around themes of a nefarious "deep state" working to undermine Donald Trump and an impending redemption for him against claims of conspiracy with Russia. Among their claims was that Robert Mueller was secretly working to expose rampant pedophilia among members of the "deep state" and that there would soon be tribunals to bring those people to justice. See Justin Bank, Liam Stack, and Daniel Victor, "What Is QAnon: Explaining the Internet Conspiracy Theory That Showed Up at a Trump Rally," *New York Times*, August 1, 2018, https://www.nytimes.com/2018/08/01 /us/politics/what-is-qanon.html.

20. This tweet and the one below from the personal account of President Trump, both continuations from a longer string of tweets, frame US financial support to NATO as an arrangement that is unfair to the United States.

21. This tweet, sent from the official account of NATO on the anniversary of its founding, includes a video celebrating its creation and promoting its cause.

22. This tweet, from the account of Guy Verhofstadt (then a member of the European Parliament), expresses solidarity with the British people after the poisoning attack on the Skripals. It links to an article in *Washington Post* that claimed the attack was likely to have been orchestrated by the Russian government.

23. This tweet, sent by CNN reporter Zachary Cohen, contains a quote from then US secretary of defense Jim Mattis, characterizing Putin's anti-NATO strategy.

24. This tweet, which we anonymized because the author is not a highly visible public figure, recounts recent actions and rhetoric by Donald Trump toward Canada and suggests that the United Kingdom should be worried about how Trump may treat it in the future.

25. We have further anonymized this account by listing it as [anon] in the graph and tables.

26. This tweet, which we anonymized because the author is not a highly visible public figure, criticizes NATO and its allies for their inaction in a conflict between Turkey and Kurdish forces in Afrin.

27. This tweet, by an anonymous online activist group that supports the Kurds in Syria, contains criticism of NATO and its allies and a call to action for other online activists to help garner attention regarding the current conflict in Afrin.

28. This tweet and the one below, both anonymized because the authors are not highly visible public figures, criticize the United States and NATO for their inaction in the conflict between Turkey and Kurdish forces in Afrin.

29. This tweet, sent from an activist account we anonymized, opportunistically leverages the narrative about NATO inaction in Afrin as an opportunity to criticize NATO.

30. Arif, Stewart, and Starbird, "Acting the Part."

31. Starbird et al., "Ecosystem or Echo-System?"; Wilson, Zhou, and Starbird, "Assembling Strategic Narratives."

Appendix A: Temporal Patterns (Tweets per Hour) by Cluster

My researchers created graphs of tweets volume over time (tweets per hour) for the accounts in each cluster. The timelines are colored according to cluster. The gray dotted line represents overall tweet volume (all tweets, including tweets from accounts in all clusters and tweets from accounts outside one of the main clusters).

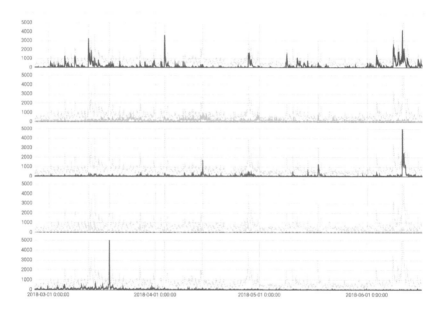

Appendix B: Top Most Retweeted Accounts by Cluster

For each cluster, we identified the accounts that were most retweeted *by* accounts in this cluster. Please note that this does not mean that those accounts are *in* this cluster, as some accounts are highly retweeted by accounts in multiple clusters.

Blue	Green	Red	Yellow	Pink
brianklaas	sahouraxo	realDonaldTrump	NATO	<anonymized>
davidfrum	RT_com	SharylAttkisson	NATOpress	KurdsCampaign
MalcolmNance	AWAKEALERT	VeteransBritain	jensstoltenberg	<anonymized>
kurteichenwald	ShehabiFares	RichardGrenell	USNATO	<anonymized>
McFaul	<anonymized>	AP	NATO_MARCOM	<anonymized>
MarkHertling	<anonymized>	charliekirk11	USAmbNATO	GissiSim
jimsciutto	<anonymized>	VP	StateDept	<anonymized>
RNicholasBurns	MaxBlumenthal	JackPosobiec	guyverhofstadt	<anonymized>
krassenstein	timand2037	<anonymized>	statedeptspox	<anonymized>
MollyJongFast	crimesofbrits	PressSec	BritishArmy	<anonymized>
funder	Partisangirl	WiredSources	AFP	<anonymized>
Kasparov63	VanessaBeeley	sahouraxo	<anonymized>	<anonymized>
mattmfm	ShoebridgeC	<anonymized>	USArmyEurope	<anonymized>
peterbakernyt	SputnikInt	<anonymized>	spectatorindex	<anonymized>
SteveSchmidtSES	BenjaminNorton	<anonymized>	USNavyEurope	<anonymized>
olgaNYC1211	<anonymized>	StateDept	brianklaas	<anonymized>
AmbassadorRice	Russ_Warrior	<anonymized>	GermanyNATO	<anonymized>
counterchekist	ClarkeMicah	<anonymized>	NATO_ACT	<anonymized>
ChrisMurphyCT	<anonymized>	FoxNews	ResoluteSupport	<anonymized>
ZcohenCNN	NinaByzantina	<anonymized>	<anonymized>	<anonymized>

Appendix C: Top Most Tweeted Domains by Cluster

Using URL links embedded in tweets and retweets (and after resolving these to their original location), we identified the most tweeted web domains in the data. Domains are displayed with the most retweeted at the top.

Blue	Green	Red	Yellow	Pink
washingtonpost .com	rt.com	dailybrian.com	nato.int	anfenglishmobile .com
m.spiegel.de	youtube.com	conservativedailypost .com	youtube.com	youtube.com
cbsnews.com	sputniknews.com	breitbart.com	washingtonpost .com	ahvalnews.com
snappytv.com	globalresearch.ca	youtube.com	reuters.com	washingtonpost.com
observer.com	zerohedge.com	washingtonexaminer .com	facebook.com	www.reuters.com
nato.int	theguardian.com	rt.com	rand.org	washingtonexaminer .com
abcnews.go.com	fort-russ.com	foxnews.com	state.gov	ahvalnews2.com
cnn.com	almasdarnews .com	express.co.uk	flickr.com	change.org
reuters.com	independent .co.uk	zerohedge.com	politico.eu	thetimes.co.uk
smartdissent.com	facebook.com	nato.int	foreignpolicy .com	facebook.com
nytimes.com	reuters.com	whitehouse.gov	rferl.org	hawarnews.com
thehill.com	nato.trendolizer .com	reuters.com	economist.com	hellasjournal.com
bbc.co.uk	theduran.com	truepundit.com	stripes.com	theguardian.com
mobile.twitter .com	off-guardian.org	dailycaller.com	defensenews .com	rt.com
youtube.com	haaretz.com	thehill.com	defenseone.com	kurdistan24.net
merriam-webster .com	telesurtv.net	tacticalinvestor.com	defense.gov	thecanary.co
newsweek.com	mirror.co.uk	facts4eu.org	wsj.com	nytimes.com
theguardian.com	21stcenturywire .com	jpost.com	ac.nato.int	bloomberg.com
rawstory.com	tass.com	veteransforbritain.uk	nytimes.com	gatestoneinstitute .org
msnbc.com	atlanticcoulcil.org	russia-insider.com	theguardian.com	wsj.com

Appendix D: Most Frequent Terms in Account Profiles (User Descriptions)

This is a list of the terms that appear most frequently in account profile descriptions. These descriptions are short, user-generated text fields. We ran this analysis on distinct accounts for each cluster, meaning that we counted each account once. In creating this list, we removed common terms (i.e., "stopwords") such as articles, pronouns, conjunctions, and some prepositions.

Blue   resist (8003), love (6513), theresistance (6254), lover (5260), trump (4676), mom (4449), fan (4384), politics (4289), proud (4250), life (4192), fbr (3941), liberal (3901), resistance (3858), writer (3793), retired (3400), wife (3265), world (3098), political (2999), mother (2996), music (2973), own (2926), people (2787), time (2493), democrat (2436), husband (2377), news (2316), what (2279), father (2249), science (2221), progressive (2196), one (2184), good (2055), american (2005), things (1972), former (1970), rights (1934), sports (1912), animal (1910), artist (1888), teacher (1888), human (1838), living (1832), opinions (1817), country (1734), truth (1708), family (1701), social (1654), junkie (1651), 2 (1645), history (1634), follow (1625), here (1610), more (1604), tweets (1592), justice (1587), advocate (1539), activist (1537), views (1534), new (1533), author (1531), twitter (1515), dog (1513), always (1450), dad (1445), veteran (1440), go (1430), live (1429), never (1410), old (1363), member (1347), art (1331), state (1295), only (1278), feminist (1272), right (1262), man (1246), married (1224), animals (1202), blue (1198), enthusiast (1197), books (1186), know (1184), neveragain (1182), america (1181), back (1170), was (1169), lists (1154), believe (1146)

Green   love (2434), world (1778), anti (1725), life (1698), politics (1568), fan (1328), people (1291), truth (1205), music (1120), proud (1072), one (1044), own (1034), political (1033), lover (1025), pro (1014), news (1007), time (990), free (989), writer (962), god (962), social (955), human (896), man (873), endorsement (852), follow (837), peace (830), socialist (805), student (799), tweets (797), activist (764), only (763), live (752), history (747), good (736), justice (736), views (727), more (726), twitter (707), media (703), member (692), rights (677), war (671), here (646), endorsements (633), always (632), never (630), supporter (629), there (627), engineer (622), right (620), father (618), know (614), things (603), freedom (601), when (600), maga (594), new (560), art (552), account (544), pakistan (535), against (532), science (523), family (520), artist (517), journalist (511), real (498), left (496), everything (491), muslim (488), labour (486), trump (482), living (478), born (475), see (472), enthusiast (470), old (464), support (462), party (460), ex (459), hate (457), non (457), business (456), international (450), american (446), too (442), some (440), husband (440), christian (434), believe (429), back (429), country (428), retired (428), think (423), first (423), day (422)

Red   maga (12684), trump (8195), conservative (6733), love (6221), god (4974), proud (3745), christian (3660), country (3428), american (3104), life (3090), nra (3061), 2a (3014), patriot (2969), family (2939), america (2784), supporter (2774), president (2665), pro (2545), that (2361), retired (2155), fan (2090), wife (2043), father (1971), politics (1881), married (1789), husband (1744), military (1669), http (1601), veteran (1575), usa (1572), follow (1566), jesus (1563), mom (1561), kag (1550), lover (1529), great (1476), truth (1454), support (1453), news (1404), mother (1395), people (1385), constitution (1371), one (1355), member (1344), world (1343), freedom (1312), vet (1309), trump2020 (1270), time (1265), own (1228), back (1226), political (1219), free (1191), deplorable (1150), anti (1137), trumptrain (1123), potus (1123), army (1110), israel (1095), lists (1069), americafirst (1067), 1a (1049), right (1031), draintheswamp (1029), business (1014), man (971), first (971), music (969), buildthewall (964), only (959), good (944), loves (942), prolife (930), former (916), brexit (898), born (881), owner (875), views (871), years (864), government (861), go (847), always (838), qanon (831), believe (819), history (792), again (779),

Yellow   own (2812), views (2515), politics (2313), security (1974), news (1900), endorsement (1887), tweets (1800), love (1748), world (1696), fan (1563), international (1538), life (1300), ou (1376), political (1320), proud (1263), policy (1229), former (1193), history (1145), european (1133), writer (1089), endorsements (1086), account (1074), lover (1058), journalist (1048), opinions (1041), director (1037), personal (1020), affairs (1001), music (990), official (969), military (953), student (946), uk (931), editor (901), foreign (897), science (896), people (871), university (863), member (860), father (827), follow (823), social (822), author (819), one (818), pro (816), husband (809), time (801), law (790), europe (789), ex (789), media (779), global (771), fbpe (768), brexit (767), human (760), business (743), retweets (733), research (733), interested (712), things (712), army (705), new (685), more (664), only (653), retired (652), fellow (645), relations (645), public (637), defence (626), good (616), liberal (613), analyst (612), rights (610), citizen (603), here (600), f (597), working (597), british (593), man (574), senior (569), enthusiast (567), american (565), embassy (564), phd (564), family (562), officer (559), national (559), conservative (554), dad (549)

Pink   en (485), love (436), kurdistan (411), politics (371), world (329), human (324), news (323), kurdish (312), pro (297), anti (292), life (285), tweets (277), endorsement (275), rights (274), kurd (245), people (238), political (236), freedom (230), proud (230), journalist (228), history (228), non (216), free (215), student (214), twitter (205), one (205), own (202), views (197), fan (190), activist (187), writer (183), turkey (183), lover (181), music (181), social (174), israel (174), international (172), time (161), man (159), english (157), east (155), endorsements (153), truth (152), university (149), peace (148), conservative (146), science (146), god (145), middle (145), only (143), art (134), media (134), eu (134), good (133), things (132), van (132), ma (128), engineer (126), right (122), member (122), maga (121), rojava (120), live (120), phd (120), interested (118), former (118), support (117), law (115), father (115), new (114), american (114), christian (113), more (112), editor (111), ex (110), im (109), author (109), justice (109), supporter (106), account (105), never (103), islam (101), retweets (101), war (100), personal (100), come (99), syria (99), against (97), greek (97), born (97), democracy (96), anarchist (96), trump (94), business (94), atheist (94)

Appendix E: Most Frequent Terms in (Unique) Tweets by Cluster

This is a list of the terms that appear most frequently in tweets. For this analysis, we excluded retweets and exact copies, meaning that we counted each textual version of a tweet only once (aggregating by cluster). In creating this list, we removed common terms (i.e., "stopwords") such as articles, pronouns, conjunctions, and some prepositions.

Blue   trump (20347), putin (14340), russia (11897), allies (8139), @realdonaldtrump (6183), russian (5054), more (4618), war (4290), president (4017), attack (3839), trade (3594), against (3516), america (3513), military (3505), world (3414), united (3285), europe (3200), one (3052), eu (2945), countries (2911), states (2862), uk (2586), sanctions (2551), country (2249), alliance (2204), only (2146), much (2111), people (2052), foreign (2041), gop (2039), iran (2021), pay (1996), germany (1988), article (1983), time (1952), other (1923), still (1890), usa (1887), ally (1845), korea (1801), nerve (1780), fbi (1780), any (1774), security (1758), potus (1713), canada (1704), over (1683), deal (1677), new (1673), good (1633), think (1597), american (1542), many (1522), nothing (1521), european (1515), same (1485), right (1482), agent (1466), syria (1465), said (1446), state (1423), cia (1411), western (1366), china (1359), weaken (1358), defense (1345),

Green   russia (23909), syria (19177), war (13614), uk (10570), eu (7583), russian (7397), military (7327), israel (7139), usa (6895), turkey (6801), against (6597), trump (6438), world (6194), more (6177), people (5682), iran (4973), countries (4639), libya (4601), attack (4585), one (4516), over (4427), putin (4382), france (4223), only (4203), europe (4152), ukraine (4119), assad (4111), syrian (4101), terrorists (3988), weapons (3936), country (3784), saudi (3695), other (3624), state (3396), news (3364), isis (3349), years (3344), any (3333), allies (3312), @realdonaldtrump (3307), iraq (3275), time (3227), new (3198), west (3154), support (3125), forces (3098), army (3066), western (2986), chemical (2969), china (2775), afghanistan (2746), think (2741), states (2708), terrorist (2694), never (2656), bombing (2596), peace (2549), propaganda (2505), media (2505), international (2464), skripal (2458), germany (2442), must (2403), backed (2365), yemen (2356)

Red   russia (3558), eu (3439), trump (3261), turkey (3112), europe (2101), germany (2019), pay (1965), uk (1894), military (1817), syria (1748), war (1717), realdonaldtrump (1714), more (1675), gdp (1534), trade (1528), allies (1472), iran (1398), russian (1367), european (1331), israel (1323), president (1269), putin (1235), against (1232), defence (1134), countries (1118), much (1106), world (1053), over (1049), only (990), good (983), defense (960), attack (947), time (938), spending (936), pays (924), erdogan (906), protect (884), one (870), need (858), great (831), must (829), new (829), cost (798), chief (791), country (767), people (766), states (764), france (755), alliance (744), america (742), own (734), member (716), news (703), change (693), off (688), makes (684), potus (677), believe (672), ally (661), usa (657), merkel (647), coming (645), towards (643), state (642), years (640), sense (635), many (634), security (624), same (623), weapons (596),

Yellow russia (14766), eu (11011), russian (6376), more (6366), military (6117), trump (5798), turkey (5698), allies (5437), security (5384), war (5023), uk (4984), putin (4976), ukraine (4735), new (4349), europe (4313), syria (4241), against (3966), one (3711), defence (3603), defense (3559), support (3553), alliance (3513), over (3158), world (3085), countries (3076), today (3059), germany (2995), attack (2932), forces (2912), european (2907), general (2821), @jensstoltenberg (2707), #wearenato (2674), secretary (2572), time (2535), only (2534), country (2533), member (2532), president (2526), news (2489), first (2364), states (2313), must (2311), good (2252), people (2248), poland (2240), usa (2214), afghanistan (2208), state (2109), part (2107), @realdonaldtrump (2069), great (2057), peace (2019), meeting (1994), air (1961), very (1957), 2018 (1952), years (1912), cyber (1891), members (1889), iran (1854), read (1839), ally (1833), macedonia (1801)

Pink turkey (20517), afrin (12612), erdogan (7197), syria (5994), turkish (5705), kurds (5565), isis (5469), russia (4193), eu (4159), against (3569), member (3144), ally (3134), army (2997), kurdish (2965), statedept (2957), war (2909), people (2863), world (2849), ypg (2562), civilians (2326), potus (2192), @realdonaldtrump (2103), stop (2089), more (1958), #breaksilenceonafrin (1955), hrw (1850), state (1786), usa (1758), time (1742), @jensstoltenberg (1691), @brett_mcgurk (1682), support (1679), military (1635), @emmanuelmacron (1607), allies (1602), one (1577), only (1568), genocide (1562), terrorist (1538), new (1484), jihadist (1475), nytimes (1470), @centcom (1435), @senjohnmccain (1404), #twitterkurds (1399), terrorists (1391), greece (1352), turks (1342), over (1319), efr (1292), @azadirojava (1291), rojava (1283), whitehouse (1278), killing (1278), city (1277), @washingtonpost (1266), efrin (1254), uk (1251), country (1246), trump (1234), jihadists (1230),

Appendix F: Percentage of Retweets from Retweeter Cluster (rows) to Retweeted Cluster (columns)

Color	Blue	Green	Red	Yellow	Pink
Blue	**0.887902**	0.005026	0.004013	0.037752	0.0018162
Green	0.009202	**0.903791**	0.015211	0.024088	0.0149524
Red	0.010467	0.037217	**0.816407**	0.054987	0.0109995
Yellow	0.077831	0.019858	0.024381	**0.836243**	0.0080863
Pink	0.009564	0.034057	0.012557	0.023755	**0.8829999**

Chapter 6

Of Wars and Rumors of Wars:

Extra-factual Information and (In)Advertent Escalation

Kelly M. Greenhill

> People who understand how crises escalate . . . [know] it is absolutely alarming that the president uses [Twitter] . . . [and that] perhaps we would stumble into a nuclear conflict with North Korea. . . . He's got one finger on Twitter, one finger on the nuclear weapon. I think most Americans walk around in the ignorant but secure belief that somehow there's a considered way to launch a nuclear weapon. And that's not the case. [Trump] has immediate access to this awesome destructive power and he loves to emote reckless bravado, and it makes this scenario that much more likely.
>
> —*Former CIA operative Valerie Plame Wilson on US President Donald J. Trump*, Newsweek, *August 24, 2017*

President Donald Trump's declarations on Twitter that North Korea could face "fire and fury the likes of which the world has never seen" and that "if Iran wants to fight, that will be the official end of Iran" have been widely interpreted as threats backed by the uniquely destructive power of the US nuclear arsenal.[1] But what should one make of these very public and singularly apocalyptic escalatory threats? Are they part of a visionary, if unconventional, bargaining strategy destined to generate unprecedented payoffs, or a dangerous, even potentially catastrophic, folly that could catalyze a costly war or wars neither side really wants?

Trump supporters assert that his inflammatory rhetorical bellicosity is calculated and has the potential to create diplomatic openings and beget more fruitful negotiations with longtime adversaries than those more sober, tempered, and private approaches have been able to achieve.[2] Indeed, the argument goes, Trump may simply be following the precepts of the so-called madman theory, which posits that looking a "little crazy" may be an effective way to induce an adversary to concede or stand down in a crisis.[3] The issuance of dramatic threats may also, it has been suggested, provide clarity about US intentions and red lines, both of which can be hard to discern and easy to misinterpret.[4]

Many nuclear and diplomatic experts are skeptical, however, and far less sanguine about Trump's resort to apocalyptic escalatory rhetoric. They fear that whatever his underlying motives, Trump does not fully appreciate or possibly even understand the dangers inherent in so cavalierly threatening to annihilate other states.[5] When asked about the risks of openly talking about the use of nuclear weapons during the 2016 presidential campaign, for instance, Trump responded: "Then why are we making them? Why do we make them?"[6] This response—as well as the policies subsequently adopted, and rhetoric since brandished, by his administration—suggests to many close observers of international politics that Trump does indeed believe there is, as Plame Wilson put it, "a considered way to launch a nuclear weapon."[7]

Ultimately, whether those threatened believe Trump thinks it is possible to use nuclear weapons in a considered way matters at least as much as whether he actually believes it himself. Even then, however, whether such beliefs would give rise to the desired results is far from a foregone conclusion. The strategy of appearing to be crazy enough to start a war (nuclear or otherwise) in order to get one's way is a risky strategy with a mixed record of success.[8] Indeed, escalatory moves infused with dramatic, arguably unhinged, and hyperbolic bravado may be just as likely to provoke an adversary, generating resistance and catalyzing further escalation rather than concession and compliance.[9] Under such conditions, parties can end up stumbling into costly and even catastrophic conflicts that neither side desired or intended.

This chapter explores how and why these escalation dynamics can emerge. After providing basic background on the concept and variations of escalation, the chapter focuses in particular on the role that unverified and unverifiable information, such as rumors, propaganda, so-called fake news, and other forms of what I collectively call *extra-factual information* (EFI) can play in heightening the risk of conflict escalation. I explore EFI's double-edged influence on rhetorical escalation dynamics and the material effects thereof.

The crux of the argument is as follows: on one hand, public EFI-imbued rhetorical escalation can be a powerful, nonviolent method of simultaneously mobilizing support among audiences at home and signaling resolve to adversaries abroad—the joint consequences of which should be to make unwanted wars *less likely*. On the other hand, however, infusing rhetorical escalation with EFI-laden messages is risky and can backfire, making both inadvertent and accidental escalation *more likely*. This is because, by publicly stoking fear, hostility, and distrust of adversaries, states, and other actors may inadvertently transform previously unresolved adversaries into committed and resolved enemies while at the same time potentially making face-saving de-escalation by both sides more difficult. Furthermore, these selfsame double-edged behaviors concomitantly create conditions whereby even wholly unsubstantiated rumors and other kinds of threatening EFI are more likely to be believed and then acted upon. While these dynamics are not remotely new, the very public and reiterative nature of modern communications arguably magnifies the potential effects of escalation dynamics and their incumbent dilemmas. The issues raised herein are perhaps particularly salient given the unusually volatile dispositional traits of certain world leaders today.

Escalation: A Primer

Following political scientist Forrest Morgan et al., I define escalation as an increase in the intensity or scope of a crisis or conflict that crosses a threshold or thresholds considered significant by one or more of the participants. Such increases in conflict scope and intensity can be intentional, inadvertent, or accidental. As such, escalation is both a strategic bargaining tool to be employed (or deterred) and a potential risk to be managed (and defused).[10]

As its name suggests, intentional escalation refers to situations when a state or actor crosses an escalatory threshold in a conflict or a confrontation more or less deliberately. Intentional escalators knowingly undertake threshold-crossing actions to gain advantage, send a signal, obtain information about an adversary, or avoid defeat.[11]

Inadvertent escalation refers to situations when an actor or state's actions are unintentionally escalatory. This kind of escalation usually occurs when an actor crosses a threshold that matters to an adversary but seems insignificant or invisible to the initiator.[12] This is to say, the initiator may recognize that his behavior is sending a signal, but does not intend—and may not even recognize—that said behavior has crossed what is viewed as a threshold by the other side.[13]

Accidental escalation refers to undesirable consequences of actions or events that were never supposed to happen in the first place, such as bombing unintended targets or inadvertently straying into another state's sovereign territory—be they understood or foreseeable ahead of time or not. Such actions may be real or they may simply be perceived to be real—i.e., actors or states may counterescalate in response to rumors rather than verified facts.

Escalation can take both violent (kinetic) and nonviolent forms. In terms of kinetic manifestations, employing different classes of weaponry or attacking new kinds of targets in the midst of ongoing military operations is referred to as "vertical escalation" while expanding the geographic scope of a conflict is known as "horizontal escalation." The term "political escalation," in contrast, refers to nonmilitary shifts in scope and intensity whereby states or actors adopt more aggressive rhetoric, articulate more expansive war aims, or announce decisions to relax or otherwise shift the prevailing rules of engagement.[14]

Not every increase or expansion of threats or use of force is escalatory, however. Escalation only transpires when at least one of the actors or states perceives there to have been a substantive change as a result of a kinetic or rhetorical shift in scope or intensity. While some actions will appear escalatory to virtually any observer, actions perceived as escalatory by one actor are often not understood to be thus by others.[15] Initial perceptual asymmetries become irrelevant, however, if the party that infers escalatory intent counterescalates, thus initiating a conflict spiral that begets war. Unfortunately, such situations are all too common. The inherently subjective nature of escalation, and particularly the difficulty of accurately inferring the intent of one's adversary, have been enduring challenges for those seeking to control and to manage escalation, whether to prevent it from occurring or to use the threat of it as an instrument of coercion.[16] Indeed, uncertainty has long been understood to be a major cause of war. Uncertainty about relative resolve has frequently led states, and actors within them, to stumble or even sprint into wars that neither side initially wanted.[17]

Signaling Resolve through the Tying of Hands

One method by which states or actors seek to attenuate resolve-related ambiguity is to employ what economist Thomas Schelling called the "tying-hands mechanism."[18] Loosely speaking, the tying of hands refers to situations in which states or actors seek to increase the credibility of their threats and demands by taking actions that would increase their costs of backing down should an adversary counterescalate but which would otherwise entail few or no costs. A common method of hand tying is for an actor or state to "go public" with its threats and demands. Doing so directly engages relevant (foreign and domestic) audiences, raises the salience of the conflict, and, at least in theory, places the personal and national prestige of the implicated actors on the line. It demonstrates a state or actor's political commitment to the issue in dispute and, in turn, reveals meaningful information to its allies as well as its adversaries.[19]

Like escalation more broadly, public hand tying can take multiple forms. It can be physical and kinetic—e.g., mobilizations, deployments, shows of force. It can also be nonphysical and political—e.g., rhetorical threats of punishment, whose primary objective is to probe or erode an adversary's will to fight while also building domestic support for war.

In contemporary twenty-first-century politics, these kinds of publicly conveyed threats are instantaneously transmitted around the globe. They are then further disseminated in print and on television, radio, and the internet. Simultaneously, they are frequently repeated (and retweeted) via social media. Thus, in today's globally interconnected, 24/7 information ecosystem, hand-tying signals in international crises are more than just publicly transmitted; they are in effect "shouted" through worldwide megaphones. How and why this might matter for international conflict-escalation dynamics is explored in the sections that follow.

Extra-factual Information and Rhetorical Escalation

In theory, rhetorically escalatory moves may take the form of sober, tempered, no-nonsense communications designed to signal commitment and, by extension, to deter or compel an adversary.[20] In practice, however, this flavor of rhetorical escalation constitutes the exception rather than the rule. This is because to be effective, escalatory pronouncements have to accomplish multiple disparate objectives simultaneously: they must not only signal credible willingness to fight to the adversary but also build support at home for costly military operations while at the same time convincing the adversary that such support will be forthcoming. This is an ambitious undertaking.

To ask one's population (and one's allies) to bear the financial, human, and psychological costs of war and to contribute muscle, mind, and money to the successful prosecution of the war is no small feat. But, at the same time, it is also "an arena no government can afford to ignore" in the midst of crisis escalation that may well result in a costly war.[21] To generate necessary support to expend blood and treasure, leaders need to mobilize hostility toward the adversary; convince their publics of the justness and necessity of the cause; build material and political support for that cause; and bolster the support of allies.[22] In order to accomplish these tasks, states and actors often invoke mythical representations of real or fictional national figures and material symbols of nationhood to strengthen feelings of national identity and promote patriotism at home. At the same time, they employ similar tactics in order to harden in-group versus out-group attitudes and prejudices to delegitimize, dehumanize, and heighten grievances against an adversary.[23] As former US defense secretary William J. Perry put it: "You don't go to war with people unless you demonize them first."[24]

To activate audience emotions and galvanize support, rhetorical escalation tends to be couched in terms of "us versus them" narratives, characterized by dramatic and emotive flourishes, and frequently peppered—or even larded—with language and information that is not strictly (or at all) factual, but rather "extra-factual." Extra-factual information (EFI) is information that is either unverified or unverifiable at the time of transmission using secure standards of evidence, but which nevertheless can serve as an actionable source of knowledge about the world both for those who believe it to be true and for those who exploit the fact that others believe it to be true. In other words, EFI is composed of a variety of types of claims that transcend widely accepted facts. Common sources include, but are not limited to, rumors, conspiracy theories, myths, propaganda, and so-called fake news.[25]

Like other influence operations, EFI-infused communications are intended to change or to reinforce and bolster the opinions and behavior of their audiences and to help mobilize support for policies that promise to be costly in both financial and human terms and for which fact-based appeals fail to muster sufficient backing. Methods used to affect audience behavior include a wide array of what might be usefully thought of as "cognitive hacking" techniques—i.e., the use of tools designed to manipulate audience perceptions and emotions by exploiting psychological proclivities and vulnerabilities. These include but are not limited to priming, strategic framing, and fear appeals.[26]

Whether meant as bluff or in earnest, such "plussed-up" rhetorical signaling can be efficacious as a straightforward signaling device and as a tool of deliberate, intentional escalation. Under conditions of incomplete information, signaling via hand-tying rhetorical escalation can allow states or actors to update their assessments of each other's levels of resolve and make more informed decisions about whether to concede the stake in question, to back down, or to further escalate, even without firing a shot. Thus, to paraphrase the old saw, a tweet may be mightier than a sword.

These kinds of public actions and the rhetorical embroidery that often accompany them can also backfire, making inadvertent escalation and unwanted war more likely. This is because making public threats carries domestic political consequences for defenders as well as for challengers, both of whom have domestic political audiences who observe how crises play out and evaluate the performance of their leaders.[27] Political scientist Jim Fearon has observed, for instance, that when a state "public declaration creates [political] costs for the opponent as well, the state is risking provocation."[28] Also consider the following observation made in *The Economist* as this book was going to press:

> Neither Mr Trump, nor America's allies, nor Iran wants a big new war in the Middle East. Yet Mr Trump's strategy of applying "maximum pressure" on Iran is making the prospect more likely—because each side, issuing ever-wilder threats, could end up misreading the other's red lines. The president's room for manoeuvre is shrinking. As Iran turns more belligerent, calls for action will grow, not least from his own party. ... [President] Rouhani has suggested that the White House is "mentally handicapped"—after which Mr Trump threatened "obliteration."[29]

Of course, war is not inevitable, and, as *The Economist* went on to note: "When he is not threatening to annihilate the mullahs, Mr Trump is offering to talk without preconditions and to 'make Iran great again.'"[30] Nevertheless, while bringing in the public via rhetorical hand tying can facilitate information transmission that convinces less resolved actors to back down or concede the stakes under dispute, it also has the potential to catalyze significant escalatory effects, especially if EFI comprises a component of the signaling: adding insults and EFI to threats of injury may intensify enemy hostility and suspicions, generate resolve where it did not previously exist, and spur counterescalation.[31] Once provoked, and after personal animus, countercommitment, and national honor and prestige are all activated and engaged, de-escalation in turn can become more difficult, albeit not impossible—and indeed rhetorical de-escalation is easier to actualize than action-based counterparts.[32] Still, as Morgan et al. note, rhetorical brinkmanship is potentially escalatory in a crisis, particularly, but not exclusively, "one with a conventionally inferior adversary who may feel that its nuclear [as well as conventional] capability is vulnerable to a disarming first strike."[33] In the section that follows, I explain why.

Problematic Provocations

Provocations are actions or incidents believed to be relatively insignificant by one actor or state, but which are construed as escalatory by the other and which stimulate resolve to defend and retaliate against perceived transgressions.[34] They may thus be thought of as a very particular kind of inadvertent escalation: not only has a threshold been unintentionally crossed by an initiator but also the defender—now angry, insulted, or agitated by the provocation—decides that he cares about something about which he previously possessed little or no resolve and decides to counterescalate.

Provocations can stem from what are known as dispositional factors, situational factors, or an interaction of both.[35] Dispositional characteristics are internal, individual traits, like personality, temperament, and genetics, that influence a leader's behavior and actions, such that different dispositions can lead to radically different styles of leadership and crisis management. (Presidents Obama and Trump, as has frequently been observed, are in many ways dispositionally polar opposites, for instance.[36]) In contrast, situational factors are external and derive from the environment in which leaders operate. They include anticipated domestic and international reputational and political costs of backing down and anticipated costs and potential benefits of war.[37]

On the individual level, provocation can heighten anger, which, in turn, can raise risk tolerance, intensify impatience, and increase the perceived reputational costs of backing down. Political scientists Glenn Snyder and Paul Diesing, for instance, warned of the dangers of "emotionally provoking an opponent's leadership into rash behavior."[38]

At the state level, provocation may increase resolve by raising the (perceived) public costs of backing down as well as by reducing the political costs of war—either by creating a pretext to escalate or by triggering a "rally 'round the flag" effect.[39] The aggregate and interactive effects of these two sets of factors can be to turn even a previously unresolved adversary into a committed actor ready for war.[40]

On the societal level, the very public (and inflammatory) nature of EFI-infused rhetorical escalation—and its further transmission and broad dissemination—can also anger, insult, and provoke populations who view their country's reputation and honor as impugned.[41] EFI-laden threats and exchanges do not of course make conflict inevitable, nor do they make flip-flopping or backing down impossible—as Trump has demonstrated on numerous occasions—but they are unlikely to be particularly peace-inducing either. As US diplomat and former ambassador to South Korea (as well as Iraq, Poland, and Macedonia) Christopher Hill put it, when engaging with potential adversaries, "avoid the personal invectives" because "they never help. . . . My sense from four years of those talks [with the North Koreans] is that getting personal is not helpful."[42]

Of course, these sorts of crisis dynamics and their potentially deadly consequences are not new or unique to the Twitter era. It is widely understood, for example, that a history of provocations and pre-activated stereotypes of the enemy helped finally push Europe over the brink and into war in 1914, a conflict that destroyed four empires, resulted in the deaths of nearly twenty million people, and was—even in a pre-radio, -TV, and -internet era—chock full of dramatic, emotive, and largely fact-free atrocity propaganda.[43]

Moreover, then as now, elites who engage in EFI-laden rhetorical escalation may also come to believe—or drive those around them to believe—the rumors, conspiracy theories, and other forms of EFI they are peddling, even in cases in which they knew the information was unverified, embroidered, or even false when first introduced, if actors come to believe the worst about the intentions, motives, and characters of those with whom they need to negotiate a stand-down.[44] Thus, even if both sides in a conflict are unresolved at the outset, public provocations that result from inflammatory and insulting EFI-laden escalation could inadvertently "tie the hands" of one's adversary and potentially, but not inevitably, lead to war.[45]

Thus, echoing security dilemma logic—wherein steps that states take to enhance their security leave both sides less secure—we might conceive of analogous and equally problematic "escalation dilemmas."[46] The logic is as follows: states or actors might attempt to increase their security by signaling and testing resolve via rhetorical escalation, with the expectation that adversaries will concede to articulated demands or back down from their own demands, leaving them better off. But if rhetorical escalation instead catalyzes resolve in an adversary that did not previously exist, escalation can make war more, not less, likely, and both sides less secure. As nonproliferation expert Jeffrey Lewis put it at the height of the heated and tense late-2017 war of words between the United States and North Korea:

> I think [Trump administration officials] are bluffing. They are, to borrow a Soviet phrase, just trying to "rattle the pots and pans," hoping to frighten North Korean leader Kim Jong Un and China's Xi Jinping. Of course, they may still get us all killed.[47]

Thankfully, cooler heads prevailed, and war, whether it had been threatened as a madman's bluff or in earnest, was averted. However, eighteen months on and several summits later, North Korea has not given up its nuclear weapons, nor has it agreed to give up its nuclear weapons, nor has it even indicated willingness to surrender a single nuclear warhead or missile. This situation could most certainly change, but as of this writing, while the dangers and potential consequences of escalation in late 2017 appeared very clear and real, the ultimate sagacity and potential payoffs are far more opaque.[48]

Nevertheless, as noted at the outset of this chapter, Trump appears to have drawn different conclusions about the consequences of the 2017 escalatory exercise with North Korea and to have drawn from the same playbook when issuing his analogous May and June 2019 threats of total destruction to Iran.[49] While it is too early to tell how either of these specific cases will ultimately play out, history makes clear that provocation can, but need not, alter actors' and states' incentives and strategic calculations and, in turn, influence crisis dynamics in dangerous ways. What ultimately determines how escalation dynamics play out is explored in the next section.

Cognitive Complications and De-escalation Difficulties

Actors' ultimate ability to successfully navigate escalatory dynamics is largely determined by how well they understand the situations in which they find themselves. A history of hostility, abetted by EFI-infused information campaigns, makes it more likely that a climate of distrust will prevail, further contributing to inaccurate perceptions of crisis dynamics. When individuals grow anxious, as is a normal response to an escalating international crisis that may result in a costly war, they are motivated to seek out information that will either confirm their fears about potential dangers (the default mode) or, in the face of mounting disconfirming evidence, help them change their minds.[50] Higher levels of threat perception increase attention both to the source of the threat and to sources of information about it.[51] However, this information-seeking tendency can backfire when facts are in short supply and the only available information is unverified. While anxiety can motivate fact finding, extreme anxiety stymies individuals' capacities to engage in a rational assessment of the knowledge they have gathered, which in turn can lead to a heightened susceptibility to threatening interpretations of otherwise ambiguous events or data.[52] Moreover, the instinct to seek information tends to be suppressed when anxiety reaches very high levels.[53]

Under such circumstances, individuals are not only potentially more open to persuasion but also less likely to interrogate the logic or plausibility of rumors and other EFI.[54] Moreover, in seeking to alleviate anxiety and risk, they may also be more willing to err on the side of caution and accept the costs of type I (false positive) rather than type II (false negative) errors.[55] (A false positive finding erroneously accepts a claim as true or correct while a false negative erroneously rejects a claim as false or wrong.) Emotions such as distrust and anxiety influence the kinds of evidence that people seek out, remember, or reject. As a result, anxiety and fear can influence how people assess capabilities and dangers and how they respond to perceived threats.

Thus, it is also far more likely that EFI that imputes bad intentions or actions to the adversary in the midst of a crisis will be taken seriously and not questioned. It is similarly more likely that worst-case scenarios will be viewed as plausible. These tendencies could in turn make both inadvertent and accidental escalation much more likely, especially if actors opt to respond and counterescalate before or absent verification of alleged hostile actions. As has been observed regarding North Korea, specifically, Julie Hirschfeld Davis wrote in the *New York Times*:

> Veterans of diplomacy and national security and specialists on North Korea fear that, whatever their intended result, Mr. Trump's increasingly bellicose threats and public insults of the famously thin-skinned Mr. Kim could cause the United States to careen into a nuclear confrontation driven by personal animosity and bravado.
>
> "It does matter, because you don't want to get to a situation where North Korea fundamentally miscalculates that an attack is coming," said Sue Mi Terry, a former intelligence and National Security Council specialist who is now a senior adviser for Korea at Bower Group Asia. "It could lead us to stumble into a war that nobody wants."[56]

Deadly missteps, such as described in the feared scenario above, may be particularly likely if said rumors are also being widely disseminated via social media and other modern communications conduits, which should perhaps engender further concern in light of reportage that both Kim and Trump get a good deal of their information from open-source intelligence (read media outlets and social media).[57]

Furthermore, although the context is radically different, the deadly effects of unverified rumors spread in India via WhatsApp as well as in Rwanda via radio and in Kenya via SMS are sobering in this regard, particularly when actors with access to nuclear codes are not always known for cautious, measured, evidence-based decision making.[58] False claims spread via WhatsApp in India in the summer of 2018 led to mob violence and a spate of killings and lynchings. Fabricated claims of ethnically motivated attacks that were spread via SMS in the lead-up to, and shortly after, the 2008 presidential election in Kenya served first as a trigger (and later as a justification) for violence that caused more than one thousand deaths and the internal displacement of between three hundred thousand and five hundred thousand people. Utterly specious rumors spread via radio in Rwanda in the early 1990s helped catalyze and then rationalize the genocide of between five hundred thousand and eight hundred thousand Rwandan Tutsis and moderate Hutus in the spring of 1994.[59]

Once reputation and honor are perceived to be on the line, whether as a consequence of an EFI-inflected provocation or otherwise, a state's or leader's ability to concede or back down may also be impeded, as such actions could be domestically politically or reputationally costly.[60] An array of historical and some recent experimental evidence, for instance, suggests that publics strongly disapprove of government inaction in the face of provocative actions.[61] (At the same time, however, the evidence on how publics respond when their leaders back down—and what scholars make of this evidence—is decidedly mixed.) So while not determinative, the proposition that EFI can further interfere with de-escalation is intuitively straightforward and comports with conflict-escalation models that take issues of rhetoric, language, and so-called othering of the adversary into account, as well as models that focus on the importance of misperceptions and other psychological mechanisms.[62]

Consistent with the discussion of "us versus them" and in-group versus out-group dynamics above, conflict researcher Friedrich Glasl, for instance, argues that once escalation is under way, "stereotypes, clichés, image campaigns and rumors are all employed. . . . The opponent is to be annihilated in his identity by means of all kinds of allegations [and] the like . . . [through] public and direct personal attacks."[63] Moreover, as conflicts escalate, EFI-infused stereotypes and images of the adversary developed before escalation tend to become more manifest, especially among those who are receptive to the EFI on offer.[64] For instance, reported behaviors that, before activation, might have been viewed as neutral are construed as suspect, dangerous, or hostile, while rumors that previously would have been treated as unverified information until or unless corroborated and verified are assumed to be true.

In general, stereotypes are defined both by their substantive content and by the out-group to which they are attached. While "us versus them" is a nearly universal feature of violent conflict, the relevant out-groups and the stereotypes assigned to them will be context-specific and influenced by the particular worldviews and threat perceptions of individual audience members.[65] In the case of North Korea, for instance, Americans are often "depicted as sadistic, war-mongering barbarians," while in the United States, North Koreans are stereotyped as "a monolithic, brainwashed population in thrall to a demagogic madman."[66]

A further and potentially dangerous consequence of "chumming the waters" with EFI in the midst of crisis escalation is the creation of an environment of heightened anxiety, distrust, and fear, in which additional (even rather dubious) EFI about one's adversary is more likely to be treated as fact, making de-escalation more difficult and politically costly. Paradoxically, by attempting to signal resolve and reduce the likelihood of conflict by painting an adversary in the worst light and similarly interpreting his behaviors—whether instrumentally or earnestly—actors may create self-fulfilling prophecies and heighten the probability of war.[67] It bears recalling, for instance, that it was an array of EFI-laden arguments—founded on rumors about nuclear programs, conspiracy theories about cooperation with al-Qaeda, and lies about responsibility for 9/11—coupled with stereotypes of an "irrational, illogical and unpredictable" "undeterrable enemy" that helped justify the ill-fated invasion of Iraq.[68] This war at the time of its launch was even cast as a preemptive war, suggesting the Bush administration viewed itself as on a much higher rung on the escalation ladder than many outside observers understood to be the case.

Conclusion

It has been hypothesized that shifts in the global information ecosystem—and particularly the advent of social media—have changed international conflict dynamics. In theory, the transparency (due to enhanced capabilities to "fact check" in real time, for instance) and reach of the internet and other technological advances in communications *could* permit radical reductions in the kind of uncertainty that have led states and actors to start unwanted wars. However, as Kurizaki notes, citing the observations of Louis XIV centuries ago (still true today), "Public diplomacy feeds bargainers with incentives for manipulative political 'posturing': 'Open negotiations . . . incline negotiators to consider their own prestige and to maintain the dignity . . . with undue obstinacy and prevent them from giving way to the frequently superior arguments of the occasion.'"[69] Thus, crisis bargaining on the world stage may not always be the peace-inducing phenomenon it is theorized to be. This is especially the case when the rhetorical escalation techniques employed by the states and actors involved rely on derogatory, provocative, and inflammatory EFI directed toward the adversary. Thus, while public rhetorical escalation can have salutary, peace-inducing effects and lead to the successful settlement of crises short of war, it can just as likely have destabilizing, escalatory effects, especially in the hands of actors inclined to provoke, insult, and dehumanize their adversaries abroad to gain support at home, whether willfully or simply cavalierly ignorant of the dangers of inadvertent and accidental escalation.

In sum, EFI-infused rhetorical escalation is a double-edged sword. It can be enormously effective at mobilizing domestic audiences (and at signaling active and latent resolve to potential adversaries). But it does so at the risk of antagonizing, insulting, and generating newfound resolve by said adversaries (and their publics) as well as generating blowback within one's own society, thereby heightening the risk of creating self-fulfilling prophecies.[70] This may be especially, albeit far from uniquely, true in today's global information ecosystem. While these propositions are firmly grounded in existing literature and supported by my earlier research, further theorizing and fine-grained case-study research is necessary to more finally hone and then test the propositions outlined herein.

Notes

1. Peter Baker and Choe Sang-Hun, "Trump Threatens 'Fire and Fury' Against North Korea if It Endangers U.S.," *New York Times*, August 8, 2017; Donald Trump, "If Iran wants to fight, that will be the official end of Iran. Never threaten the United States again!" Twitter, May 19, 2019, 1:25 p.m., https://twitter.com/realdonaldtrump/status/1130207891049332737.

2. See, e.g., Tom O'Connor, "Donald Trump Needs 'Similar' North Korean Diplomacy with Iran, Says Expert Praised by the President," *Newsweek*, July 1, 2019, https://www.newsweek.com/us-korea-north-iran-trump-1446935; Fred Fleitz, "Trump Knows His Iran Strategy Is Working. Now the Ball Is in Tehran's Court," *FoxNews*, June 25, 2019, https://www.foxnews.com/opinion/fred-fleitz-trump-iran-drone-jcpoa-middle-east.

3. Herman Kahn, *Thinking about the Unthinkable* (New York: Horizon Press, 1962). To be clear, Kahn did not advocate the use of the madman strategy, he just noted that it was important to recognize that it might be employed by others. Trump himself has suggested, at least after the fact, that this was his plan all along when dealing with North Korea. See, e.g., James Hohmann, "Trump Suggests

His Embrace of the 'Madman Theory' Brought North Korea to the Table," *Washington Post*, February 26, 2019, https://www.washingtonpost.com/news/powerpost/paloma/daily-202/2019/02/26/daily-202-trump-suggests-his-embrace-of-the-madman-theory-brought-north-korea-to-the-table/5c7422741b326b71858c6c33/?utm_term=.599d2b416b07.

4. See, e.g., Alex Ward, "Trump Vows to Bring About 'the Official End of Iran' If It Threatens the US Again," *Vox*, May 20, 2019, https://www.vox.com/2019/5/20/18632247/trump-iran-end-threat-twitter-north-korea.

5. See, e.g., interviews conducted with (nuclear) policy expert in Greg Sargent, "Could Trump Help Unleash Nuclear Catastrophe with a Single Tweet?" *Washington Post*, December 26, 2016, https://www.washingtonpost.com/blogs/plum-line/wp/2016/12/26/could-trump-help-unleash-nuclear-catastrophe-with-a-single-tweet/?utm_term=.7227ca8857b7.

6. Quoted in Anthony Zurcher, "Donald Trump's Nuclear Fixation—From the 1980s to Now," BBC News, August 10, 2017, https://www.bbc.com/news/world-us-canada-40879868.

7. On the question of Trump's understanding of nuclear weapons, see, e.g., Zach Beauchamp, "Donald Trump's Very Confusing Thoughts on Nuclear Weapons, Explained," *Vox*, January 18, 2017, https://www.vox.com/world/2017/1/18/14310168/trump-nuclear-policy-inauguration-explained; and on the question of how and for what nuclear weapons may be used (and how significantly the Trump administration has departed from the last four Republican and Democratic administrations), see, e.g., Lynn Rusten, "The Trump Administration's 'Wrong Track' Nuclear Policies," *Arms Control Today*, March 2018, https://www.armscontrol.org/act/2018-03/features/trump-administrations-wrong-track-nuclear-policies.

8. For instance, in 1969, in the midst of negotiations with North Vietnam, then US president Richard Nixon sent a squadron of nuclear-armed B-52s toward Moscow and initiated a global nuclear readiness alert in an attempt to appear sufficiently unhinged that the Soviets would pressure North Vietnam to cave to Washington's demands. "I want the North Vietnamese to believe I've reached the point where I might do anything to stop the war," Nixon reportedly told chief of staff H. R. Haldeman. Did Nixon's ploy work? The answer depends on how one defines success. As Jonathan Stevenson recently put it, "The Soviet Union was taken aback, but then again the American role in the war lasted three and a half more years." Quoted in Jonathan Stevenson, "The Madness Behind Trump's 'Madman' Strategy," *New York Times*, October 26, 2017, https://www.nytimes.com/2017/10/26/opinion/the-madness-behind-trumps-madman-strategy.html.

9. Consider, for instance, the Iranian regime's public response to Trump's threats to destroy Iran: Foreign Minister Javad Zarif wrote on Twitter "@realdonaldTrump hopes to achieve what Alexander, Genghis & other aggressors failed to do. Iranians have stood tall for millennia while aggres-

sors all gone. EconomicTerrorism & genocidal taunts won't 'end Iran'. . . NeverThreatenAnIranian. Try respect–it works!" Later that same day, President Hassan Rouhani added that, while he favored talks and diplomacy, they would be impossible in the current environment: "Today's situation is not suitable for talks and our choice is resistance only." Quoted in Patrick Wintour, "Iran Hits Back at Trump for Tweeting 'Genocidal Taunts,'" *The Guardian*, May 20, 2019, https://www.theguardian.com/world/2019/may/20/iran-trump-tweet-genocidal-taunts.

10. Forrest E. Morgan, Karl P. Mueller, Evan S. Medeiros, Kevin L. Pollpeter, and Roger Cliff, *Dangerous Thresholds: Managing Escalation in the Twenty-First Century* (Santa Monica, CA: RAND Corporation, 2008).

11. Ibid., chapter 2; see Robert J. Art and Kelly M. Greenhill, "Coercion: An Analytical Overview," in *Coercion: The Power to Hurt in International Politics*, ed. Kelly M. Greenhill and Peter Krause (New York: Oxford University Press, 2018), 11–12, for a discussion of why challengers may choose to deliberately escalate crises.

12. See, e.g., Barry R. Posen, *Inadvertent Escalation: Conventional War and Nuclear Risk* (Ithaca, NY: Cornell University Press, 1991).

13. For instance, in the midst of heightened tensions between NATO and the Russian Federation, actions taken to shore up NATO's deterrent posture in Eastern Europe could be inadvertently interpreted by Moscow as the start of a military offensive, which then triggers counterescalation by Russia. For additional information and other examples, see, e.g., "Three Escalation Scenarios," in Ulrich Kuhn, *Preventing Escalation in the Baltics*, Carnegie Endowment for International Peace, March 2018, https://carnegieendowment.org/2018/03/28/three-escalation-scenarios-pub-75882.

14. Morgan et al., *Dangerous Thresholds*, chapter 2.

15. Michael Brecher, "Crisis Escalation: Model and Findings," *International Political Science Review* 17 (2) (1996): 215–30.

16. Ibid.; Art and Greenhill, "Coercion."

17. On uncertainty as a cause of war, see, e.g., Geoffrey Blainey, *The Causes of War*, 3rd ed. (New York: Free Press, 1988). On uncertainty about resolve—which is to say, the willingness of an actor to bear costs (Art and Greenhill, "Coercion," 10)—as a cause of war, see, e.g., Robert Powell, *In the Shadow of Power: States and Strategies in International Politics* (Princeton, NJ: Princeton University Press, 1999); Robert Powell, "War as a Commitment Problem," *International Organization* 60, no. 1 (January 2006): 169–203.

18. Thomas C. Schelling, *Arms and Influence* (New Haven, CT: Yale University Press, 1966).

19. See, e.g., James D. Fearon, "Signaling Foreign Policy Interests, Tying Hands versus Sinking Costs," *Journal of Conflict Resolution* 41, no. 1 (1997): 68–90; Bahar Levenotoğlu and Ahmer Tarar, "Prenegotiation Public Commitment in Domestic and International Bargaining," *American Political Science Review* 99,

no. 3 (August 2005): 419–33; Shuhei Kurizaki, "Efficient Secrecy: Public versus Private Threats in Crisis Diplomacy," *American Political Science Review* 101, no. 3 (August 2007): 543–58; see also Paul G. Lauren, "Coercive Diplomacy and Ultimata: Theory and Practice in History," in *The Limits of Coercive Diplomacy*, 2nd ed., eds. Alexander L. George and William E. Simons (Boulder, CO: Westview Press, 1994); James D. Fearon, "Rationalist Explanations for War," *International Organization* 49, no. 3 (Summer 1995): 379–415.

20. See, e.g., Art and Greenhill, "Coercion."

21. Ben D. Mor, "Public Diplomacy in Grand Strategy," *Foreign Policy Analysis* 2, no. 2 (April 2006): 157; see also Kelly M. Greenhill, "Public Mobilization and Opinion Management," in *Oxford Handbook of Grand Strategy*, ed. Ronald Krebs and Thierry Balzacq (Oxford: Oxford University Press, forthcoming).

22. David Welch, *Propaganda, Power and Persuasion: From World War I to Wikileaks* (London: I. B. Tauris, 2013); Kelly M. Greenhill, *Fear and Present Danger: Extra-factual Sources of Threat Conception and Proliferation* (forthcoming).

23. Welch, *Propaganda, Power and Persuasion*.

24. Quoted in Cynthia Schneider, "The Sound of Music in Pyongyang," Brookings Institution, February 28, 2008, https://www.brookings.edu/opinions/the-sound-of-music-in-pyongyang.

25. Greenhill, *Fear and Present Danger*; Kelly M. Greenhill and Ben Oppenheim, "Rumor Has It: The Adoption of Unverified Information in Conflict Zones," *International Studies Quarterly* 61, no. 3 (2017).

26. See, e.g., Kelly M. Greenhill, "Scary Stories: Threat Narratives, Extra-factual Information and Foreign Policy," *Swedish Institute for International Affairs* (May 2014); Kelly M. Greenhill, "How Trump Manipulates the Migration Debate: The Use and Abuse of Extra-factual Information," *Foreign Affairs* (July 5, 2018), https://www.foreignaffairs.com/articles/united-states/2018-07-05/how-trump-manipulates-migration-debate; Greenhill, *Fear and Present Danger*.

27. Kurizaki, "Efficient Secrecy."

28. James Dana Fearon, "Threats to Use Force: Costly Signals and Bargaining in International Costs" (PhD thesis, UC–Berkeley, 1992), 173.

29. "As America and Iran Inch Closer to War, New Talks Are Needed," *The Economist*, June 29, 2019, https://www.economist.com/leaders/2019/06/29/as-america-and-iran-inch-closer-to-war-new-talks-are-needed.

30. Ibid.

31. See also Todd Hall, "On Provocation: Outrage, International Relations, and the Franco-Prussian War," *Security Studies* 26, no. 1 (2017): 1–29.

32. See, e.g., Kurizaki, "Efficient Secrecy"; and the excellent Joshua D. Kertzer, *Resolve in International Politics* (Princeton, NJ: Princeton University Press, 2016). Trump's de-escalation of the crisis with North Korea in early 2018 is a case in point of how de-escalation is of course possible.

33. Morgan et al., *Dangerous Thresholds*, 105.

34. Kertzer, *Resolve in International Politics*; Joshua D. Kertzer, "Resolve, Time, and Risk," *International Organization* 71, Supplement S1 (2017): S109–36.

35   Ibid.; also see Hall, "On Provocation."

36. See, e.g., Mark Murray, "Analysis: Contrast Between Obama and Trump Is 'Unprecedented,'" NBC News, January 19, 2017, https://www.nbcnews .com/storyline/inauguration-2017/analysis-contrast-between-obama-trump -unprecedented-n708456; Dan McAdams, "The Mind of Donald Trump," *The Atlantic*, June 2016, https://www.theatlantic.com/magazine/archive/2016/06 /the-mind-of-donald-trump/480771.

37. Hyun-Binn Cho, "Provocation, Crisis Escalation, and Inadvertent War" (paper presented at Harvard International Security Conference, Cambridge, MA, October 14–15, 2017, 3 and passim).

38. Glenn H. Snyder and Paul Diesing, *Conflict among Nations: Bargaining, Decision Making, and System Structure in International Crises* (Princeton, NJ: Princeton University Press, 1978), 235.

39. See, e.g., John Mueller, *War, Presidents and Public Opinion* (New York: Wiley, 1973).

40. Fearon, "Signaling Foreign Policy Interests"; Kurizaki, "Efficient Secrecy"; Hall, "On Provocation."

41. See, e.g., Barry O'Neill, *Honor, Symbols, and War* (Ann Arbor, MI: Michigan University Press, 1999).

42. Quoted in Julie Hirschfeld Davis, "Is Trump All Talk on North Korea? Uncertainty Sends a Shiver," *New York Times*, September 24, 2017.

43. Welch, *Propaganda, Power and Persuasion*.

44. See, e.g., Jack Snyder, *Myths of Empire: Domestic Politics and International Ambition* (Ithaca, NY: Cornell University Press, 1993); Greenhill, "How Trump Manipulates the Migration Debate"; Greenhill, *Fear and Present Danger*; and Jeffrey Lewis, chapter 8 in this volume.

45. Alexander L. George, ed., *Avoiding War: Problems of Crisis Management* (Boulder, CO: Westview Press, 1991).

46. The term "security dilemma" refers to a situation in which actions by a state that are intended to heighten its security, such as increasing its military strength, committing to use weapons, or founding alliances, can lead other states to respond in kind, producing increased tensions that create conflict, even when no party actually desires it. See, e.g., Robert Jervis, "Cooperation under the Security Dilemma," *World Politics* 30, no. 2 (January 1978): 167–74.

47. Quoted in Daniel W. Drezner, "This North Korea Business Will Get Out of Control," *Washington Post*, January 3, 2018.

48. See, e.g., Kori Schake, "What Total Destruction of North Korea Means," *The Atlantic*, September 19, 2017, https://www.theatlantic.com/international /archive/2017/09/north-korea-trump-united-nations-kim-jong-un-nuclear -missile/540345.

49. See Hohmann, "Trump Suggests."

50. David P. Redlawsk, Andrew J. W. Civettini, and Karen M. Emmerson, "The Affective Tipping Point: Do Motivated Reasoners Even 'Get It'?" *Political Psychology* 31, no. 4 (August 2010): 583–93; Stephan Lewandowsky, Ullrich K. H. Ecker, Colleen M. Seifert, Norbert Schwarz, and John Cook, "Misinformation and Its Correction: Continued Influence and Successful Debiasing," *Psychological Science in the Public Interest* 13, no. 3 (2012): 106–31.

51. See, e.g., George E. Marcus, Michael MacKuen, and W. Russell Neuman, *Affective Intelligence and Political Judgment* (Chicago: University of Chicago Press, 2000).

52. Prashant Bordia and Nicholas DiFonzo, "Psychological Motivations in Rumor Spread," in *Rumor Mills: The Social Impact of Rumor and Legend*, ed. Gary A. Fine, Veronique Campion-Vincent, and Chip Heath (Piscataway, NJ: Transaction Publishers, 2007); see also Colin D. MacLeod and Ira L. Cohen, "Anxiety and the Interpretation of Ambiguity: A Text Comprehension Study," *Journal of Abnormal Psychology* 102, no. 2 (May 1993): 238–47.

53. See, e.g., Leonie Huddy, Stanley Feldman, Charles Taber, and Gallya Lahav, "Threat, Anxiety, and Support of Antiterrorism Policies," *American Journal of Political Science* 49, no. 3 (July 2005): 593–608; Michael Shermer, *The Believing Brain: From Spiritual Faiths to Political Convictions: How We Construct Beliefs and Reinforce Them as Truths* (New York: St. Martin's Press, 2012).

54. See, e.g., Ted Brader, *Campaigning for Hearts and Minds: How Emotional Appeals in Political Ads Work* (Chicago: University of Chicago Press, 2006); Shana Kushner Gadarian, "The Politics of Threat: How Terrorism News Shapes Foreign Policy Attitudes," *Journal of Politics* 72, no. 2 (April 2010): 469–83; Mark V. Pezzo and Jason W. Beckstead, "A Multilevel Analysis of Rumor Transmission: Effects of Anxiety and Belief in Two Field Experiments," *Basic and Applied Social Psychology* 28, no. 1 (April 2006): 91–100.

55. Mieneke W. H. Weenig, Arieneke C. W. J. Groenenboom, and Hank A. M. Wilke, "Bad News Transmission as a Function of the Definitiveness of Consequences and the Relationship between Communicator and Recipient," *Journal of Personality and Social Psychology* 80, no. 3 (March 2001): 449–61; Greenhill, *Fear and Present Danger*.

56. Davis, "Is Trump All Talk."

57. See, e.g., Tom O'Connor, "Like Trump, North Korea's Kim Jong Un Gets His News from TV and Twitter," *Newsweek*, November 3, 2017.

58. See, e.g., Sargent, "Could Trump Help Unleash Nuclear Catastrophe."

59. See Greenhill and Oppenheim, "Rumor Has It."

60. Fearon, "Signaling Foreign Policy Interests"; Kurizaki, "Efficient Secrecy."

61. See, e.g., Jessica Chen Weiss and Allan Dafoe, "Authoritarian Audiences, Rhetoric and Propaganda in International Crises: Evidence from China," *International Studies Quarterly* 63, no. 4 (December 2019): 963–73; Kertzer, *Resolve in International Politics.*

62. See, e.g., Robert Jervis, *Perceptions and Misperceptions in International Politics* (Princeton, NJ: Princeton University Press, 1978).

63. Friedrich Glasl, *Confronting Conflict: A First-aid Kit for Handling Conflict* (Gloucestershire, UK: Hawthorn Press, 1999).

64. Ibid.; Jervis, *Perceptions and Misperceptions*.

65. John Sides and Kimberly Gross, "Stereotypes of Muslims and Support for the War on Terror," *Journal of Politics* 75, no. 3 (July 2013): 583–98.

66. UCLA's Suk-Young Kim, quoted in Reed Johnson, "Before Going to War in North Korea, Try Understanding the Place First," UCLA Newsroom, October 25, 2017, http://newsroom.ucla.edu/stories/before-going-to-war-in-north-korea-try-understanding-the-place-first; see also Hugh Gusterson, "Paranoid, Potbellied Stalinist Gets Nuclear Weapons: How the U.S. Print Media Cover North Korea," *Nonproliferation Review* 15, no. 1 (May 12, 2008): 21–42. Gusterson found that North Korea is most often portrayed as backward, its leaders as narcissistic, paranoid, and malicious, and the regime as untrustworthy.

67. See Jervis, *Perceptions and Misperceptions*, on fundamental attribution bias and other psychological predispositions

68. Ewan MacAskill, "Irrational, Illogical, Unpredictable—24 Years On, the World Awaits Saddam's Next Move," *The Guardian*, March 18, 2003; Kenneth Pollack, *The Threatening Storm: The Case for Invading Iraq* (New York: Random House, 2002).

69. Quoted in Kurizaki, "Efficient Secrecy."

70. See, e.g., Greenhill, *Fear and Present Danger*; Greenhill, "Public Mobilization."

Chapter 7

Crisis Stability and the Impact of the Information Ecosystem

Kristin Ven Bruusgaard and Jaclyn A. Kerr

"Loss of control," writes political scientist Richard Ned Lebow, "is a principal theme . . . of crisis management."[1] Yet crisis stability presumes that control can be retained in war and that conditions can be construed so as to ensure that nuclear weapons are not used. The Cold War debate on crisis stability deliberated how particular military capabilities, military doctrines, and misperceived communication were sources of instability in a crisis that could trigger escalation. The current information environment presents additional challenges for retaining stability in crisis. New tools of misinformation and disinformation and the abundance of data available to decision makers via the global information ecosystem (a significant proportion of which may be unverified) enhance the problem of understanding the capabilities, doctrines, and intentions of the adversary. The risk of misperception during a crisis may increase significantly as a result, contributing to risks of escalation and inadvertent war. The deliberate manipulation of information may be used to influence decision makers as well as public opinion before or during a crisis. Such manipulation of the political process may also significantly affect crisis decision making. This chapter addresses what the sources of crisis instability are given this new information ecosystem.

Traditionally, crisis stability was defined as a situation where no party has an incentive for nuclear first strike or preemption. Its focus was on the size of the gap between the payoffs for striking first and striking second with nuclear weapons.[2] This stemmed from the central

concern that nuclear war could result from "the reciprocal fear of surprise attack."[3] This delineation is important, as the central concern of
crisis stability is *not* to avert or deter or stabilize conflict per se but to
avert the escalation of a *nuclear* crisis.[4]

The relationship between crisis stability and deterrence is intimate
but complex. Deterrent relationships determine whether crises arise
and leaders' perceptions of their opportunities to influence a crisis once
it is a fact. Effective deterrence depends on the credibility of nuclear
threats, which suggests a contradiction between deterrence and crisis
stability: efforts to preserve crisis stability could undermine the credibility of deterrence. If there were ever to be perfect crisis stability—and
thus a perfect absence of risk of a crisis resulting in nuclear use—then
nuclear weapons would serve no useful purpose as a deterrent and, in
the absence of other forms of deterrence, aggressive states would have
no reason to fear undertaking aggressive subnuclear military action.[5]
Uncertainty as to whether lower-level actions might trigger nuclear
escalation is meant to exert a deterrent force prompting aggressive
states to avoid aggression.

But assurance of and transparency with adversaries can also be critical to avoiding or stabilizing crises. Incorrectly gauging the motivations
of another state—whether assuming these to be more or less aggressive than in fact intended—can lead to unintended escalation. While
appeasing a revisionist state can invite further aggression, threats and
punishment of a state that is fearful for its own security can trigger
a security-dilemma-fueled escalatory spiral. Strategic relationships
between potential adversary states require a balanced awareness of
both escalatory dynamics. They also require continuous insight and
feedback as to the more appropriate understanding of the other state's
motivations and potential next actions.

Information about capabilities and intentions and its correct interpretation thus plays a critical role in all strategic decision making: from
the slow-moving calculations of arms development and deployment
to the faster timescales of alerts and nuclear-weapons-use decisions
during crises.[6] Information is vital to assess the actions, motives, and

likely responses of other states and provides available options for decision makers. Flows of information affect decision-making dynamics, reinforce or undermine biases, confuse or clarify analysis, and dampen or amplify pressures through public feedback or panic. The accurate relaying of undistorted information is likewise critical to command and control, and its failure can lead to breakdowns in the chain of command with catastrophic consequences. Changes in the information ecosystem thus directly affect the sources and potential of instability in a crisis.

Traditional Sources of Instability in a Crisis

Nuclear strategy expert Colin S. Gray describes the very concept of crisis stability as "far more often advanced and cited than defined."[7] The debate on crisis stability traditionally has been largely focused on seeking to reduce incentives for capabilities or doctrines associated with nuclear preemption. A range of capabilities associated with such incentives, such as vulnerable silo-based ICBMs, was deemed more unstable than more survivable forces due to the temptation to use them preemptively and avoid decapitation. Although the emergence of full American and Soviet nuclear triads was considered "stabilizing," the potential for further cuts kept the debate on arsenal composition and crisis stability alive.[8]

Strategic defensive systems were also traditionally perceived as destabilizing, offering the possibility of blocking retaliatory action.[9] In particular, the interaction of vulnerable forces on one side with counterforce and defensive capabilities on the other was seen by experts as contributing to crisis instability.[10] In such situations, the incentives for preemption would be strong: the only thing worse than starting a counterforce war would be having to fight one after receiving the first blow. Western academics entertained the idea of a Soviet preemptive doctrine and Soviets entertained the same idea with regard to US strategy.[11] Khrushchev's decision to place Soviet missiles in Cuba in 1962 — helping to precipitate the Cuban Missile Crisis—was in part a reaction to intelligence reports that the Kennedy administration had considered a preemptive strike plan during the Berlin Crisis the previous year.[12]

Doctrines of nuclear first use for limited objectives were also traditionally deemed highly destabilizing. Limited nuclear strikes could offer opportunities for a quick end to conflict or more favorable accord than to continue the conventional fight. Strategists deliberated potential benefits associated with nuclear escalation, such as enhancing credibility for subsequent nuclear strikes or instilling fear in a target audience.[13] It was (and still is) possible to envisage a range of operational or tactical incentives for nuclear first strikes that could produce an operational benefit. If an actor believes that the benefit of aggression outweighs the cost or that retaliation is uncertain, secure retaliation is no deterrent.

Today, we are seeing a proliferation of destabilizing capabilities and doctrines. Both Russia and the United States are currently reinvesting in new subnuclear weapons and dual-capable platforms. The vulnerabilities of command, control, and communications (C3) systems have been partially overcome by technological solutions such as permissive action links.[14] But other challenges linked to the entanglement of nuclear and conventional C3 systems have emerged.[15] Many analysts claim that Russia and North Korea (and possibly China) could consider the limited use of nuclear weapons in order to try to stem the escalation of a conflict to a level they cannot handle conventionally.[16] Russia's military doctrine explicitly states it would consider a nuclear response to large-scale conventional military aggression.[17] First-use doctrines contradict the ideal of crisis stability: that there is some way of ensuring that conventional conflict between nuclear-armed adversaries remains conventional.

In addition to potentially destabilizing nuclear capabilities and doctrines, other aspects of nuclear crisis may induce instability. Nuclear crisis stability, like deterrence theory, presumes rational actors capable of "understanding their environment and coordinating their policy instruments" in a legible way through the fog of war.[18] And yet, several academics point out how "most statesmen realize that whenever violence is set in motion, no one can be sure where it will end up. Because events can readily escape control, limited responses carry with them some probability that the final, although unintended, consequence will be all-out war."[19] Absence or misinterpretation of information, failures of communication, accidents, and emotion can all play potentially catastrophic roles setting off cascades of events. During the Cuban Missile Crisis, US military leaders learned how difficult it was to control military activity with the aim of preventing gratuitous provocations of the Soviet Union.[20] Soviet submarines that the US Navy tried to signal to surface during the Cuban crisis were armed with nuclear defensive systems and misinterpreted the depth charges used by the US vessels as a possible attack. Only the persistent opposition of a single Soviet officer on board one of the submarines precluded a Soviet nuclear response to these depth charges at the height of the crisis. Such use of a defensive nuclear weapon would very likely have triggered a substantial US response.[21]

The decisions made by leaders in crisis will be based on their interpretations and perceptions of their adversaries' capabilities, doctrines, and perceived intentions—all of which are products of the information ecosystem they are a part of. Deterrence is a psychological theory about manipulating the behavior of others, which means that leaders' personalities and preferred modes of decision making play a role.[22] Their willingness to go to the brink of war will differ based on knowledge, information, cognition, and perception of what is at stake. If an actor perceives the consequences of not going to war as intolerable, no capability, doctrine, or communication may preserve crisis stability.[23] On the other hand, if a viable off-ramp is available, escalation may be avoided.

Other factors such as time pressure, internal government politics, relationships with allies and partners, media attention, and public feedback can further complicate the decision-making process. During the Cuban Missile Crisis, both President Kennedy and Premier Khrushchev had aggressive initial reactions but came to prefer more cautious approaches. Both faced intense pushback from significantly more hawkish advisers or partners. In spite of, and even because of, the slowness of direct communication, each leader faced enormous time pressure: for fear of public (over)reaction should the news become widely known, at the risk of further unintended escalation or of losing the opportunity for a way out. Neither leader, however, faced the early media scrutiny that might have been possible in an age of social media. The White House was able to convince the *New York Times* and the *Washington Post* to delay publication on the crisis until after Kennedy's address—dynamics that would be unlikely today.[24] Today's information ecosystems constitute a radically different environment for policy deliberation, public debate, and decision making.

Characteristics of Contemporary Information Ecosystems

In recent years, the national and international information ecosystems have undergone significant changes and continue to develop at a rapid pace. The information and media environment today bears little resemblance to that during the Cuban Missile Crisis. In the early 1960s, earth-orbiting satellites were a new phenomenon and U-2 planes were still used for aerial photographic intelligence gathering. Televised presidential addresses and debates had been gradually redefining the relations between politicians and publics. Emerging information technologies had yet to significantly affect the velocity of information flows for the purposes of political or diplomatic communication, media coverage, or intelligence gathering. American warships enforcing the blockade in Cuba were able to "bounce messages off the moon," but it took "many hours to decipher a top secret communication" and "high-priority traffic between the Pentagon and the warships . . . routinely [was] delayed."[25]

The rapid technological changes that have taken place in the period since the Cuban Missile Crisis have transformed the information ecosystem within which political crises today might unfold. Each new technology has brought new affordances; enabled distinct mechanisms for communication and for the sharing of information or its gathering and organizing; and altered the overall environment for media, public discourse, collective action, intelligence, and diplomatic and political communications. The digitization of information, lowered costs, and increased resilience of high-speed information sharing, disintermediation of information flows on the national and transnational levels, and the emergence of tools for searching, filtering, and sorting information flows have had profound effects on forms of civic engagement, state-society relations, and the media and public spheres of most countries.

In the 2000s and early 2010s, new information technologies played a critical role in events such as the Occupy Wall Street protests that sprang up in the United States in the wake of the 2008 global financial crisis, the 2009 Iranian Green Movement that protested what was widely regarded as a fraudulent presidential election, and the Arab Spring, beginning in 2011, that toppled autocratic governments across the Middle East. Some observers hailed information communication technologies as "liberation technologies" strengthening the hand of collective action against stronger state organizations, pointing to the ease and low cost of asynchronous communications across great distances, the ability to aggregate small inputs rapidly, and the ways that individuals could leverage these tools without the need for hierarchical organizations and centralized leadership.[26] The internet's ability to facilitate mass levels of rapid preference revelation and information cascades was credited for undermining authoritarian regime types with their enforced silence of dissenting views.[27] Blogs, online media outlets, "citizen journalism," and social media emerged as alternatives to the mainstream press and challenged the information monopolies of highly censored or propagandistic government media outlets. The anonymity of online speech, for a while, permitted less risky forms of hard-to-attribute engagement or self-expression.

Over time, states have learned to leverage the new information environment to their advantage. While the use of information and communication technologies (ICT) by terrorist networks and illicit businesses bolstered the case for increased digital surveillance within democracies, authoritarian states struggling to address "regime security" dilemmas developed techniques to maintain political control despite *and through* online flows of information. China developed technically sophisticated forms of nearly ubiquitous censorship for online content.[28] Russia experimented with tailored content production for the purpose of manipulating public opinion and narratives—techniques now increasingly utilized as tools of foreign policy and aggression as well.[29] New techniques and laws for control have been shared and emulated across regimes and technologies.

Meanwhile, the changes in the information environment have had profound effects on the public spheres and commercial cultures of even the most robust democracies. Mechanisms of "homophily" and "sorting" online (emerging from search- and user-centered design paradigms) combined with the low cost of "digital shelf space" permitted individuals to easily find others with unusual tastes or views and for content producers to cater to the "long tail" of diverse interests rather than steering everyone toward the most popular topics or cultural products.[30] Public discourse has become increasingly fragmented, no longer dominated by a few trusted mainstream sources or a single authoritative narrative as had mostly been the case in the heyday of television broadcast news.

As individuals self-segregate across disparate and often polarized echo chambers, this has allowed previously fringe viewpoints—from hateful extremism to conspiracy theories—to gain wider audiences and a more visible public representation. This fragmentation of the public sphere and the loss of universally trusted media outlets coincided with a period of profound political polarization, leaving many democratic populations vulnerable to intentional information operations.[31] Meanwhile, decision makers are subject to the accelerating minute-by-minute news cycle and the changing pressures of public opinion, often facing political pressure to respond to events before accounts can be confirmed or fact-checked.[32]

While significant attention has been paid to the role of these new dynamics in mass protest movements or efforts to influence foreign elections, there has been less scrutiny of the potential impact of the changes in the information environment on events that could precipitate nuclear crises today and the dynamics of such crises as they would unfold.

Potential Impact of Current Information Environment on Crisis Stability

Could a crisis similar to the 1962 Cuban Missile Crisis emerge today? The placement of vulnerable, first-strike-capable missiles, first in Italy and Turkey by the United States, then in Cuba by the Soviet Union, prompted a global nuclear crisis once existence of the latter was uncovered by US intelligence. This discovery, combined with each side's inadequate intelligence concerning the other's intentions and some indications of preemptive-strike plans, played roles in the crisis as each leader grappled with pressures from within their own governments and the prospect of public scrutiny once the discovery of Soviet missiles in Cuba was announced.

Today, a nuclear crisis scenario similar to the emergence of the Cuban Missile Crisis seems less likely given the vastly increased availability of satellite imagery that would allow each side to detect the deployment of significant military assets abroad at an earlier stage. But despite vast increases in some forms of intelligence, other types of intelligence failures can still be significant concerns.[33] The significant possibility for misinterpreting adversary intention remains, as do risks of destabilizing nuclear or conventional capabilities, doctrines, plans, and procedures. Indeed, Russian officials are currently warning of the potential for a standoff comparable to the 1962 Cuban Missile Crisis if the United States deploys land-based missile systems near Russia's borders.[34]

The inherent characteristics of the current information environment and the forms of deliberate manipulation that it enables contribute to an environment in which miscalculation and misperception is
likely, despite improved capabilities for information and communications. Whether these are characteristics of the current information
ecosystem or have resulted from the convergence with other economic,
social, and political conditions, many contemporary dynamics in democratic societies—including the polarization of public opinion, the
increased role of fringe groups in public life, and the increasing role of
populism—encourage destabilizing dynamics before or during a crisis.

The Impact of Information on Crisis Emergence

Information and its interpretation have always been vital to preventing
crisis and maintaining stable deterrent relationships. The greater the
shortage of correctly interpreted intelligence or trustworthy channels
of communication, the greater the potential for misperceiving an adversary's motives and miscalculating the balance between threatening and
conciliatory postures. One might assume that the current abundance
of intelligence sources and communication channels would limit such
risks, but this would mistake the speed and abundance of information
with the likelihood of its correct interpretation. While it is difficult to
assess the likelihood of correct interpretation, it is possible to identify
dynamics in the current information environment that can affect decision making.

   Within government, emerging information ecosystems have spurred
the politicization of policy. While there have always been hawks and
doves on matters of national security, policy decisions that were traditionally relatively apolitical have become less so. Political positions are
increasingly subject to real-time scrutiny, and diminished trust in media
institutions makes it increasingly hard to find national consensus even
on topics of grave security concern. Relationships with other countries
are also subject to more turbulent domestic political forces. In such an

environment of politicization, unbiased analysis and agreement on an adversary's motives may be harder to generate. Polarization and politicization risk a perpetual shifting of strategic postures toward potential adversaries and allies, undercutting the ability of governments to form lasting and stable relationships and binding agreements on matters of importance to strategic stability. This produces less predictability in the eyes of adversaries, who may in turn respond with destabilizing actions of their own.

The direct one-to-one and one-to-many communication channels available to contemporary populist leaders further risk subjecting significant strategic decisions to real-time public opinion pressures and interpersonal dynamics without the input of expert intelligence and strategic communities. As we have seen in 2017 with US presidential tweets directed at North Korean leader Kim Jong Un, such technology, while offering a seemingly rapid and transparent communication channel between leaders, can also encourage an extreme approach to the balance between threats and conciliation.

The role of and emphasis on different sources of information is further compounded in the contemporary information environment. While intelligence may be more plentiful than before, intelligence analysis may be the subject of politicization as described above or may suffer from competing with the myriad of other information sources, such as social media. Leadership style may directly affect the role and relevance of intelligence assessments in leadership decision making. Whereas the current US president's appetite for intelligence is seemingly low, the Russian president allegedly absorbs little other information than that provided by his intelligence agencies.[35] While information ecosystems may affect national leaders differently, the impact on dynamics between states may still be significant.

Adding to this is the potential for manipulating the current information environment and new forms of low-level interstate conflict using such methods. Russia's utilization of hard-to-attribute forms of "cross-domain coercion" was exhibited by the advanced use of cyber, information, and kinetic military tools in the 2014 war in Ukraine.[36] Russia's use of "cyber-enabled information conflict" was demonstrated through Russia's interference in the 2016 US presidential election.[37] Together, these have prompted significant discussion of ways to increase Western deterrence posture, while diminishing trust in Russian claims of (potentially real) security concerns. At the same time, the use of these techniques—which leverage precisely the forms of ambiguity, division, and extreme views just described to influence the internal situation in other countries—has potential for significant miscalculation and potentially undesired effects. These could take the form of escalation from an ongoing conflict or slower tectonic effects in public opinion that might affect strategic posture or crisis decision making.

The Impact of Information on Crisis (In)Stability

While the current information environment poses serious risks for overall stability of deterrent relationships, the risks resulting from the new information environment may be even more intense during crises. Both unintended effects of the current information ecosystem and the intended and unintended effects of intentional manipulation of that ecosystem can affect decision making.

   While Cold War decision makers also faced intense pressure to rapidly and correctly gauge the intention and likely reactions of adversaries, the current information environment may tighten the time window and increase audience costs for decision making during crises. At the same time, political and cognitive pressures may be larger than before due to the potential overflow of information from classified and open sources. The rapid flows of information combined with lowered reliability of many information sources and polarization mean that individuals faced with crisis decisions may be more likely to fall victim to misperceptions caused by cognitive biases and heuristics at work. This risk increases when individuals rapidly process large quantities of material under stressful conditions.[38] This can affect primary decision makers, but it can also influence analysts, journalists, military officers, and others involved in processing the information that will ultimately inform decision making. The overall tone of such biases may be affected by the slower processes of politicization discussed previously.

The leakiness of digital information and politicization of radical transparency combine with the disintermediation of news reporting, twenty-four-hour news cycles, and the social media environment to limit decision makers' ability to handle crises in the relative calm of closed-door sessions and diplomatic channels. As opposed to the six days of deliberation and maneuvering by the Kennedy administration in 1962 prior to the president's public address, the public today might know about a crisis as soon as—or before—decision makers. Leaders might never get the chance to introduce a crisis with a framing or agenda-setting narrative but would instead be chasing an already politicized and fragmented cascade of rumors, fears, and conspiracy theories. Increasingly politicized media coverage further reduces the possibility of unified public support.[39] Such dynamics add pressure and subject decision makers to constant real-time public opinion feedback and second-guessing. This could have particularly deleterious repercussions for thin-skinned leaders who are incapable of mounting internal buffers against the emotional sting and urge to respond to criticism. It poses a serious challenge for leaders whose electoral legitimacy depends on the popularity of their actions.[40] Increased public scrutiny of, or conspiracies about, a crisis may complicate issues that can affect crisis outcomes, such as saving face, preserving credibility, and taking revenge.[41] Decision makers must deal simultaneously with the nuclear crisis itself and potential secondary domestic or international crises resulting from public panic or the cascades of false information or extremist reactions.

Another dynamic that might further exacerbate public relations problems and constrain decision makers' freedom to maneuver and negotiate is the many-to-many transparency of public discourse between countries. In the past, decision makers have had some ability to represent a unified position on behalf of their country during moments of tense diplomacy. The greater external visibility of internal divisions in the current information environment could undermine the negotiating power of unpopular or polarizing leaders. What is more, the publics in each country involved in a crisis would have greater ability to see into the internal events and discourse of the other countries in real time, although this would not necessarily be paired with greater understanding. While this might serve to humanize the adversary, it could also further exacerbate tensions and serve to empower marginalized voices within or across borders.[42] Furthermore, each of these dynamics could be manipulated and used for advantage by foreign actors.

Of perhaps greatest concern in the current information environment is the lack of reliable signals or channels of trusted communication through which to defuse crises. Of course, the problems of communication during the Cuban Missile Crisis were of a different nature. It took hours or days for private communications between national leaders to be relayed and translated. Events on the ground could easily outpace the speed of such communications. Today, with very few exceptions, channels of communication exist or can be quickly established. But the prior politicization of strategic relationships and the recent increase in the use of misinformation as a tool of aggression between strategic adversaries could undermine or hinder such communication. While information and psychological operations played a role during the Cold War as well, the increased use of such techniques in the new digital environment and as a tool of conflict is a dynamic with characteristics that are not yet well understood.[43] The increased strategic use of (sometimes implausible) denial has potential to undercut trust in diplomatic communications, even during crises. Such trust will be vital to retain stability in any conventional crisis that had best not escalate.

Finally, the contemporary information environment offers unprecedented opportunity for manipulating the adversary during crisis. Such manipulation can be targeted at politicians and the process that informs their decision making, and also at the adversary country's public at large. Traditional deception methods could be used to, for example, skew the intelligence collection and analysis of the adversary, through utilizing what is known about the other side's patterns and sources of intelligence collection. Information operations could be aimed at making one's own retaliatory capability more credible in the eyes of the adversary through disinformation or through real information regarding actual capabilities. Reports of Russian inflatable fighter jets demonstrate how state actors continue to see value in traditional and unsophisticated deception.[44] Information operations could also be used to reduce the confidence of the adversary in its own systems or retaliatory capability by targeting individuals or systems that form part of that capability.[45] Social media offer new opportunities to target the individuals who make up the systems an adversary relies on. This was demonstrated during the Ukraine crisis, when individual cell phones were subject to targeted information operations.[46] These types of information operations are a novel aspect of modern war and would add a fog of war that remains untested in severe nuclear crises.

An adversary could seek to influence the political preferences or biases of individual decision makers through long-running campaigns to alter personal preferences or through targeted operations to sway or coerce individuals during crisis. An adversary could also seek to affect decision making by influencing the public debate and reactions of the target state in order to foment pressures to sue for peace or delegitimize war means or goals. Russia has engaged in targeted public diplomacy campaigns in several NATO countries regarding the destabilizing impact of NATO's missile defense in Europe in order to influence both public discourse and individual policy makers.[47]

Any large-scale conflict between major powers today would entail active information campaigns from the warring parties to legitimize their own war aims and military actions as well as efforts to delegitimize the goals and methods of the adversary. In a nuclear conflict, one could, for example, envisage a propaganda war where accurate or inaccurate information regarding war methods and consequences would be used actively to legitimize or delegitimize use of force or indeed nuclear weapons use. Unverified reporting of a nuclear detonation in contested territory could be one example of information that could affect leadership decision making and public opinion in rapid and direct ways, which consequently could have severe repercussions for crisis dynamics. Third-party actors (be they associated with state actors or not) could instigate information operations to foment nuclear crisis or use by spreading false information regarding issues related to the conflict. This could create political, military, or public pressures on state leaders to take actions they would otherwise not have taken.

Conclusion

The sources of crisis instability are inexorably linked to the interpretation and processing of information by decision makers. The contemporary information environment has exacerbated several of the cognitive challenges connected with processing information and created some entirely new ones for any decision maker faced with a nuclear crisis in the modern era.

The changed information ecosystem does not alter the basic premise that most decision making in crisis and war is characterized by uncertainty, incomplete information, and risk. The information available to policy makers today may be more plentiful and, at times, of better quality than before. Although this could reduce uncertainty regarding certain technical facts, the increased availability of information may also enhance the cognitive challenges of decision making. For some leaders, the immediate availability of information and the social media feedback loop augments the information they acquire via other channels. Alternate sources of information may supplant the critical role intelligence information has had in crisis decision making. A more complex information environment places greater demands on identifying clear signals from noise, a process made more difficult when the signals may contain noise deceptively orchestrated by an adversary.

The changed information ecosystem does entail some relatively new dynamics that may place novel pressures on decision makers in nuclear crises. Individual leaders and collectives responsible for decision making are likely to be affected by unprecedented exposure to new and potentially disparate sources of information. The public is likely to play a larger part in nuclear crises through access to information and outlets to let its voices be heard. The preferences of both decision makers and the public may be influenced by the shaping efforts of several actors, including the warring parties as well as other benign or malign actors with agendas of their own. This will potentially introduce unprecedented public deliberation of crisis dynamic and policy options and might affect decision making.

In such a changed information ecosystem, it seems prudent to raise questions regarding how or whether nuclear war will remain "special" or "different" in the public or policy domain and how public pressures will affect decision making. To more fully answer questions regarding how the contemporary information ecosystem will affect crisis stability, we need more information about, and research on, how the emerging information environment affects decisions regarding war and peace and how it may affect preference formation and alteration before as well as during a crisis. Finally, we need to understand how the information ecosystem affects decision making in different political systems. Such insight will be critical to assessing more fully whether and how crisis stability can be achieved in a conventional war between nuclear powers and what measures must be taken to foster such stability.

Notes

1. Richard Ned Lebow, "Clausewitz and Nuclear Crisis Stability," *Political Science Quarterly* 103, no. 1 (Spring 1988): 81–110.

2. Robert Jervis, "Arms Control, Stability, and Causes of War," *Political Science Quarterly* 108, no. 2 (Summer 1993): 239–53.

3. Thomas C. Schelling, *Arms and Influence* (New Haven, CT: Yale University Press, 1966), chapter 6.

4. Forrest E. Morgan, *Crisis Stability and Long-Range Strike: A Comparative Analysis of Fighters, Bombers, and Missiles* (Santa Monica, CA: RAND Corporation, 2013).

5. For a discussion of the iteration between crisis stability and arms control and the relation to the stability-instability paradox, see Jervis, "Arms Control."

6. James M. Acton, "Crisis Stability," *Adelphi Series* 50, no. 417 (2010): 57–70.

7. Colin S. Gray, "Nuclear Strategy: The Case for a Theory of Victory," *International Security* 4, no. 1 (Summer 1979): 54–87; Jean-Pierre P. Langlois, "Rational Deterrence and Crisis Stability," *American Journal of Political Science* 35, no. 4 (November 1991): 801–32.

8. Acton, "Crisis Stability."

9. Lawrence Freedman, *The Evolution of Nuclear Strategy*, 2nd ed. (Basingstoke, UK: Palgrave Macmillan, 1989), 165.

10. Acton, "Crisis Stability"; Jervis, "Arms Control."

11. Nate Jones, ed., *Able Archer 83: The Secret History of the NATO Exercise That Almost Triggered Nuclear War* (New York: New Press, 2016); Jan Hoffenaar and Christopher Findlay, *Military Planning for European Theatre Conflict during the Cold War: An Oral History Roundtable, Stockholm, April 24–25, 2006*, Center for Security Studies, 2007.

12. Acton, "Crisis Stability."

13. The problem with this logic is that encountered by Soviet strategists in the 1980s, who concluded that nuclear battlefield strikes produced few battlefield advantages.

14. Bruce G. Blair, *The Logic of Accidental Nuclear War* (Washington, DC: Brookings Institution, 1993).

15. Alexey Arbatov, Vladimir Dvorkin, and Petr Topychkanov, "Entanglement as a New Security Threat: A Russian Perspective," Carnegie Moscow Center, November 8, 2017, 25–26.

16. On the contemporary logic of limited nuclear war, see John K. Warden, "Limited Nuclear War: The Twenty-First-Century Challenge for the United States" (lecture, NSI, Boston, September 12, 2018).

17. Voennaia doktrina rossiiskoi federatsii (Military Doctrine of the Russian Federation), December 26, 2014, http://static.kremlin.ru/media/events/files /41d527556bec8deb3530.pdf.

18. Robert Jervis, Richard Ned Lebow, and Janice Gross Stein, *Psychology and Deterrence* (Baltimore: Johns Hopkins University Press, 1989).

19. Jervis, "Arms Control."

20. Graham T. Allison and Philip Zelikow, *Essence of Decision: Explaining the Cuban Missile Crisis* (Boston: Little, Brown, 1971); Scott D. Sagan, "Nuclear Alerts and Crisis Management," *International Security* 9, no. 4 (1985): 99–139.

21. Daniel Ellsberg, *The Doomsday Machine: Confessions of a Nuclear War Planner* (London: Bloomsbury, 2017); Michael Dobbs, *One Minute to Midnight: Kennedy, Khrushchev, and Castro on the Brink of Nuclear War* (New York: Random House, 2008).

22. Jervis, "Arms Control."

23. Richard Ned Lebow, "The Deterrence Deadlock: Is There a Way Out?" *Political Psychology* 4, no 2 (June 1983): 333–54.

24. Dobbs, *One Minute to Midnight*, 38.

25. Dobbs, *One Minute to Midnight*.

26. Jennifer Earl and Katrina Kimport, *Digitally Enabled Social Change: Activism in the Internet Age* (Cambridge, MA: MIT Press, 2011); Henry Farrell, "The Consequences of the Internet for Politics," *Annual Review of Political Science* 15 (2012); Patrick Meier, "Do 'Liberation Technologies' Change the Balance of Power Between Repressive Regimes and Civil Society?" (PhD dissertation, Stanford University, 2010); R. Kelly Garrett, "Protest in an Information Society: A Review of Literature on Social Movements and New ICTs," *Information, Communication & Society* 9, no. 2 (2006): 202–24; Clay Shirky, "The Political Power of Social Media: Technology, the Public Sphere, and Political Change," *Foreign Affairs*, January/February 2011: 28–41; Philip N. Howard, "How Digital Media Enabled the Protests in Tunisia and Egypt," Reuters, January 29, 2011; Leon Aron, "Nyetizdat: How the Internet Is Building Civil Society in Russia," AEI (American Enterprise Institute), June 28, 2011.

27. Timur Kuran, *Private Truths, Public Lies: The Social Consequences of Preference Falsification* (Cambridge, MA: Harvard University Press, 1997).

28. Gary King, Jennifer Pan, and Margaret Roberts, "How Censorship in China Allows Government Criticism but Silences Collective Expression," *American Political Science Review* 107, no. 2 (May 2013): 1–18; Jonathan Sullivan, "China's Weibo: Is Faster Different?" *New Media & Society* 16, no. 1 (2014): 24–37, https://doi.org/10.1177/1461444812472966.

29. Andrei Soldatov and Irina Borogan, *The Red Web: The Struggle between Russia's Digital Dictators and the New Online Revolutionaries* (New York: Public Affairs, 2015); Keir Giles, *Handbook of Russian Information Warfare* (NATO Defence College Research Division, November 23, 2016); Thomas Rid, "Disinformation: A Primer in Russian Active Measures and Influence Campaigns," *Hearing before the Select Committee on Intelligence, US Senate, 115th Congress*, March 30, 2017.

30. Farrell, "The Consequences of the Internet for Politics"; Chris Anderson, "The Long Tail," *Wired*, October 1, 2004.

31. Shawn Powers and Markos Kounalakis, eds., "Can Public Diplomacy Survive the Internet? Bots, Echo Chambers, and Disinformation," US State Department Advisory Commission on Public Diplomacy, May 2017; Kate Starbird, "Examining the Alternative Media Ecosystem through the Production of Alternative Narratives of Mass Shooting Events on Twitter" (presentation at Eleventh International AAAI [Association for the Advancement of Artificial Intelligence] Conference on Web and Social Media, Montreal, May 15-18, 2017).

32. The Obama administration's 2010 firing of and subsequent offer of a new position to Agriculture Department official Shirley Sherrod as a result of a doctored video excerpt released by Breitbart News from a longer consciousness-raising speech she had given to the NAACP about prejudice is indicative of the

types of problems that can result from rapid news-cycle-based decision-making pressures. Sheryl Gay Stolberg, Shaila Dewan, and Brian Stelter, "With Apology, Fired Official Is Offered a New Job," *New York Times*, July 21, 2010.

33. Robert Jervis, *Why Intelligence Fails: Lessons from the Iranian Revolution and the Iraq War* (Ithaca, NY: Cornell University Press, 2010); Christopher Andrew and Vasili Mitrokhin, *The Sword and the Shield: The Mitrokhin Archive and the Secret History of the KGB* (London: Hachette UK, 2000); Raymond L. Garthoff, *Soviet Leaders and Intelligence: Assessing the American Adversary during the Cold War* (Washington, DC: Georgetown University Press, 2015).

34. "Russia Warns of Repeat of 1962 Cuban Missile Crisis," Reuters, June 24, 2019, https://news.yahoo.com/1-russia-warns-repeat-1962-124007200.html.

35. Kimberly Marten, "Explaining Russia's Schizophrenic Policy toward the United States," PONARS Eurasia, policy memo 501, January 19, 2018, http://www.ponarseurasia.org/memo/explaining-russias-schizophrenic-policy-toward-united-states.

36. Dmitry Adamsky, "Cross-Domain Coercion: The Current Russian Art of Strategy," *Proliferation Papers*, FRI Security Studies Center, November 2015.

37. Herbert Lin and Jaclyn Kerr, "On Cyber-Enabled Information Warfare and Information Operations," in *Oxford Handbook of Cybersecurity* (Oxford: Oxford University Press, forthcoming), https://papers.ssrn.com/abstract=3015680; Alicia Wanless and Michael Berk, "Participatory Propaganda: The Engagement of Audiences in the Spread of Persuasive Communications," *Proceedings of the Social Media and Social Order*, Cultural Conflict 2.0 Conference, Oslo, December 1, 2018; Samuel C. Woolley and Philip N. Howard, "Computational Propaganda Worldwide: Executive Summary," Working Paper 2017.11, Project on Computational Propaganda, Oxford University, June 2017.

38. Lin and Kerr, "On Cyber-Enabled Information Warfare"; Daniel Kahneman, *Thinking, Fast and Slow* (New York: Farrar, Straus and Giroux, 2011); Martin F. Kaplan, L. Tatiana Wanshula, and Mark P. Zanna, "Time Pressure and Information Integration in Social Judgment," in *Time Pressure and Stress in Human Judgment and Decision Making*, eds. Ola Svenson and A. John Maule (Boston: Springer, 1993), 255–67, https://doi.org/10.1007/978-1-4757-6846-6_17; Carsten K. W. De Dreu, "Time Pressure and Closing of the Mind in Negotiation," *Organizational Behavior and Human Decision Processes* 91, no. 2 (July 2003): 280–95, https://doi.org/10.1016/S0749-5978(03)00022-0.

39. Christopher Gelpi, "Democracies in Conflict: The Role of Public Opinion, Political Parties, and the Press in Shaping Security Policy," *Journal of Conflict Resolution* 61, no. 9 (2017): 1925–49.

40. As the digital and social media environment makes more of the words and deeds of leaders searchable in real time, such dynamics also can subject leaders to increased "rhetorical entrapment" pressures—possibly foreclosing some policy alternatives. For earlier development of this concept, see Frank Schimmelfennig,

"The Community Trap: Liberal Norms, Rhetorical Action, and the Eastern Enlargement of the European Union," *International Organization* 55, no. 1 (Winter 2001): 47–80.

41. Rose McDermott, Anthony C. Lopez, and Peter K. Hatemi, "'Blunt Not the Heart, Enrage It': The Psychology of Revenge and Deterrence," *Texas National Security Review* 1, no. 1 (November 2017): 68–89.

42. How would public opinion react to images of flag-burning protesters or cheering crowds following escalatory events? How would internal social media debates concerning crisis risks influence the faith of ally populations in extended deterrence assurances during crisis? How would such dynamics constrain the political options for the leaders of allied countries?

43. Richard H. Shultz and Roy Godson, *Dezinformatsia: Active Measures in Soviet Strategy* (Oxford, UK: Pergamon Press, 1984); Brian D. Dailey and Patrick J. Parker, eds., *Soviet Strategic Deception* (Lanham, MD: Lexington Books, 1987).

44. Andrew E. Kramer, "A New Weapon in Russia's Arsenal, and It's Inflatable," *New York Times*, October 12, 2016, https://www.nytimes.com /2016/10/13/world/europe/russia-decoy-weapon.html.

45. Here the use of (dis)information campaigns could clearly be combined with utilization of cyberweapon systems, seeking to undermine opponents' confidence in their technological preparedness. Elements of such an approach (though not during crisis) are evident, for example, in US efforts with regard to Iranian nuclear capabilities and North Korean missile systems. See David E. Sanger, *The Perfect Weapon: War, Sabotage, and Fear in the Cyber Age* (New York: Broadway Books, 2019).

46. Vladimir Sazonov, Kristiina Müür, and Holger Mölder, eds., *Russian Information Campaign Against the Ukrainian State and Defence Forces*, NATO Strategic Communications Centre for Excellence, 2016.

47. See, for example, Hege Eilertsen, "Russia's Ambassador Warns: Missile Shield Will Endanger Norway's Borders," *High North News*, Feb. 22, 2017, https://www.highnorthnews.com/en/russias-ambassador-warns-missile-shield -will-endanger-norways-borders.

Chapter 8

Bum Dope, Blowback, and the Bomb:

The Effect of Bad Information on Policy-Maker Beliefs and Crisis Stability

Jeffrey Lewis

How might bad information affect crisis stability? We like to imagine that elites—military officials, politicians, and experts—will be immune to the kind of rumor, disinformation, and propaganda with which the internet is awash. This chapter explores that notion, with a nod to political scientist Stephen Van Evera's notion of blowback—the idea that propaganda can, in fact, warp elite perceptions. Van Evera was concerned about psychological blurring between rhetoric and sincere belief while others, like Jack Snyder, another expert on international relations, emphasized the risk that policy makers might become trapped by political rhetoric.[1]

This chapter is principally concerned with this idea: that bad information, even deliberate disinformation knowingly planted by some cynical elites, might "blow back" (or echo) through a wider range of elites and worsen a nuclear crisis. It examines two contemporary case studies of bad information, both of which help illustrate how such information—to use George P. Shultz's colorful phrase, "bum dope"—could undermine crisis stability.[2]

I conclude that the same pathologies seen in online discourse could undermine stability, even in a serious crisis involving nuclear weapons. In short, policy makers tend to engage in public rhetoric that, in turn, shapes their own thinking. Often such statements are propagandistic in their initial formulation. But as they become part of the public discourse, policy makers tend to believe them. This carries additional risk in an era of social media. There is a casual assumption that elites are immune to the bad information on social media, particularly involving issues relating to nuclear weapons and nuclear war. This confidence seems misplaced.

Bad Information

An interesting feature of our current era is what appears to be a sudden surge in the prevalence and power of fake news, disinformation, and conspiracy theories—bad information. This is merely a surmise, of course, one that reflects what the moment *feels* like. It is rather difficult, in practice, to measure the prevalence or the influence of such ideas in a body politic. One study, which simply looked at letters to the *New York Times*, found that between 1890 and 2010 the number of letters espousing conspiracy theories has generally declined—although there were distinct spikes following the financial panic of 1890 and during the "Red Scare" in the 1950s.[3] There are limits to such a methodology—many aspects of journalism have changed significantly over 120 years—but the main takeaway is fairly obvious: conspiracy theories have been with us for a long time and they are more intense in some periods than others.

A growing body of research is now available on how widespread internet access, and the social media platforms that depend upon that access, has shaped the dissemination of bad information, particularly conspiracy theories. "Partisan misinformation and conspiracy theories have seemingly increased in recent years," wrote the authors of one survey of research on this field, "in tandem with intensifying elite ideological polarization and widespread affective polarization at the mass level."[4]

Public-policy concerns drive this interest. The widespread belief that survivors of mass shootings are, for example, crisis actors appears intended to prevent the government from considering certain policy responses to gun violence.[5] There is also a pervasive sense that "fake news" on social media platforms like Facebook—in particular, Russian-supplied disinformation—may have altered the outcome of the 2016 election, although the relationship is difficult to establish.[6]

Whatever challenges we face in measuring the overall popularity or impact of bad information, there is an interesting body of research that suggests that the internet and social media are helpful for the spreading of "bum dope." This research tends to emphasize the ability of users to create homogenous online communities, communities that then collectively "process information through a shared system of meaning and trigger collective framing of narratives that are often biased toward self-confirmation."[7]

In general, however, our concern that bad information might inhibit effective public policy has focused on mass communication and political participation. There is a frequent, if unstated, assumption that political elites are immune to such thoughts. The argument goes something like this: sure, the base might be motivated by conspiracy theories, but those in positions of power know this is simply something to wind up the rubes. One example was the tendency of George H. W. Bush and GOP consultant Lee Atwater to refer to those elements in the Republican Party easily inclined to believe conspiracies—in this case about an arms-control deal with the Soviet Union—as "extra-chromosome" conservatives, a cruel comment about people with Down syndrome for which President Bush later publicly apologized.[8] More recently, then senator Robert Corker dismissed concerns about a tweet by President Trump that referenced a false conspiracy theory about the expropriation of lands and killing of white farmers in South Africa, a popular talking point among racists in the United States, as "a base stimulator."[9] Both of these comments are examples of how Republican elites distance themselves and, by implication, elite discourse from the false and often absurd views of some of their supporters— even though the available research suggests that conspiracy theories are far more common than many may realize.[10]

The idea that elites know better is, of course, a reassuring thought when it comes to nuclear weapons. After all, the base does not get to make decisions about nuclear war. An unstated assumption of popular discourse is that elites—those who would be responsible for handling a nuclear crisis—are somehow immune to the effects of bad information and would not likely be influenced by disinformation or conspiracy theories.

But why should this be the case? Perhaps, as self-styled elites, we like to think we are above all this. Looking at the situation objectively, however, as a group, those in positions of political power might actually be more susceptible to the cognitive processes that power bad information. For example, a substantial body of research suggests that "partisan stimuli have the power to activate motivated reasoning."[11] Motivated reasoning is a common human cognitive bias that leads people to select, trust, and make decisions based on information that agrees with their previous beliefs rather than rationally or objectively.[12] Partisanship is, one might say, a hell of a drug. And perhaps less kindly, one might point to a recent paper—one that admittedly requires replication—that suggests that excessive confidence, or explanation hubris (perhaps a hallmark of elites), correlates with a tendency to believe in conspiracy theories.[13]

In fact, the political science literature is replete with examples of propaganda or disinformation that became ingrained among elites. Van Evera first used the term "blowback" to describe the phenomenon by which military propaganda, intended for the public at large, instead influences the views of political leaders. As Snyder noted in discussing blowback, "The blurring of sincere belief and tactical argument has been common, and it would not be surprising if the elites purveying such arguments were unable to maintain the distinction between valid strategic concepts and opportunistic strategic rhetoric."[14]

There is even a well-known instance of blowback relating to nuclear weapons, one that occurred during the so-called war scare of 1983. As head of the KGB, Yuri Andropov had the ability to manipulate intelligence reports to shape discussions within the Politburo. Indeed, the dissemination of intelligence information was a major element of Andropov's power within the Politburo, as other members had few sources of information to counter Andropov's seemingly factual assessments about the threat environment or the efficacy of Soviet policies. Oleg Kalugin, then serving as a KGB officer, recalled receiving "what I can only describe as a paranoid cable from Andropov warning of the growing threat of a nuclear apocalypse."[15]

KGB officers felt obligated to shape their own assessments to match Andropov's views. "When, for example, Andropov concluded that the first Reagan administration had plans for a nuclear first strike against the Soviet Union," Christopher Andrew and Vasily Mitrokhin wrote, "none of the probably numerous sceptics in KGB residencies around the world dared to breathe a word of open dissent."[16] In particular, Andropov, positioning himself to succeed the ailing Brezhnev, instituted an intelligence-gathering operation known as RYAN that sought to detect American preparations for a surprise attack but that in fact resulted in fabricated reports that served to confirm paranoid fears in the Soviet leadership about the possibility of an American surprise attack.

And it was Andropov—having succeeded Brezhnev and himself in failing health and having internalized those concerns—who presided over the period of tension now known as the war scare.[17]

Nuclear Weapons in Romania

Throughout the Cold War, the Soviet Union frequently used disinformation campaigns to undermine the North Atlantic Treaty Organization (NATO) and the United States. A particularly noteworthy example was the campaign by the KGB and East Germany's Stasi secret police to spread what then secretary of state George Shultz called "bum dope about AIDS." This was a conspiracy theory that HIV was a biological weapon that had escaped from a US government laboratory.[18] In recent years, the Russian Federation has resumed these efforts, for example spreading disinformation about the destruction of Malaysia Airlines flight 17 over Ukraine in July 2014 despite overwhelming evidence that Russian-backed separatists shot down the aircraft with a Russian-supplied surface-to-air missile system.[19] Rather than simply accepting responsibility for the tragic mistake, the Russian government has released doctored photographs, including satellite images, to muddy the waters.

One frequent target of Russian disinformation campaigns is cohesion in NATO, discussed in broad terms by Kate Starbird in chapter 5 of this volume. In one specific case targeting NATO, in 2016 a Russian disinformation campaign spread rumors that the United States had moved nuclear weapons to a former air base in Deveselu, Romania. The site, officially known as Naval Support Facility Deveselu, is the first of two missile defense sites that are being constructed by the United States in Romania and Poland as part of the European Phased Adaptive Approach (EPAA), a missile defense system that is intended to defend NATO allies in Europe against ballistic missile attacks. The EPAA, as well as Romania's participation in NATO, are both frequent targets of Russian ire. After the site was declared operational in May 2016, Russian officials bitterly criticized it as "part of the military and political containment of Russia" that "can only exacerbate an already difficult situation."[20]

The disinformation campaign—which was intended to raise political opposition to Romania's participation in the EPAA—began in August 2016 at an annual public forum that features important Romanian politicians.[21] An anonymous person at the forum asked Traian Băsescu, a former president of Romania and at the time the leader of an important political party in the country, for "information about a possible intention of US to move its nuclear facilities from Incirlik, Turkey." At that time, there was no such information in the Romanian press. The question appears to have been planted in the hopes that an answer from an important political figure would in itself be newsworthy enough to generate coverage of the issue.

The dumbfounded former president said that he doubted the United States would remove nuclear weapons from Turkey and that, in any case, nuclear weapons should not be stationed in Romania.[22] The exchange was written up in a Romanian newspaper, however, which served to distribute the idea.

A second report soon followed, this time by Georgi Gotev, a Bulgarian journalist based in Brussels, writing for an obscure new site called Euractiv.[23] Gotev claimed that the transfer was, in fact, under way and had been "very challenging in technical and political terms." The sourcing for this story was unusually thin—he cited only "two independent sources" with no indication of how they might know such a thing—and the Romanian government denied it. Moreover, the notion made no sense at all. Deveselu was no longer an air base—there are no aircraft there that could deliver the gravity bombs stored in Turkey. Moreover, satellite images clearly showed that there are no facilities at Deveselu for storing nuclear weapons and no construction under way.[24]

Russian media, including Sputnik and RT, immediately seized on the story. Sputnik published no fewer than four stories on the report in the days that followed. RT, Izvestia, and other Russian sources also spread the rumors.[25] When accused of conducting a coordinated disinformation campaign, Sputnik media personalities claimed to be simply asking legitimate questions about whether the story was true or not. Meanwhile, the story spread through Twitter and entered the wider media ecosystem through publications like *Haaretz* in Israel and Breitbart News in the United States.[26]

The evidence of Russian involvement is, of course, circumstantial. But the story had many aspects of a disinformation campaign. Like the AIDS story, it was laundered through an obscure publication, which Russian media could then spread without taking responsibility for it. The prominence of the idea among Twitter accounts bears many of the hallmarks of Russian bots. And finally, some US experts later noted that they had been contacted by Russian journalists *in advance* of the publication by Euractiv, suggesting that Russian media were generally aware of the coming campaign.

What is more interesting, however, is the question: Do the Russians know their own disinformation is false? The answer to this question is not obvious.

The disinformation campaign was part of a continuing effort to paint US missile defense systems to be deployed in Poland and Romania as systems that could be converted to house offensive missiles, armed with nuclear weapons, and used to decapitate the Russian leadership. There was also a similar campaign in Poland during June 2016 following joint military exercises.[27]

But what if the Russians believe it? What if the Russians believe that there is, in fact, a conspiracy to convert missile defense interceptors into nuclear-armed offensive missiles? And what if they come to believe that nuclear weapons are, in fact, covertly stationed around the world?

There is a fair amount of evidence that the Russians believe *precisely* that. For example, in 2009 then secretary of defense Robert Gates explained that "the Russians believed, despite our best efforts to dissuade them, that the ground-based interceptors in Poland could be fitted with nuclear weapons and become an offensive weapon like a Pershing and a weapon for which they would have virtually no warning time."[28] The then deputy undersecretary of defense Jim Miller later told a meeting at the Arms Control Association that he was shocked to hear Gates say that in an unclassified setting. During the negotiations over the New START treaty, Russian officials insisted on treaty language prohibiting the emplacement of offensive systems in missile defense silos. This was a significant point of disagreement between the two parties that Russia raised repeatedly and ultimately succeeded in including in the treaty text. Russian leader Vladimir Putin himself has made the point repeatedly. Putin told writer Oliver Stone that "the launching pads of these antiballistic missiles can be transformed within a few hours [into] offensive missile launching pads. Look, if these antiballistic missiles are placed in Eastern Europe, if those missiles are placed on water, patrolling the Mediterranean and Northern Seas, and in Alaska, almost the whole Russian territory would be encircled by these systems." In addition, he told a meeting of defense industry officials that "the launchers, to be deployed after the radar stations in Romania and Poland go on stream, can easily be used for the deployment of intermediate and short range missiles. The conversion can actually happen in a very short time, and we will not even know what is happening there."[29] The last sentence is particularly worrisome—if the Russians believe that the conversion can take place without their knowledge, then in a crisis they may well experience a kind of analytic slippage, going from "a conversion might have taken place" to a belief that "a conversion had taken place."

It seems bizarre. There are no nuclear weapons in Poland or Romania, nor are there plans to convert these missiles to offensive purposes. The problem is that such a conversion is feasible, and it is the kind of thing that American officials occasionally propose. For example, the report accompanying the Senate version of the FY 2018 National Defense Authorization Act included language calling for "evaluating existing U.S. missile systems for modification to intermediate range and ground-launch, including Tomahawk, Standard Missile-3, Standard Missile-6, Long-Range Stand-Off Cruise Missile, and Army Tactical Missile System." The SM-3, of course, is the missile deployed in Poland and Romania.[30]

Of course, we know that there is no secret plan to convert the missile defenses in Poland and Romania into offensive nuclear-armed intermediate-range missiles. But the Russians do not know that—and that is the point. The Russians have pushed this particular conspiracy theory so long—maybe cynically at first, to recreate the Euromissile crisis of the 1980s—that now they might very well believe it. After President Donald Trump announced that the United States would withdraw from the 1987 Intermediate-Range Nuclear Forces Treaty, Vladimir Putin announced that Russia would target with nuclear weapons any countries in Europe that hosted US intermediate-range missiles. "The European countries that agree to [host future US missiles]," Putin explained, "must realize that they will put their own territory at risk of a retaliatory strike." Putin singled out Romania, explaining, "The Aegis launchers can be used for offensive missiles, not anti-missiles.

They only need to update the software and that's it. This can be done in hours. We will not even be able to guess what is happening, we will not be able to see it from the outside." There is no way to know whether Putin really believes this, but Van Evera's theory of blowback suggests he very well might. And that might be very dangerous in a crisis.

Escalate to De-escalate

The United States has its own myths about Russia, just as Russia has about us. Consider the idea, widespread in the United States, that Russia has a nuclear strategy that involves a limited use of nuclear weapons. "The dominant narrative about Russia's nuclear weapons in Western strategic literature since the beginning of the century," French political scientist Bruno Tertrais wrote, "has been something like this: Russia's doctrine of 'escalate-to-de-escalate' and its large-scale military exercises show that Moscow is getting ready to use low-yield, theatre nuclear weapons to stop NATO from defeating Russia's forces, or to coerce the Atlantic Alliance and end a conflict on terms favourable to Russia."[31] Other American officials have gone further, asserting that they believe that Russian military doctrine contemplates the first use of a small number of nuclear weapons in the midst of a conventional conflict to compel NATO to accept a settlement favorable to Russia. "I don't think the Russian doctrine is escalate to de-escalate," General John E. Hyten, commander of US Strategic Command, told a conference of reporters. "To me, the Russian doctrine is to escalate to win."[32] This narrative dominates conversations at conferences and appears in official US documents, including the 2018 Nuclear Posture Review.[33]

It is worth noting how little evidence there is to support this view. A full examination is beyond the scope of this chapter, but it is worth noting two dissents. Russia expert Olga Oliker concludes that assertions that Russia has an escalate-to-de-escalate strategy "do not track with what I know of Russian nuclear strategy, nor with how Russians talk about it, for the most part."[34] For Tertrais, "All the elements of this narrative, however, rely on weak evidence—and there is strong evidence to counter most of them."[35] For nuclear security expert Kristin Ven Bruusgaard, "The evidence for a lowered Russian nuclear threshold is getting weaker by the day."[36]

It is true, of course, that some Russian officials have discussed using nuclear weapons first—in precisely the same way that it is also true that some US officials have discussed giving the SM-3 an offensive role. Proving such an assertion requires more than curating selected statements from Russian officials. For most outside observers, the idea of escalate-to-de-escalate seems like a bit of a Beltway fad, a Team B exercise that slipped out of the Washington, DC, think-tank "fever swamp" and has gone viral. Tellingly, when pushed to explain why Russian writings and exercises have clearly moved away from such strategic concepts, proponents of the escalate-to-de-escalate narrative have invoked the notion that Russia's classified doctrine must be different from the public one.[37]

Despite the thin evidence to support this approach, the escalate-to-de-escalate narrative remains the dominant view in American strategic circles, much as the view that the United States has a covert plan to convert missile defense interceptors to offensive weapons is dominant among Russians strategists. Perhaps some will object to the comparison. *Their* concerns may be a conspiracy theory, but *ours* reflect a reasonable debate among viewpoints. Here I might note that sincerity of belief is hardly relevant, since we are concerned here precisely with the prospect that motivated reasoning might harden into sincere, if wrong-headed, conviction. For all its sincerity, the indignation that would meet the claim that escalate-to-de-escalate is little more than a conspiracy theory would seem little different to an outside observer than the indignation that would be heard in Moscow if someone denied that NATO were covertly converting missile defenses in Poland and Romania to nuclear-armed offensive roles.

Crisis Stability

These two ideas, even if false, could have real implications for crisis stability—especially if they interact with one another. Four years after the collapse of the Soviet Union and the end of the Cold War, there was a scare. It all started innocently enough. In 1995, a group of American and Norwegian scientists launched a sounding rocket from the Andøya Rocket Range off the northwest coast of Norway. This was all quite normal—there have been more than one thousand rocket launches from this site over the decades. Following standard protocol, Norwegian authorities informed their Russian counterparts of the launch.

Yet, as the sounding rocket headed up and away from Russia, Russia's Olenegorsk early-warning radar in Murmansk saw it. The radar operators thought the speed and flight pattern resembled not a sounding rocket but something more ominous: a single US Trident ballistic missile, launched from a submarine and heading toward Russia.

The sounding rocket was headed out to sea, away from Russia. But the radar operators saw something else. The radar operators saw a US ballistic missile, not a sounding rocket, and concluded that it was headed toward Russia, not away from it. Russian military officials looked at the lonely missile streaking toward their country and began to worry that the United States had fired it to black out Russian early-warning radars, with the main nuclear attack to fly past the blinded radars a few moments later.

So, a warning was passed up the chain of command, reaching all the way to Russian president Boris Yeltsin. He was informed of the impending attack and presented with Russia's "nuclear briefcase"—the *cheget*—which was activated for the very first time. All that was left was for Yeltsin to order a retaliation. And then? Nothing.

There was in fact no US nuclear-tipped missile headed for Russia. Yeltsin, fortunately, did not order Russian strategic forces to retaliate preemptively. This was four years after the end of the Cold War. US-Russian relations were as good as ever. Yeltsin simply did not think his friend Bill Clinton would launch a surprise nuclear attack (also, he was sober). Happily, we survived.

Now, let us consider our current moment. The Nuclear Posture Review proceeds on the basis that, unlike in the 1990s, a nuclear war with Russia is very much a possibility. It imagines a scenario in which the United States and Russia are at war, for example with conventional weapons in the Baltics, when Vladimir Putin "escalates-to-de-escalate." According to the Nuclear Posture Review, Moscow might use a small number of nuclear weapons under the "mistaken expectation that coercive nuclear threats or limited first use could paralyze the United States and NATO and thereby end a conflict on terms favorable to Russia."[38]

So this time there is no misunderstanding—the authors of the Nuclear Posture Review propose to "modify a small number of existing SLBM warheads to provide a low-yield option," modifying the weapons so that they explode with far less destructive power. This would allow the United States to respond to a limited first nuclear use by Russia—in other words, the escalate-to-de-escalate scenario—by responding with a low-yield strike of its own. Put simply, they propose to replay the most frightening nuclear scare of the past thirty years, but for real—by deliberately launching a nuclear-armed Trident ballistic missile toward Russia with the expectation that Russian radars will see it, Putin will be informed, the *cheget* will be opened, and then Putin will decide to wait. And that once it explodes, Putin will wait for a report on its yield, that report will be accurate, and Putin will take no further action.

There are two contrary data points. First, Russian doctrine is not to wait for a nuclear warhead to detonate. Russia's policy is a kind of "launch on warning"—although Putin, in an effort to be reassuring, has added that "warning" includes not merely detection of the launch but also the calculation of its trajectory. "A decision about using nuclear weapons can be made only if our missile warning system recorded not only the launch of missiles," he has explained, "but also gave an accurate prediction of flight trajectories and the time when the warheads fall on Russia."[39] Second, Putin has also made clear that he would not distinguish between different yields. "I believe it is my duty to say this: any use of nuclear weapons of any yield—small, medium, or whatever—against Russia or its allies will be regarded as a nuclear attack against our country. Retaliation will be instant with all the ensuing consequences."[40]

Perhaps Putin is just bluffing. Maybe there really is a secret Russian nuclear doctrine to ride out an attack. Perhaps Putin is exaggerating his concerns about US missile defenses in Poland and Romania to score propaganda points. These are major assumptions on which to base US policy, especially since they may be based on motivated reasoning—"bum dope."

Let us consider the alternative believed by Russian nuclear analysts: that the United States might covertly convert missile defense installations to give them offensive capabilities. Let us imagine that the Russian denial is sincere, that Moscow does not have an escalate-to-de-escalate strategy. If that is so, then Russian policy makers are likely to conclude that the Nuclear Posture Review is simply an elaborate justification to allow the United States to adopt the very strategy of which it accuses Moscow. And they will have evidence to support this view—from, of all places, Twitter.

Here is how one of the architects of the US Nuclear Posture Review responded when an expert at a Russian think tank tried to make a rhetorical point about the absurdity of "escalate-to-de-escalate." He asked if, given the low standard for evidence adopted by US proponents, Russia should not worry that the United States might not have such a strategy. "Should Russia be worried that when US is faced with a loss in a conventional conflict with Moscow," wrote Moscow consultant Andrey Baklitskiy, "Washington would use limited nuclear strike to 'de-escalate' the situation and cease hostilities on US terms?"

His American colleague responded: "Yes!!!!!!!"[41]

The point, of course, is that information has consequences. The United States believes that Russia has an escalate-to-de-escalate strategy and is taking actions—the development of a low-yield SLBM option—to respond to it. And we accept that Russia should worry that we will do the same. It is not controversial to observe that what the late economist Thomas Schelling called the reciprocal fear of surprise attack might be destabilizing. But it should be jarring to observe how little such fears need to be grounded in reality to pose a real danger.

Conclusion

It is uncomfortable to consider the fact that American and Russian elites are just as vulnerable to bad information as our relatives on Facebook are. Yet there is ample evidence that leaders in Moscow have made—and are making—decisions based on ideas about us that we find ridiculous. It would be extraordinary arrogance to imagine that we do not suffer some of the same problems. As Moscow and Washington drift back into an arms race, officials and politicians in both countries are spreading myths about the other with the high-minded purpose of creating the political will to keep up. This is how political systems function. "If we made our points clearer than the truth," US statesman Dean Acheson later said of the first wave of Cold War propaganda, "we did not differ from most other educators and could hardly do otherwise."[42]

The problem, of course, is that clarity might well lead us into deeper crisis. Yet, unlike Acheson, we have hindsight. We do not have to wait for our own crisis like Berlin or Cuba to learn that false strategic concepts—like the missile gap—might lead us into oblivion. We also have experience with the tools—arms-control agreements—that can provide transparency, stability, and predictability. If the problem is that Russia believes there may be nuclear weapons, then we might imagine allowing Russian inspectors access to the sites. And if the United States believes that Russia is developing a covert nuclear doctrine, then we might imagine US military officials being invited to attend exercises and allowed to interact with their counterparts on the Russian general staff. These problems are old ones—ones we know how to manage, if not quite solve.

Notes

1. Stephen Van Evera as quoted in Jack Snyder, *Myths of Empire: Domestic Politics and International Ambition* (Ithaca, NY: Cornell University Press, 2013).

2. Norman Kempster and William J. Eaton, "State Dept. Report Angers Soviet Leader: Shultz-Gorbachev Talks Turn Heated," *Los Angeles Times*, October 24, 1987, https://www.latimes.com/archives/la-xpm-1987-10-24-mn-4106-story.html.

3. Joseph E. Uscinski and Joseph M. Parent, *American Conspiracy Theories* (New York: Oxford University Press, 2014).

4. Joshua Tucker, Andrew Guess, Pablo Barberá, Cristian Vaccari, Alexandra Siegel, Sergey Sanovich, Denis Stukal, and Brendan Nyhan, "Social Media, Political Polarization, and Political Disinformation: A Review of the Scientific Literature," Hewlett Foundation, March 2018.

5. Saranac Hale Spencer, "No 'Crisis Actors' in Parkland, Florida," *FactCheck. Org*, February 22, 2018, https://www.factcheck.org/2018/02/no-crisis-actors-parkland-florida; Michael M. Grynbaum, "Right-Wing Media Uses Parkland Shooting as Conspiracy Fodder," *New York Times*, February 20, 2018, https://www.nytimes.com/2018/02/20/business/media/parkland-shooting-media-conspiracy.html.

6. Hunt Allcott and Matthew Gentzkow, "Social Media and Fake News in the 2016 Election," *Journal of Economic Perspectives* 31, no. 2 (2017): 211–36; Andrew Guess, Brendan Nyhan, and Jason Reifler, "Selective Exposure to Misinformation: Evidence from the Consumption of Fake News during the 2016 U.S. Presidential Campaign," European Research Council, January 8, 2018.

7. Michela Del Vicario, Alessandro Bessi, Fabiana Zollo, Fabio Petroni, Antonio Scala, Guido Caldarelli, H. Eugene Stanley, and Walter Quattrociocchi, "The Spreading of Misinformation Online," *Proceedings of the National Academy of Sciences* 113, no. 3 (January 29, 2016): 554–59.

8. The usage by Bush and Atwater was reported by John Brady in his biography of Atwater. Bush used the phrase in public in 1987 and later apologized for the reference. "Bush Offers Apology for Remark About 'Extra Chromosome,'" *Los Angeles Times*, December 18, 1987, https://www.latimes.com/archives/la-xpm-1987-12-18-mn-20078-story.html.

9. Jennifer Williams, "Trump's Tweet Echoing White Nationalist Propaganda about South African Farmers, Explained," *Vox*, August 23, 2018, https://www.vox.com/policy-and-politics/2018/8/23/17772056/south-africa-trump-tweet-afriforum-white-farmers-violence.

10. J. Eric Oliver and Thomas J. Wood, "Conspiracy Theories and the Paranoid Style(s) of Mass Opinion," *American Journal of Political Science* 58, no. 4 (October 2014): 952–66, https://doi.org/10.1111/ajps.12084. Oliver and Wood

find that belief in conspiracy theories is associated not with ideology but rather with predisposition to believe in unseen but intentional forces manipulating the world and with Manichean narratives.

11. Adam M. Enders and Steven M. Smallpage, "On the Measurement of Conspiracy Beliefs," *Research & Politics* 5, no. 1 (March 15, 2018).

12. Ziva Kunda, "The Case for Motivated Reasoning," *Psychological Bulletin* 108, no. 3 (1990): 480–98.

13. Jessecae K. Marsh and Joseph A. Vitriol, *Explanation Hubris and Conspiracy Theories: A Case of the 2016 Presidential Election*, Proceedings of the 38th Annual Conference of the Cognitive Science Society, Madison, WI, July 25–28, 2018.

14. Van Evera, in Snyder, *Myths of Empire*, 41–42.

15. Oleg Kalugin, *Spymaster: My Thirty-Two Years in Intelligence and Espionage Against the West* (New York: Basic Books, 2009).

16. Christopher Andrew and Vasily Mitrokhin, *The World Was Going Our Way: The KGB and the Battle for the Third World; Newly Revealed Secrets from the Mitrokhin Archive* (New York: Basic Books, 2006).

17. Ibid.

18. Kempster and Eaton, "State Dept. Report Angers Soviet Leader."

19. "The JIT concludes that flight MH17 was shot down on 17 July 2014 by a missile of the 9M38 series, launched by a BUK-TELAR, from farmland in the vicinity of Pervomaiskiy (or: Pervomaiskyi). At that time, the area was controlled by pro-Russian fighters. Furthermore, the investigation also shows that the BUK-TELAR was brought in from the territory of the Russian Federation and subsequently, after having shot down flight MH-17, was taken back to the Russian Federation." Joint Investigation Team, "Presentation Preliminary Results Criminal Investigation MH17," Public Prosecution Service, the Netherlands, September 28, 2016, https://www.om.nl/onderwerpen/mh17-crash/@96066/presentation.

20. Robin Emmott, "U.S. Activates Romanian Missile Defense Site, Angering Russia," Reuters, May 12, 2016, https://www.reuters.com/article/us-nato-shield-idUSKCN0Y30JX.

21. Each year, the central Romanian town of Izvorul Muresului hosts a "Summer University of the Romanians in the Diaspora" in which representatives of Romanian communities around the world can ask questions of important politicians.

22. "Băsescu: Nu cred că teritoriul României trebuie să devină unul pe care să fie şi un arsenal nuclear" [Basescu: I do not think that the territory of Romania is one that should become a nuclear arsenal], Jurnalul.ro, August 17, 2016, https://www.digi24.ro/stiri/actualitate/basescu-nu-cred-ca-pe-teritoriul-romaniei-trebuie-sa-fie-si-arsenal-nuclear-550611.

23. Georgi Gotev and Joel Schalit, "US Moves Nuclear Weapons from Turkey to Romania," Euractiv, August 18, 2016.

24. Jeffrey Lewis, "Russia's Nuclear Paranoia Fuels Its Nuclear Propaganda," *Foreign Policy*, *Voice* (blog), August 22, 2016, http://foreignpolicy.com/2016/08/22 /russias-nuclear-paranoia-fuels-its-nuclear-propaganda.

25. Sam Meyer, "Fake News, Real Consequences: The Dangers of WMD Disinformation," Nuclear Threat Initiative, December 18, 2017, https://www.nti .org/analysis/articles/fake-news-real-consequences-dangers-wmd-disinformation.

26. "Report: U.S. Transfers Nukes From Turkish Airbase to Romania," *Haaretz*, August 18, 2016, https://www.haaretz.com/middle-east-news/report-u -s-transfers-nukes-from-turkish-airbase-to-romania-1.5426668. As reposted from Breitbart, Raheem Kassam, "Claim: U.S. Moving Nuclear Weapons from Turkey to Romania," *Middle East Forum* (blog), August 18, 2016, https://www.meforum .org/6201/us-nuclear-weapons-turkey.

27. Lewis, "Russia's Nuclear Paranoia."

28. US Department of Defense, "DoD News Briefing with Secretary Gates and Gen. Cartwright from the Pentagon," news release, September 17, 2009, https://archive.defense.gov/transcripts/transcript.aspx?transcriptid=4479.

29. "Meeting on Defence Industry Development," news release, President of Russia, May 13, 2016, http://en.kremlin.ru/events/president/news/51911.

30. National Defense Authorization Act for Fiscal Year 2018, Report 115-125 to accompany S.1519, Committee on Armed Services, *To Authorize Appropriations for Fiscal Year 2018 for Military Activities of the Department of Defense, for Military Construction, and for Defense Activities of the Department of Energy, to Prescribe Military Personnel Strengths for Such Fiscal Year, and for Other Purposes*, 115th Congress, 1st Session (July 10, 2017), 304, https://www.congress.gov/115/crpt /srpt125/CRPT-115srpt125.pdf.

31. Bruno Tertrais, "Russia's Nuclear Policy: Worrying for the Wrong Reasons," *Survival* 60, no. 2 (2018): 33–44.

32. John E. Hyten, keynote speech, Military Reporters and Editors Association Conference, Arlington, VA, March 31, 2017, http://www.stratcom .mil/Media/Speeches/Article/1153029/military-reporters-and-editors -association-conference-keynote-speech.

33. US Department of Defense, "Nuclear Posture Review," Office of the Secretary of Defense, 2018.

34. Olga Oliker, "No, Russia Isn't Trying to Make Nuclear War Easier," *National Interest*, May 23, 2016, https://nationalinterest.org/feature/no-russia-isnt -trying-make-nuclear-war-easier-16310.

35. Tertrais, "Russia's Nuclear Policy."

36. Kristin Ven Bruusgaard, "The Myth of Russia's Lowered Nuclear Threshold," *War on the Rocks* 22 (September 2017).

37. Mark Schneider, "Escalate to De-Escalate," *U.S. Naval Institute Proceedings* 143, no. 2 (February 2017): 1368.

38. US Department of Defense, "Nuclear Posture Review," 30.

39. Putin made the comment in the documentary *World Order 2018* at 1:21:43, on YouTube, https://www.youtube.com/watch?v=bWoIE1CWYbQ.

40. "Putin Vows Instant Retaliation Against Any Nuclear Attack on Russia or Its Allies," TASS, March 1, 2018, https://tass.com/politics/992246.

41. The exchange can be found on Twitter at https://twitter.com/Elbridge Colby/status/1057277124128763904.

42. As quoted in Snyder, *Myths of Empire*, 42.

Chapter 9

The Impact of the Information Ecosystem on Public Opinion during Nuclear Crises:

Lifting the Lid on the Role of Identity Narratives

Ben O'Loughlin

Public Opinion Is Embedded in Identity Narratives

How do strategic narratives function in an information ecosystem to influence constituencies during international crises? And how does an information ecosystem marked by increasing use of social media affect public opinion during such crises? In this chapter I argue, first, that nuclear crises allow the public articulation of narratives about how international order works and that narratives about the identities of the key protagonists often remain central to the reaction of public opinion. Second, I argue that we cannot expect social media to greatly affect how public opinion works in crises. Decades of scholarship on political communication have shown that news, entertainment, and other media formats have influenced what issues and events publics think about but not what positions they hold toward issues or events. Instead of simply asking what impact social media have, it is more useful to ask first *whether* social media, via the relationships they enable and the content they convey, play a significantly new or different role on public opinion during international crises.

As this chapter outlines, changes to the information ecosystem will not make substantial changes to public opinion during international crises such as nuclear standoffs. Many decades of research in political communication have shown that public opinion is very difficult to change. This is confirmed by recent research exploring the narratives citizens hold about international affairs and global media events. Certainly, social media intensify the speed and potential public participation in global media events, but there is no evidence to suggest they change opinions. Instead, it is more useful to examine the longer-term narratives that citizens and publics hold about international affairs, how those enduring narratives shape expectations about how global crises are likely to unfold, and how they should be managed.

Social Media, Identity, and Strategic Narratives

Social media have been viewed across scholarly and policy debates as a potential source of chaotic, participatory exuberance. This is deemed to mark a moment of transformation in how public opinion functions. And yet, a more realistic view is possible. Digital technologies that allow anyone a public voice have simply lifted the carpet on the range of already existing and diverse viewpoints for all to see.[1] And many are horrified! It is not that social media have led to greater polarization about, or emotional reactions to, international affairs. US public feeling about nuclear conflict, for instance, was intense and divergent in the early days of the Cold War.[2] Rather, those divisions and responses were offline, face to face, and not immediately turned into data that are archived, cherry-picked, and sensationalized. A sanitized "mainstream" idea of public opinion could be constructed in the post–World War II era, a period characterized by relatively few national news media outlets covering international affairs, polling geared around the issues covered by those outlets, and, in the West, a democratic politics geared toward compromise and stability after the upheavals of the early twentieth century.[3]

We now see much more clearly the role of identity in the long-term narratives held by ordinary people about their own country and its role in international affairs. This is to some degree a function of the methodologies that let us research public opinion. In marketing, digital traces of ordinary people's conversations provide firms with new ways to segment populations by sentiment and interest, renewing attention to identity groups—what consultancy firm KPMG labeled digital "tribes."[4] Communication becomes tribal, too, in the sense that social media enable instantaneous conversation or "chat" such that many scholars argue we are witnessing a return to an oral public culture. After a "Gutenberg parenthesis" in the twentieth century, when periodic written texts were central to public life, digital media enable a return to a pre-twentieth-century orality based around storytelling.[5] This encourages easy expression and contestation of identities. But how can we understand this in a systematic and rigorous way?

I define strategic narratives as a means by which political actors attempt to construct a shared meaning of international politics to shape the behavior of domestic and international actors.[6] Critically, I argue that three types of narrative are pivotal to explaining how the meaning of international affairs is generated, including the meaning of nuclear politics:

- *System narratives* describe how the world is structured, who the players are, and how it works. For example: Is there a global bipolar international order led by a G2 consisting of the United States and China, or is there a multipolar system in which the European Union, India, and Russia join the United States and China as great powers? Is the system governed by states or by some mix of states, firms, and international organizations?
- *Identity narratives* set out what the story of a political actor is, what values it has, what its character and reputation are, and what goals it has.[7] One's system narrative determines what constitutes an appropriate role or function that a state with certain characteristics can play. Thus, system narratives play an important and often primary role in shaping what identity narratives these states project.[8] For instance, if we inhabit a G2 system, this would entail China and the United States taking equal responsibility as leaders tackling global problems.
- *Issue narratives* set out a problem and why a policy is needed and (normatively) desirable, and how it will be successfully implemented or accomplished. For example, depending on how we narrate the origins and causes of climate change as an issue, this will then shape the

design of solutions (for example, whether to focus on adaptation or mitigation) and the distribution of responsibility for implementing them (whether the major polluters should bear the greatest costs or all should contribute to addressing them).

The study of narrative in international affairs has become a recurring theme in international relations recently, particularly to explain how communities of consensus on an issue can be built such that actors feel they are moving toward a shared problem diagnosis and solution. Political scientist Jack Snyder has argued that, through analyzing strategic narratives, we can see how political actors attempt to persuade others of their political vision.[9] He argues that narratives make possible the "conceptual integration of facts and values (of 'is' and 'ought') in strategic persuasion and the political integration of diverse perspectives among partners in a strategic coalition."[10] The use of narrative is a tool to organize the identities of political communities and international organizations.[11] Narratives are also seen as having force to coerce others to do the will of the powerful in international affairs, since confident great or emerging powers can point to and exacerbate the contradictions or hypocrisies in another actor's proclaimed identity and empirical actions.[12] Hence, we find in nuclear politics efforts to shame or embarrass parties to the Nuclear Non-proliferation Treaty (NPT) who do not meet commitments on disarmament and nonproliferation, and to stigmatize and securitize non-NPT states who seek nuclear technologies. Nuclear politics is mediated by narrative characterizations of key actors. Those characterizations determine expectations about how those actors are likely to act and thus how they should be engaged. In other words, through identity narratives, communication is used to shape behavior.

Nuclear Crises Are Standoffs That Must Be Narrated

We can further understand the role of narrative in nuclear crises if we treat them as instances of a standoff. A standoff involves two antagonistic parties at deadlock in a conflict. Following sociologist Robin Wagner-Pacifici, I treat standoffs as "action in the subjunctive mood": witnesses hypothesize about likely outcomes and their speculation is tinged with emotion—doubt, hope, fear.[13] A spectator may think, "I dread that my country will be bombed and we will suffer" or, "I fear our leaders will launch an unjustified attack." Standoffs let us identify how regularities and norms of behavior are invoked and thus what opinions publics hold about international affairs. What is the appropriate way for the international community to manage such crises and dilemmas? And what is the most effective and useful way for journalists to report on such events? There is a duration to these moments of crisis, when fate hangs in the balance, and in that duration we can focus on how actors respond to the contingency of that moment.[14]

The centrality of expectations and projections of possible outcomes necessitates the analysis of public opinion in the forms of narratives rather than simply public attitudes or sentiments toward ongoing events. I would expect to see cultural variations in how different nations and their leaders respond to nuclear standoffs. Wagner-Pacifici writes, "In the action-oriented culture of the United States, there is an exaggerated *horror vacui*—the horror of nothingness, of doing nothing—that exerts pressure on the standoff. Nobody wants to do nothing."[15] A country like Germany will approach the standoff differently, given that past instances of acting—of doing something—led to the crimes of the Nazi period. India and Pakistan could bring different approaches again to a nuclear standoff within the context of their rivalry and entangled history.[16] Digital media will enable citizens from such different countries to debate the relative merits of action or inaction during a crisis, but this conversation is unlikely to alter opinions on either side. Let us now examine why.

The Problem of "Impact"

There is a tendency among pundits and policy makers alike to believe that communication influences publics. This is the concept of the "third-person effect"—that while *our* minds are made up, the minds of *others* are influenced and their behavior changed by exposure to media. The validity of the third-person effect has been a subject of recurring debate. Based on years of ethnographic fieldwork, Professor Sarah Maltby has documented how military communications teams have a mindset of "imagined influence": if they project content (videos, leaflets, sweets for children), those on the receiving end must "get the message," surely? This leads to efforts to communicate more and "smarter" but rarely to any research with those target audiences to see if they actually welcome these communications.[17] (The same could be said for science communication on vaccines, climate change, and so on.) As political scientist Joanna Szostek is showing in her ongoing research in Ukraine, the presumption that enemy media are influencing "your" public spurs state efforts to control the information battlefield—which is also the public sphere and the space of democracy.[18] But *are* people influenced by propaganda? *Does* the enemy "implant" conspiracies in "our" population—and *how*? The longevity of presumed media influence is embedded in more long-standing assumptions about the malleability of human hearts and minds and, normatively, what the *right* and *normal* responses of individuals *should* be.

Yet, scholars of political communication continue to argue that exposure to a narrative is not the same as being persuaded by a narrative, let alone altering one's behavior based on being persuaded by a narrative. Hence, we face a paradox. On the one hand, we have never had more efforts to influence others in political campaigns, at home and abroad. A study of the presence of disinformation campaigns by political parties in forty-eight countries found that parties in *every one* of these countries are now using these techniques.[19] On the other hand, there is no evidence these techniques have made any difference in voter behavior. A recent metastudy of the effects of voters' exposure to political campaigns across forty-nine field experiments showed an average of *zero* effect on voters' candidate choices.[20] This does not rule out voters at opposite poles becoming more polarized, even if the net effect is zero. But comparative research demonstrates that this polarization is by far the most evident in the United States, such that the debate about the persuasiveness of disinformation campaigns is being driven by an outlier.[21] Even within the United States there is uncertainty about media effects. Internal testing of the persuasive effects of political ads on American citizens by one firm discovered that "not only did the group find zero correlation between engagement and persuasion; in some cases, the most engaging videos persuaded people in the wrong direction."[22] The consensus view in scholarship on political communication is that shaping citizens' opinions is extremely difficult and that a citizen's position on an issue is explained more by feelings of identity than by any "rational" processing of information.[23]

Robin Brown, a historian of international communication, contends that strategic narratives projected through public diplomacy programs only succeed to the extent that these communications become interwoven within existing social networks and communities.[24] Previous public diplomacy programs have failed because they have neither penetrated existing social networks nor generated new networks. He argues that doing so today is potentially feasible, methodologically, to the degree that social networks are constituted through digital media. But not all communication is online. Many of the networks public diplomats would target are face-to-face or proceed through nondigital media. Nevertheless, the spread of mobile telephony, the internet, and thus social media in the developing world will afford opportunities to trace how states' strategic narratives about nuclear weaponry and norms of countries' behavior during standoffs or crises are received, negotiated, and sustained or challenged in local contexts. But because narratives are embedded in long-term social networks and tied to perspectives on the identities of one's own state and others, it is unlikely that a narrative about a nuclear crisis arriving from outside a community will shift that community's view of the matter. If the effects of communication depend on how narratives enter into and circulate in communities, we would need to employ offline methods to trace how such narratives and norms are present in those communities and how online and offline communications work. The temptation to study online communities is high because social media data are relatively freely available and much cheaper than the costs of fieldwork in offline communities. Ultimately, however, such effort and collaboration across locations are needed if we are to understand how narratives about nuclear crises are received and interpreted and how any influence may operate.

A key finding of much research of audience engagement with global crises in past decades is that ordinary people feel a great deal of uncertainty and ambiguity about how issues like cyberattacks, nuclear proliferation, or radicalization actually work.[25] This is often in part because journalists have difficulty explaining them.[26] Hence there is the tendency to fall back upon long-established identity narratives that hold in one's community and that precede digital communication. Are changes to the information ecosystem likely to alleviate such uncertainty? Will the diffusion of information allow citizens to enjoy more meaningful engagement with matters of international security?

Changes to the Information Ecosystem

Too much footage and information from contemporary wars and conflicts leave us unsure what we are being shown or what we are hearing.[27] Since 2015 the post-truth debate has stirred invocations of a crisis of journalism and of democracy precisely because of uncertainty about communication. Communication poses a problem because it is simultaneously ubiquitous and black-boxed; it constitutes all relations and yet is beyond our grasp, our "literacy." From Syria we have unprecedented digital content yet maddening opacity.[28] Russia's interventions in US elections and Ukraine are said to show the brittleness and fragility of mass communication and the institutions supposed to uphold it. Content from open-source outlets and citizen journalists may allow verification when a crisis unfolds, but it is often slow and may not receive wide publicity in mainstream media that would allow publics to reconsider the event. Even when we see, we cannot discern the motivation of those who publish content. Trust collapses. Events in international affairs seem important and could possibly affect us, but they reach audiences in ways that offer a picture that is unclear, contested, and ambiguous—indeed, often deliberately so in the case of a news organization like Russia's RT.

By 2018, a recurring claim about the information ecosystem was that it intensifies and polarizes emotional positions of publics. Professor of journalism Silvio Waisbord writes:

> Recent political events . . . have magnified social and communicative rifts driving post-truth politics. Truth becomes a matter of personal and group convictions rather than something that resembles the scientific orthodoxy of shared procedures and verifiable statements about reality.[29]

Now, we can question whether public processing and interpretation of information about international affairs ever resembled a scientific process. As I argued above, social media have rather lifted the lid on the range of epistemologies and orientations to truth that people hold. There is no evidence that social media created or increased that range of orientations. But, in a context of uncertainty about complex international affairs issues like nuclear standoffs, it is easy to see why publics would fall back upon long-standing identity narratives about the protagonists. Through characterization of familiar actors in international affairs, identity narratives offer a degree of certainty about those protagonists' likely motives based on interpretations of their past behavior.

Several insider accounts now indicate that the business model of social media rests upon cultivating a degree of emotional charge, and such emotionally charged engagements *may* work to exacerbate a focus on identity. Platforms offering campaign services to political parties in the US 2016 presidential election led to efforts "to make politics more sensational," argued one former Facebook employee.[30] A Facebook investor compared the "if it bleeds, it leads" logic of traditional news media to how Facebook uses outrage through its "2.1 billion individualized channels. . . . They're basically trying to trigger fear and anger to get the outrage cycle going, because outrage is what makes you be more deeply engaged. . . . Therefore, you're going to be exposed to more ads and that makes you more valuable."[31] This outrage cycle is structurally built into how social media generate revenue, because attention generates interactions, which can be analyzed to offer insights about user behavior, data, and insights that in turn can be sold to advertisers. Consequently, those structures must be altered if we are to expect different outcomes.

This is not the place to list recommendations to reconstruct information ecosystems so that they are more resilient for a functioning democratic culture or to ensure citizens are protected from disinformation on matters of international affairs such as nuclear crises. That debate is unfolding, and it varies in each national media and political system. Instead, we must acknowledge that, to the extent that information ecosystems are increasingly driven by commercial and platform logics that prioritize emotional engagement, this has the potential to further intensify the importance of identity narratives in the way ordinary citizens interpret international affairs.

Conclusion

Changes to the information ecosystem such as the proliferation of social media will not make substantial changes to how public opinion operates during international crises such as nuclear standoffs. Research in political communication and current work on the stickiness of narrative in communities demonstrates why this is the case. Social media do affect how debate works, speeding up the connectivity and circulation of content and enabling a greater degree of participation by members of publics around the world. However, there is no evidence to suggest they change opinions. They can focus attention upon social division that could be used to intensify opinion and feeling, but the effects of this are not yet understood. I have argued instead that social media simply lift the lid on a greater range of diverse and long-standing narratives held by publics. For this reason, it is more useful to examine the longer-term narratives citizens and publics hold about international affairs and how those enduring narratives shape expectations about how global crises are likely to unfold and how they should be managed.

If we treat crises as standoffs, Wagner-Pacifici's analysis indicates that for a standoff to be resolved there must be a restructuring of the situation so there is some overlap of meaning and time horizons.[32] At least a degree of convergence of perspectives must occur for debate to be intelligible. Participants must agree on the sequence of events being disputed, the nature of the problem, and a likely timescale for it to be resolved. Social media enable publics in different countries to be exposed to each other's perspectives and narratives as they exchange views through social media. However, this does not imply that this exposure alters those perspectives and narratives, because, as Brown argues, those are embedded in communities and it is difficult to alter the form and substance of a community's narratives.[33]

What is needed is collaborative, mixed-method, and sustained research that integrates online and offline analyses of how publics engage with nuclear issues. Exploring the rituals and practices of news engagement in moments of crisis *and* in moments *between* crises will give a far greater understanding of how social media or any other media are influencing public opinion.

Notes

1. I am grateful to Shawn Powers for this analogy.

2. Elaine Tyler May, *Homeward Bound: American Families in the Cold War Era* (New York: Basic Books, 1988).

3. Herbert Blumer, "Public Opinion and Public Opinion Polling," *American Sociological Review* 13, no. 5 (October 1948): 542–49; W. Russell Neuman, Marion R. Just, and Ann N. Crigler, *Common Knowledge: News and the Construction of Political Meaning* (Chicago: University of Chicago Press, 1992); Douglas M. McLeod and James K. Hertog, "The Manufacture of 'Public Opinion' by Reporters: Informal Cues for Public Perceptions of Protest Groups," *Discourse & Society* 3, no. 3 (July 1992): 259–75.

4. "The Tribes Explained," *The Guardian*, November 30, 2009, https://www
.theguardian.com/digital-tribes/the-tribes.

5. Lars Ole Sauerberg, "The Gutenberg Parenthesis: Print, Book and
Cognition," *Orbis Litterarum* 64, no. 2 (March 10, 2009): 79–80; Tom Pettitt,
"Containment and Articulation: Media, Cultural Production, and the Perception
of the Material World," University of Southern Denmark: Institute of Literature,
Media, and Cultural Studies, 2009; Andrew Hoskins, "The Restless Past: An
Introduction to Digital Memory and Media," in *Digital Memory Studies: Media
Pasts in Transition* (London: Routledge, 2017), 13–36.

6. Alister Miskimmon, Ben O'Loughlin, and Laura Roselle, *Strategic
Narratives: Communication Power and the New World Order* (New York: Routledge,
2014), 2.

7. K. J. Holsti, "National Role Conceptions in the Study of Foreign Policy,"
International Studies Quarterly 14, no. 3 (September 1970): 233–309, https://doi
.org/10.2307/3013584; Felix Berenskoetter, "Parameters of a National
Biography," *European Journal of International Relations* 20, no. 1 (2014): 262–88.

8. Alister Miskimmon, Ben O'Loughlin, and Laura Roselle, eds., *Forging the
World: Strategic Narratives and International Relations* (Ann Arbor, MI: University
of Michigan Press, 2017).

9. Jack Snyder, "Dueling Security Stories: Wilson and Lodge Talk Strategy,"
Security Studies 24, no. 1 (2015): 171–97.

10. Ibid., 171.

11. Catarina Kinnvall and Ted Svensson, "Hindu Nationalism, Diaspora
Politics and Nation-Building in India," *Australian Journal of International Affairs*
64, no. 3 (2010): 274–92; Mary Kaldor, Mary Martin, and Sabine Selchow,
"Human Security: A New Strategic Narrative for Europe," *International Affairs*
83, no. 2 (March 2007): 273–88; Felix Ciută, "Narratives of Security: Strategy
and Identity in the European Context," in *Discursive Constructions of Identity in
European Politics*, ed. Richard C. M. Mole (Basingstoke, UK: Palgrave Macmillan,
2007), 190–207.

12. Janice Bially Mattern, *Ordering International Politics: Identity, Crisis and
Representational Force* (New York: Routledge, 2005).

13. Robin Wagner-Pacifici, *Theorizing the Standoff: Contingency in Action*
(Cambridge, UK: Cambridge University Press, 2000), 3.

14. Ibid., 5.

15. Ibid., 80.

16. Tom Hundley, "India and Pakistan Are Quietly Making Nuclear War
More Likely," Pulitzer Center, April 2, 2018, https://pulitzercenter.org
/reporting/india-and-pakistan-are-quietly-making-nuclear-war-more-likely.

17. Sarah Maltby, "Imagining Influence: Logic(al) Tensions in War and
Defence," in *The Dynamics of Mediatized Conflicts*, ed. Mikkel Fugl Eskjær, Stig

Hjarvard, and Mette Mortensen, *Global Crises and the Media*, vol. 3 (New York: Peter Lang, 2015).

18. Joanna Szostek, "Russia, Ukraine and the Influence of Presumed Media Influence in Wartime," Media, War and Conflict Journal 10th Anniversary Conference, Florence, 2018.

19. Samantha Bradshaw and Philip N. Howard, "Challenging Truth and Trust: A Global Inventory of Organized Social Media Manipulation," Oxford Internet Institute, Oxford University, July 2018.

20. Joshua L. Kalla and David E. Broockman, "The Minimal Persuasive Effects of Campaign Contact in General Elections: Evidence from 49 Field Experiments," *American Political Science Review* 112, no. 1 (2018): 148–66.

21. Richard Fletcher, Alessio Cornia, and Rasmus Kleis Nielsen, "Is Online News Consumption Polarizing News Audiences? A 12-Country Comparison," presented at American Political Science Association Annual Convention, Boston, 2018.

22. Issie Lapowsky, "Viral Political Ads May Not Be As Persuasive As You Think," *Wired*, August 7, 2018, https://www.wired.com/story/viral-political -ads-not-as-persuasive-as-you-think.

23. Daniel Kreiss, "Micro-Targeting, the Quantified Persuasion," *Internet Policy Review* 6, no. 4 (December 31, 2017).

24. Robin Brown, "Public Diplomacy, Networks, and the Limits of Strategic Narratives," in *Forging the World: Strategic Narratives and International Relations*, ed. Alister Miskimmon, Ben O'Loughlin, and Laura Roselle (Ann Arbor, MI: University of Michigan Press, 2017).

25. Aaron Smith, "Americans and Cybersecurity," Washington, DC: Pew Research Center, January 2017.

26. Akil Awan, Andrew Hoskins, and Ben O'Loughlin, *Radicalisation and Media: Connectivity and Terrorism in the New Media Ecology* (London: Routledge, 2011).

27. Peter Chonka, "New Media, Performative Violence, and State Reconstruction in Mogadishu," *African Affairs* 117, no. 468 (July 2018): 392–414; Andrew Hoskins, "War in the Grey Zone," (keynote speech, Media, War and Conflict Journal 10th Anniversary Conference, Florence, 2018); Florian Rainer and Jutta Sommerbauer, "Grey Zone: A Journey between the Front Lines in Donbass," *ERSTE Stiftung*, May 25, 2018, http://www.erstestiftung.org/en /grey-zone-donbass.

28. Shawn Powers and Ben O'Loughlin, "The Syrian Data Glut: Rethinking the Role of Information in Conflict," *Media, War & Conflict* 8, no. 2 (2015): 172–80.

29. Silvio Waisbord, "Truth Is What Happens to News: On Journalism, Fake News, and Post-Truth," *Journalism Studies* 19, no. 13 (2018): 6.

30. Antonio Martinez cited in Noah Kulwin, "'The Organic Side, to Me, Is Scarier than the Ad Side," *New York*, April 10, 2018, http://nymag.com/intelligencer/2018/04/antonio-garcia-martinez-former-facebook-employee-interview.html.

31. Roger McNamee, cited in Noah Kulwin, "You Have a Persuasion Engine Unlike Any Created in History," *New York*, April 10, 2018, http://nymag.com/intelligencer/2018/04/roger-mcnamee-early-facebook-investor-interview.html.

32. Wagner-Pacifici, *Theorizing the Standoff*.

33. Brown, "Public Diplomacy."

Chapter 10

What Can Be Done to Minimize the Effects of the Global Information Ecosystem on the Risk of Nuclear War?

Harold A. Trinkunas, Herbert S. Lin, and Benjamin Loehrke

On August 11, 2017, President Trump tweeted: "Military solutions are now fully in place, locked and loaded, should North Korea act unwisely. Hopefully Kim Jong Un will find another path!"[1] This message followed months of escalating rhetoric and military posturing between the United States and North Korea. The crisis became acute enough that, near the height of tensions in July 2018, polling showed that 60 to 75 percent of Americans were worried about the possibility of war between North Korea and the United States within the following six months.[2] Tweets from President Trump often drove or narrated the crisis, adding fears that instantaneous, direct, 280-character threats could lead directly to nuclear war. As former acting undersecretary of defense for policy Brian McKeon testified at a Senate Foreign Relations Committee hearing on presidential nuclear authorities, "The statements the president makes through his Twitter account no doubt cause concern and confusion on the other side of the Pacific. . . . I'll be very worried about a miscalculation based on continuing use of his Twitter account with regard to North Korea."[3]

As this case illustrates, the new global information ecosystem may be having an important impact on the evolution of international crises. Widespread access to social media on a global scale has accelerated news cycles in traditional media and made it easier to spread misinformation and disinformation. Intemperate, ill-considered, and impulsive outbursts have become an important part of crisis dynamics. In the decade since the founding of Facebook and Twitter, social media have added new arenas to conflicts in the Persian Gulf region among Iran, Saudi Arabia, and their respective allies; among Russia, Ukraine, and NATO; between nuclear-armed India and Pakistan; and, as we have just considered, among North Korea, Japan, South Korea, and the United States.[4] If we were to include information operations meant to influence governments and publics, we could extend the list of cases to include Russian interference in elections in the United States, the United Kingdom, Germany, Spain, Italy, and France; operations by the Venezuelan government against its neighbors in South America; and operations between China and its neighbors in East Asia.[5] Some of these crises involve nuclear-armed powers. Were one of these crises to spin out of control, the outbreak of nuclear war could have a catastrophic impact on humanity. Even a modest exchange involving one hundred relatively small warheads has the potential for producing a nuclear winter with dramatic effects on global climate and the prospects for human survival.[6]

While disinformation and misinformation have always been part of conflict, the chapters in this volume outline how the new global information ecosystem has created conditions for the spread of disinformation, misinformation, and other malign information in ways that threaten crisis stability, even nuclear crisis stability. Scholars of crisis stability have had well-established frameworks with which to analyze deterrence, decision making, and the role of public opinion in foreign policy. These approaches principally rest on rational actor models. While they acknowledge that misperception and miscalculation can have an impact on crisis stability, they tend to assume that leaders will make policy decisions rationally and analytically, based on the best available evidence and with the national interest foremost in mind.[7]

Social media and their disruptive effects are cause to reassess how existing analytical and theoretical frameworks for understanding crisis stability might be affected by the evolution of today's information ecosystem. This volume fills a gap on whether, when, and how social media could contribute to international conflict—including deterrence failure and nuclear war. In particular, it makes four contributions.

First, it incorporates findings from cognitive psychology and decision analysis into analyses of how leaders and publics receive, process, and act on information, misinformation, and disinformation in the emerging global ecosystem. It highlights how social media have an impact on how much information individuals receive, how they receive it, and, in turn, how these factors affect and may increase the likelihood of engaging in heuristic thinking (i.e., intellectual shortcuts) to manage the overwhelming volume of information available.

Second, the authors in this volume examine how cyber-enabled influence operations may be deliberately conducted via the new tools made available in the present information environment to take advantage of human cognitive biases and affect the perceptions, preferences, and decisions of both publics and leaders in times of crisis.

Third, this volume examines how the intersection of human propensity to heuristic thinking and cognitive bias may have a dangerous impact on international crisis stability. Such mental shortcuts are common to decision making. The emerging global information ecosystem, combined with deliberate influence operations designed to affect leader and public perceptions, could further wear on leaders during crises—potentially even those involving major nuclear powers and the risk of war.

And fourth, this volume assesses the limits of what adversaries may actually be able to accomplish in the present information environment, including the risk that influence operations may cause blowback on the perpetrators. In addition, public preferences may actually be fairly resilient in the long run in the face of deliberate attempts to influence mass opinion, even if these may have an impact in the short run.

Human Cognition, Heuristic Thinking, and Implications for Crisis Stability

Digitization and global communication technologies make generating and sharing new information possible at an unprecedented speed and scale. Social media platforms provide vehicles (in many cases tailored to take advantage of human cognitive biases) via which to maximize the impact of targeted persuasion. Each year, more people around the world are part of this information ecosystem, as mobile phone penetration globally is estimated to reach five billion users in 2019 (and there is no reason to expect this trend to slow down).[8] The transformation of the global information ecosystem is not just about speed, ease, or scale of communication. It has crucially democratized information production and information dissemination. Moreover, it is increasingly apparent that the new global communications ecosystem is producing new opportunities to influence humans by playing on traditional cognitive biases that we use to process information. Audiences could be more susceptible to such efforts when faced with time pressure, high volumes of information, and appealing post-truth narratives that are preferred by significant segments of the global public instead of evidence-based journalism and policies. Taken together, these trends call into question whether traditional models of crisis stability, which assume rational decisions made by elites based on the best available evidence, are an accurate way to understand the likely evolution of future international conflicts.

In chapter 2, Rose McDermott explores the psychology of the post-truth political environment. Applied to the political environment, post-truth denotes "circumstances in which objective facts are less influential in shaping public opinion than appeals to emotion and personal belief." Absent special mental discipline, story and narrative are more important in shaping a person's views than empirical fact or logically reasoned conclusions—and this applies both to ordinary citizens and to leaders. Importantly, McDermott argues that most people will regard a plausible story as true, whether or not it is in fact true. McDermott also points out two exacerbating factors. First, the decline of public trust in institutions and expertise has left individuals on their own to gather information and to make judgments about what to believe for themselves. Second, the rise of social media as primary information sources means that those who rely on such sources do not have the benefit of intermediaries who fact-check and place information in context. In this environment, people are far more likely to fall back on their own intuitive thinking, which places much higher value on factors such as simplicity, familiarity, consistency with prior belief, and how many other people appear to believe the same things. Analytical evidence-based thinking will struggle to keep pace.

Paul Slovic and Herb Lin consider the psychology of nuclear decision making, especially during crisis. Such decisions involve the highest possible stakes. The authors point to several psychological phenomena that affect nuclear decision making. Psychic numbing refers to a devaluation of life when large numbers of deaths are contemplated—the death of one innocent civilian is regarded as a tragedy, whereas the death of a million is merely a statistic. Indeed, in some cases, the death of millions is regarded as less tragic than the death of a few. Psychological devaluation of life likely underlies the ability of nuclear planners and decision makers to proceed in ways that they believe to be consistent with laws of war that are intended to minimize harm to innocent civilians. Tribalism reflects an "us versus them" mindset, enabling "us" to hate "them." Tribalism enables the dehumanization of the enemy and treatment of the enemy in ways that do not seem to violate the laws of war. Decision makers often avoid making trade-offs between competing values, such as the value of protecting national security versus protecting noncombatant enemy civilians. Rather than finding a common currency to evaluate trade-offs, they will often prioritize different values and focus on achieving those of highest priority. Thus, a decision maker may well favor security objectives over lifesaving objectives because the former are more defensible. Combined with the affordances of social media (such as their use of short, simple messages and evocative visual and auditory content), the existence of such psychological processes means that social media messages are more likely to be processed with fast, intuitive thought rather than with reflective, deliberate thought. The same is true of leaders and decision makers who are active social media users, and they are just as likely to be pushed by their social media usage into fast, intuitive thought. Slovic and Lin conclude that where such leaders are concerned, exposure to social media may well increase the likelihood of taking rash action and of premature use of force.

Cyber-Enabled Influence Operations: The Impact of Disinformation on Leaders and Publics

The present revolution in the global information ecosystem has made propaganda cost effective again. Manipulating information with the intent to persuade is a tried-and-tested part of warfare, and skeptics are right to note that there is nothing new about propaganda per se.[9] But the current information environment substantially reduces barriers to the conduct of information operations not just for great powers but also for small and middle powers as well as for nonstate actors. Unlike offensive cyberoperations—which require substantial investments in sophisticated cybercommands, recruitment of scarce hacking talent, and maintenance of up-to-date cyberweapons based on fresh exploits—information operations are much more affordable.[10] As we learned from the investigation into Russian targeting of US elections, influence operations may cost millions of dollars, but they need not cost tens or hundreds of millions of dollars.[11] Moreover, operations can be conducted on platforms made available largely for free by major social media platforms, designed to be used by the general public with the most minimal training. Lowering costs along all dimensions enables a wide array of states, great and small, and nonstate actors such as political parties and civil society organizations to conduct influence operations cheaply. In addition, states traditionally seem to treat influence operations as falling short of the threshold of armed conflict (more akin to subversion), which means that even great powers have avoided responding to such attacks by other state actors with military force. Since costs are low, both in financial terms and in terms of the likelihood of retaliation, we should expect the widespread use of influence operations intended to affect the behavior of leaders and publics, even against the great powers and even by weaker actors in the international system.

Misinformation and disinformation on social media have the potential to contaminate information flows, which could affect behavior during crises, as Mark Kumleben and Samuel Woolley show in chapter 4. People increasingly turn to social media for information during emergency situations, which creates an opening for nefarious actors to exploit that information ecosystem. For example, during a military crisis, an adversary could use a variety of computational propaganda techniques to interrupt and confuse information flows on social media in order to encourage publics and leaders to behave in a way that suits the adversary's interests. Kumleben and Woolley explain some of the more important of those techniques and give an overview of how they have been used in political conflicts. The cases that the authors use illustrate the potential effects of misinformation and disinformation during military crises. The 2018 false missile alert in Hawaii is a useful hypothetical on how computational propaganda could provide an adversary with a cost-effective means to erode a target state's civil defenses and interrupt its ability to mobilize resources. Political leaders might also be susceptible to digital information operations during crises. The microtargeting of Jeremy Corbyn by members of his own 2017 Labour Party campaign staff shows that disinformation on social media could affect political decision making. By showing how computational propaganda has the power to affect behavior, Kumleben and Woolley highlight the strategic importance of the information ecosystem during crises.

State and nonstate actors are already engaged in information operations designed to affect interstate relations, as Kate Starbird outlines in chapter 5 in this volume. Using the techniques analyzed by Kumleben and Woolley, these actors are conducting influence operations online to influence political discourse and generate false information, most likely with the intention of generating confusion and mistrust among their adversaries and competitors. Starbird's work outlines how deliberate efforts by state actors, such as those aligned with Russia, can influence broader online conversations and activism among sympathetic audiences. In the case of NATO, both alt-right and fringe conservative voices and international far-left activists converged on a shared anti-alliance message that was influenced and driven in part by state-sponsored online actors working via social media. There is a pattern of state actors and state-backed trolls infiltrating authentic online and social media–based activist communities on both the right and the left to reshape their activities so that they unwittingly support state-sponsored messages and objectives, in this case Russia's anti-NATO activities. The long-term impact of these activities remains to be seen, but they are already shaping conversations about and among major international actors, in this case NATO, possibly shaping the future strategic environment in ways that could undermine popular support for alliance activities to deter Russia.

The Risks to International Crisis Stability from the Global Information Ecosystem

During the Cold War, government leaders of the major nuclear powers received information from military and intelligence services that, while of course vulnerable to many errors, was nonetheless subject to a process designed to produce verifiable data on which leaders could base decisions. Publics received information via gatekeepers, whether in the form of official or private media, that also subjected information to a vetting process, admittedly not always designed to produce truth but at least to produce consistency and a consensus view of reality among audiences.

Publics and leaders are today exposed to masses of unverified information produced at high speed and distributed at high volume for next to no cost. It is much easier to produce polarization in target populations, to spur storms of public opinion to influence enemy leaders, to leak information deleterious to adversaries, and to conduct influence operations designed to target the psychology of enemy publics.

Moreover, the same techniques, as Kristin Ven Bruusgaard and Jaclyn Kerr suggest, can target leaders, affecting perceptions of crises and of adversaries' intentions. We already know that major government officials pay attention to social media, and they are also subject to the same effects from the global information ecosystem as the publics they lead. This raises the real possibility that influence operations may become an additional contributing factor to growing crisis instability in the world today.

In fact, the deployment of post-truth information during crises may contribute to escalation dynamics in dangerous and unpredictable ways. In the current information environment and given human propensity for heuristic thinking, deployment of convenient half-truths, rumors, or "extra-factual information," as Kelly Greenhill argues, is attractive because it is a powerful mobilizer of public opinion and can magnify signals of resolve in international crisis. But precisely because it is so powerful and provocative, it can lead adversaries to escalate rather than back down. It can alarm public opinion among adversaries, putting opponents in the position of having to resort to their own escalation and provocation or else appear weak. In addition, as Jeffrey Lewis also documents in chapter 8, there is the possibility that both the general public and elites in the provoking country will come to believe extra-factual information, making it difficult to build off-ramps from international crises for fear of appearing weak or losing face. It may become difficult or impossible to "walk back" or discredit extra-factual information in a global information environment too prone to magnifying human heuristic thinking and spreading information that is appealing even if untrue.

The Limits of Disinformation and Influence Operations

This volume has painted a grim picture of the future of a global information ecosystem increasingly awash in large volumes of unverified misinformation and disinformation, with the attendant impact on leaders and publics—and potentially even on crisis stability. However, there are some likely limits on what information alone can achieve.

The first limit on the impact of the evolving information ecosystem on the likelihood of interstate conflict is the underlying material distribution of capabilities among states. The findings in this volume are relevant to the dimensions of international conflict that relate to misperception, miscalculation, and the risk of inadvertent war. In other words, even though the global information ecosystem now makes new capabilities available to both great and small powers, and even if it increasingly exposes global publics and leaders to misinformation, disinformation, and post-truth, the great powers remain materially more capable and are thus more able to impose their preferences on others. Smaller powers are vulnerable to international pressure in ways that great powers are not, and this may be part of the eventual solution to this threat if and when great powers begin to retaliate coercively against information operations that strike too close to home. The "mouse that roared," in which a weaker power is able to dissuade or persuade a larger state's employment of its material capabilities to achieve the smaller power's preferences, may still fall into the realm of fiction.

Another limit is the possibility that those conducting influence operations may "lose control" of the disinformation or propaganda they are using and that it will "blow back" on their own population or leaders. Lewis in this volume documents several instances in which information operations went awry, infecting the debate on issues related to deterrence, nuclear deployments, and nuclear doctrine in the Soviet Union, later Russia, and possibly the United States. This is of course more of a concern for those attempting to use influence operations to achieve particular effects than for those who simply intend to sow chaos or promote polarization—which, as has been suggested by recent Russian influence operations, may be a goal in itself. But to the extent that those conducting information operations become more aware of this possibility (i.e., if an operation goes badly wrong), this may in the future lead states to self-deter from using this capability.

There is also cause to be more contingent in asserting what effects social media might have. Ben O'Loughlin in his chapter stresses that researchers first need to answer whether social media play a new or different role in public opinion. He notes that individuals perceive the world around them through established narratives they hold about how the world works, the actors in it, and the problems at hand. Changing opinions by dislodging those narratives through political communication is extremely difficult, and it is unclear if social media are an effective means for that. O'Loughlin provides a valuable cautionary note by describing a paradox that this situation presents. While social media have enabled a new and cheaper means to influence politics—at home and abroad—he believes there is not enough evidence that political communication on social media is any better at persuasion than traditional media. It is unclear if information operations on social media would change public opinion or simply help make more apparent the opinions of certain constituencies and their long-held views. Gaining more insight into and gathering evidence on such questions would better show whether social media significantly affect public opinion and help explain what roles information operations on social media might have during international crises.

Future Trends in Crisis Stability and Avenues for Further Research

We already live in an era in which international crisis stability is being undermined by the actions of great powers. Crisis stability has traditionally derived from, in the most limited sense, the major nuclear powers having secure second-strike capabilities that assured the destruction of adversaries even in the event of a surprise attack. Such capabilities greatly diminished the incentive to strike first. In a broader sense, it has meant a different kind of stability produced by the efforts of major nuclear powers to limit arms races, facilitate crisis communication, and promote an international environment that limits the likelihood that crises will become nuclear.[12] Neither of these conditions is as true as it was in the 1970s, when both the United States and the Soviet Union were actively engaged in efforts that tended to promote crisis stability.

In the nuclear domain, the United States and Russia are recapitalizing nuclear arsenals, investing in substrategic nuclear weapons, and floating trial balloons regarding possible limited first use or use of low-yield weapons to respond to nonnuclear threats. The United States continues to invest in strategic defense against nuclear missiles, traditionally thought of as undermining crisis stability. China refuses to participate in nuclear arms-control negotiations, which is being used as an excuse by both Russia and the United States to sunset existing arms-control treaties.[13]

In addition, the nuclear weapons, conventional weapons, and associated early-warning and command-and-control systems of the major powers are becoming increasingly entangled. Emerging military technologies such as conventional long-range precision strike systems, cyberwarfare, and antisatellite weapons pose threats to the sensor and warning networks that are useful for conducting both conventional and nuclear operations. James Acton argues that this may pose a risk to crisis stability because attacks on early-warning and command-and-control systems to degrade conventional capabilities of a nuclear-armed adversary may be perceived as the preliminary moves of a nuclear first strike, encouraging the targeted nation to preemptively attack. In addition, a nuclear power engaged in a conventional war may come to believe that attacks on its long-range sensor networks in the course of military operations may degrade its ability to conduct damage limitation attacks designed to reduce the impact of an adversary's nuclear arsenal should the conflict escalate, therefore encouraging a first strike with nuclear weapons.[14]

Technological progress is also contributing to declining crisis stability by providing states with new capabilities with which to undermine the integrity and survivability of nuclear arsenals. Artificial intelligence and machine learning, combined with ubiquitous sensors, have the increasing potential to reveal the locations of once hidden second-strike capabilities such as ballistic missile submarines and ground-mobile missile launchers. These second-strike systems depend for their survival on being hard to locate.[15] There remains a lurking concern that emerging powers with small numbers of nuclear weapons may find their arsenals and their production establishments vulnerable to the use of emerging technologies, such as offensive cyberweapons to disarm them. This may lead them to favor first use or "fail-deadly" nuclear doctrines. There is even concern that the information systems of major nuclear powers are vulnerable in ways that might contribute to crisis instability.[16]

In this context of destabilizing strategic trends, it is important as ever for decision makers to think carefully and cautiously during crises. But the changes wrought by social media to the information ecosystem are making that more difficult, as tightening decision windows are met with the relentless speed and volume of information.

There are no indications that the role of the global information ecosystem in promoting crisis instability will decline in the short to medium term. There is no evidence yet that human beings are likely to become cognitively more resistant to misinformation and disinformation, nor are the platforms on which the global information ecosystem is built addressing the risks posed by human cognitive biases. For the private companies that build and deploy social media platforms, increasing consumer interaction with their products is part of their monetization strategy. This means both extending the reach of social media to new consumers, many of whom may not be on guard against online misinformation, and crafting products designed to increase the "dwell time" of existing users on platforms. Under present conditions, companies have few incentives to adjust the algorithmically selected data streams displayed via their platforms in ways that would improve the accuracy and validity of information provided but that consumers might find disagreeable. In fact, all incentives point toward algorithmically selecting experiences for platform consumers that they find agreeable and unchallenging, creating what is known as filter bubbles, rather than ones that foster reasoned thinking (or slow thinking, as discussed in chapter 3 by Slovic and Lin).

In addition, deliberate influence campaigns conducted in the present global information environment seem likely to continue to proliferate. As many as forty-eight countries have already been detected as engaging in some form of computational propaganda, according to the Oxford Internet Institute.[17] Although the rewards may not always be high, for reasons earlier discussed they are cheap and low risk, accessible to even small and middle powers. As private social media companies expand the reach of the global information ecosystem, new targets are becoming available for influence operations. And few countries have thus far retaliated against information operations, not even the United States. Under such circumstances, the incentives all point toward a continued expansion of influence operations.

But many unknowns remain, and much research has yet to be done. Here we suggest five possible research agendas:

1. What is the relationship between social media and heuristic reasoning? Popular business and journalistic narratives seem to assume there is one, suggesting that social media tend to encourage System 1, or fast, thinking, in which consumers are more prone to impulsive behavior. There is some initial evidence that this is the case, but academic studies of the relationship between social media and heuristic reasoning are still few and far between. If such a relationship is borne out by additional studies, it would support the argument that the global information ecosystem as it has currently evolved contributes to the risk of crisis instability.

2. A related question is how engagement with social media actually affects decision making in high-stakes scenarios. Some research suggests that individuals are more inclined to slow, reflective thinking when stakes are high and the individuals involved have a personal interest in the matter at hand. How and to what extent might such an inclination moderate the pressures for fast thinking induced by engagement with social media in crisis?

3. What kinds of information operations are being conducted and by whom? Increasing numbers of reports document the proliferation of influence operations by state and nonstate actors. However, data are only episodically available and are usually incomplete. More focused and systematic study of influence operations would help illuminate the boundaries between disinformation and misinformation, as well as help analysts further examine the relationship with crisis stability. Unfortunately, in the short term we will need to navigate the impasse between social media platforms and social science researchers in the wake of Cambridge Analytica's role in the 2016 US election.[18] The appropriation and misuse of large amounts of Facebook data by Cambridge Analytica for electoral purposes led to a crackdown on data sharing by social media companies which has in turn inhibited legitimate social science research on information operations globally.

4. Has mass political participation on social media affected the role of public opinion in foreign policy making? Social media have increased the velocity of information and public participation with it. For decision makers, to what degree has this caused them to become more sensitive to these information flows or to more aggressively filter out information? For publics, has this significantly changed constituent influence in foreign policy making? In some ways, public opinion is the fulcrum of an argument that social media intensify public pressure on decision makers in ways that increase risks to crisis stability. Further research into how the current information ecosystem might be changing interactions between publics and decision makers could provide better understanding of the implication for international conflict.

5. More research is needed on how societies adapt to the proliferation of technologies that democratize access to information production and distribution. The present global information environment is not the first in which traditional authorities and gatekeepers have become alarmed at technology-aided jumps in the speed of information flow and the incorporation of new users into the ecosystem. The spread of the printing press in Europe, which interacted with the Protestant reformation, so greatly alarmed the Catholic Church that it devised a new and

deliberate countermessaging strategy and organization under the rubric of the Sacra Congregatio de Propaganda Fides (Congregation for the Propagation of the Faith) in 1622. This effort by the Catholic Church to proselytize among its faithful has become known as the origin of the term *propaganda*.[19] The telegraph similarly provided a leap in availability of information to users, as eventually did radio and television. In each case, societies navigated the impact of new technology and arrived at a solution in which a means of verifying and validating ever more widely available information became available. This has not yet happened in the present global information environment.[20]

Policy Recommendations

Publics and some political leaders are increasingly aware of the role of malicious manipulation and influence operations. This is in part because of the results of the US elections in 2016, but it is also because of news of such operations involving both domestic politics—elections in India, Mexico, France, and Germany in 2017 and 2018, for example—and international crises such as India-Pakistan border clashes or Saudi Arabia and the UAE's cold war with Qatar. However, many remain unaware of the full scope of influence operations currently at work around the globe: the actors, their true intentions, cascading consequences, and implications on international security and crisis stability.

In addition, states have so far been reluctant to devise and implement policies to curtail the negative effects of influence operations in the global information ecosystem. This volume has described a number of causes for state reticence on this issue. These include the prospect that limiting influence operations may involve restrictions on speech that would run counter to the norms and laws of democratic states. Also, foreign influence operations may in fact be caught up within a state's domestic politics, benefiting one political party over others and leading the victors to be reluctant to take actions that might damage their prospects of future electoral success. The enterprise of distinguishing "good" from "bad" information and normal campaigning and advertising from malicious influence operations may be simply too political to be handled by a neutral governance or regulatory body. Indeed, there may not be much difference between some influence operations and ordinary political campaigning in a democracy. Finally, in cases raising international security concerns, influence operations have so far been seen as falling short of the threshold of armed conflict. State leaders still have not found a consensus on appropriate ways to deter such attacks or retaliate against them. In fact, they may want to avoid setting a precedent via such a retaliation to protect their own states' ability to conduct influence operations abroad.

However, there are still some things that states can do to limit the prospect of influence operations contributing to worsening international crises, particularly those involving nuclear powers. First, the social media platforms themselves may need to change. American jurisprudence suggests that regulation of speech content on social media channels is inconsistent with the First Amendment's guaranteeing freedom of speech, although legal precedents in the European Union may provide some leverage. It may prove more feasible to regulate or otherwise influence the business model rather than the content per se. For example, improved transparency and attribution of sources may be vehicles for allowing users to assess the validity of content they are receiving via social media platforms. Although social media companies are likely to resist regulation, they may welcome uniform standards that relieve them of some liability and the reputational damage inflicted on them now by the recurring scandals related to how companies handle user information. Social media companies have optimized their business models to maximize revenues, and it is these very business models that undergird the information ecosystem of today. A key research problem in this domain is to find profitable business models that are consistent with efforts to reduce the volume and velocity of malign information spread across social media.

A second lesson from this volume is the need for decision makers to engage in clear-headed and deliberative thinking when contemplating decisions about the use of nuclear weapons. Even before the emergence of the present global information ecosystem, there were reasons to be concerned about the impact of time pressure on decision making. These pressures seem to have increased. One countermeasure may be to increase the availability of sufficient time for deliberation. Since it is the half-hour timeline for the flight of Russian ICBMs toward the United States that is most stressing for US decision makers, policy attention should be devoted to extending that timeline. This could include modernizing command-and-control systems and processes to improve the time for decisions and the quality of information available to leaders. A great deal of the time pressure derives from the belief that decisions must be made about the employment of the land-based missile force, the leg of the US nuclear triad most vulnerable to degradation by a major first strike. Essentially, it is viewed by some as a "use it or lose it" element of the US nuclear arsenal, thereby encouraging not only decision making under time pressure (when humans are more vulnerable to heuristic thinking) but also a posture of "launch on warning."

By removing requirements for launch-on-warning capability, eliminating the US silo-based ICBM force, or adopting a less vulnerable ICBM basing mode such as mobile launchers, US presidents would no longer face the same time pressure to launch on warning.[21] There would be theoretically more time to ride out an initial attack and decide how and when to retaliate. Moreover, US adversaries would know this, minimizing their incentive to try to launch a sudden attack to degrade the land-based component of the US nuclear arsenal. Similarly, other nations with nuclear weapons could take steps to increase decision time. Steps may entail changes in doctrine, force structure and deployments, or early-warning capabilities.

A third possible area for policy innovation lies in altering how decisions are made about the employment of nuclear weapons. Of course, states have different approaches to making decisions around nuclear weapons use, but the evolution of the present global information environment suggests that it is time to step away from systems that place this responsibility in the hands of a single individual. Human beings vary in their propensity for "thinking fast" or heuristic reasoning. They also vary in their susceptibility to influence operations.

Such variation suggests that a higher quality of nuclear decision making would be possible if the concurrence of multiple individuals were needed to order the use of nuclear weapons. This would reduce the likelihood that a single decision maker would act impulsively in the face of time pressure, commit cognitive errors in assessing a crisis, or fall under the effects of an influence operation.[22] For example, in the case of the United States, Richard Betts and Matthew Waxman have proposed requiring the concurrence of the secretary of defense (to certify that a nuclear weapons use order is a valid military necessity) and the attorney general (to certify that a US nuclear weapons use order is legal) before a president could initiate a nuclear strike.[23]

A fourth possible area for policy innovation lies in how information is processed during crisis within the national security apparatus of states. Almost all states have intelligence communities (or something similar) that are designed to collect, process, evaluate, and analyze data about the world, presumably with the objective of providing a somewhat accurate and verified picture of the world to their leadership. In many states, this is coupled with an executive apparatus that is designed to elaborate policy proposals for decision makers to consider and to follow up on implementation of approved proposals. For example, in the United States the intelligence community would collect, verify, and analyze information for use by the National Security Council staff and other government departments to prepare policy recommendations for vetting through the interagency process. Ideally, this process should by itself minimize the impact of disinformation and misinformation through subjecting intelligence analyses and policy recommendations to vigorous questioning and evaluation. However, in the modern global information ecosystem, it is clear that new information and policy ideas can enter the decision-making process very close to the top of a decision chain and very close to the end of the process, i.e., in the final decision-making settings, even in a state leader's office. This suggests that information assessment teams should be assigned to senior decision makers to help them evaluate information inflows from outside the normal decision-making process, such as from social media, contemporaneously to those decisions being made. Such teams would be trained to understand the tactics of information warfare perpetrators (and their allies, witting or unwitting) and the psychological mechanisms that social media leverage. They would be tasked with helping senior decision makers to understand the context of new data that they are receiving and to retain the appropriate perspective and distance from their personal information feeds. So while shielding the mass of the population from influence operations may prove to be too political or trigger accusations of partisanship in many democracies, protecting senior decision makers may in the end prove to be more feasible and practical.

Overall, the analysis presented in this volume suggests that the global information ecosystem, because of the way it interacts with human cognitive biases and because of the new abilities it affords state and nonstate actors to conduct influence operations, is a potentially important threat to crisis stability. While it is difficult to imagine developing useful countermeasures at this stage of our understanding of the phenomenon, some aspects of the problem to be addressed are clear. Human cognition is unlikely to change significantly on anything less than an evolutionary scale, so that means the information ecosystem needs to be modified to minimize the impact of bad information on crisis decision making, given current human propensity to heuristic thinking. To avoid the possibility that "fast thinking" (or System 1 thinking) may lead policy makers to poor decisions, more time for deliberation needs to be built into international crises, particularly ones among nuclear powers that have the most potentially catastrophic effects. In addition, to minimize the possibility that bad information or deliberate influence operations will lead state leaders to make cataclysmic decisions involving nuclear weapons during international crises, decision-making authority should be spread out among multiple senior leaders, serving as a check on the possibility of any single individual precipitating a nuclear exchange. Finally, senior decision makers will likely need support to evaluate and curate the data flows they receive from outside the normal governmental process for providing intelligence analyses and policy recommendations. That support should likely sit as close to them as possible.

Notes

1. Donald J. Trump, Twitter, August 11, 2017, 4:29 a.m., https://twitter.com /realdonaldtrump/status/895970429734711298?lang=en.

2. A July 18 poll from ABC/Washington Post showed that 74 percent of respondents were concerned about the possibility of "full-scale war with North Korea." See Allison De Jong, "Distrust in Trump Deepens North Korea Concerns," ABC News, blog, July 18, 2017, https://www.langerresearch.com /wp-content/uploads/1189a3NorthKorea.pdf. In an August 15, 2017, poll from The Economist/YouGov, 60 percent of respondents were worried that North Korea will take military action against the United States, https://d25d2506sfb94s .cloudfront.net/cumulus_uploads/document/8binbopoey/econTabReport.pdf.

3. *Authority to Order the Use of Nuclear Weapons, Senate Foreign Relations Committee*, 115th Cong. 1, November 14, 2017 (testimony of Brian McKeon).

4. Jack Stubbs and Christopher Bing, "How Iran Spreads Disinformation around the World," Reuters, November 30, 2018, https://www.reuters.com /article/us-cyber-iran-specialreport-idUSKCN1NZ1FT; Tom Hundley, "India and Pakistan Are Quietly Making Nuclear War More Likely," Pulitzer Center, April 2, 2018, https://pulitzercenter.org/reporting/india-and-pakistan-are -quietly-making-nuclear-war-more-likely; Neha Thirani Bagri, "When India and Pakistan Clashed, Fake News Won," *Los Angeles Times*, March 15, 2019, https:// www.latimes.com/world/la-fg-india-pakistan-fake-news-20190315-story.html.

5. Larry Diamond, *Ill Winds: Saving Democracy from Russian Rage, Chinese Ambition, and American Complacency* (New York: Penguin Press, 2019).

6. Seth Baum, "The Risk of Nuclear Winter," *Federation of American Scientists* (blog), May 29, 2015, https://fas.org/pir-pubs/risk-nuclear-winter.

7. Robert Jervis, "Deterrence and Perception," *International Security* 7, no. 3 (Winter 1982/83): 3–30; Robert Jervis, *Perception and Misperception in International Politics*, new edition (Princeton, NJ: Princeton University Press, 2017).

8. Kyle Taylor and Laura Silver, "Smartphone Ownership Is Growing Rapidly Around the World, but Not Always Equally," Pew Research Center, February 5, 2019, https://www.pewresearch.org/global/2019/02/05/smartphone-ownership -is-growing-rapidly-around-the-world-but-not-always-equally.

9. Philip M. Taylor, *Munitions of the Mind: A History of Propaganda from the Ancient World to the Present Day* (Manchester, UK: Manchester University Press, 2003).

10. Max Smeets, "How Much Does a Cyber Weapon Cost? Nobody Knows," *Net Politics* (blog), Council on Foreign Relations, November 21, 2016, https://blogs.cfr.org/blog/how-much-does-cyber-weapon-cost-nobody-knows.

11. Adrian Chen, "The Agency," *New York Times*, June 2, 2015, https://www.nytimes.com/2015/06/07/magazine/the-agency.html; Samantha Bradshaw and Philip N. Howard, "Challenging Truth and Trust: A Global Inventory of Organized Social Media Manipulation," Oxford Internet Institute, Oxford University, July 2018.

12. Joshua H. Pollack, "Is Crisis Stability Still Achievable?" APS Forum on Physics & Society, July 2017, https://www.aps.org/units/fps/newsletters/201707/crisis.cfm.

13. Steven Pifer, "With US-Russian Arms Control Treaties on Shaky Ground, the Future Is Worrying," Brookings Institution, April 25, 2019, https://www.brookings.edu/blog/order-from-chaos/2019/04/25/nuclear-security-arms-control-and-the-us-russia-relationship.

14. James M. Acton, "Escalation through Entanglement: How the Vulnerability of Command-and-Control Systems Raises the Risks of an Inadvertent Nuclear War," *International Security* 43, no. 1 (August 2018): 56–99, https://doi.org/10.1162/isec_a_00320.

15. Edward Geist and Andrew Lohn, "How Might Artificial Intelligence Affect the Risk of Nuclear War?" Santa Monica, CA: RAND Corporation, 2018, https://doi.org/10.7249/PE296.

16. Andrew Futter, *Hacking the Bomb: Cyber Threats and Nuclear Weapons* (Washington, DC: Georgetown University Press, 2018).

17. Bradshaw and Howard, "Challenging Truth and Trust."

18. Matthew Rosenberg, Nicholas Confessore, and Carole Cadwalladr, "How Trump Consultants Exploited the Facebook Data of Millions," *New York Times*, March 17, 2018, https://www.nytimes.com/2018/03/17/us/politics/cambridge-analytica-trump-campaign.html.

19. Taylor, "Munitions of the Mind."

20. It is true that to a certain extent these technologies lent themselves to economies of scale that tended to facilitate the role of gatekeepers and regulators. So far, this has not been the case with the latest wave of information technology.

21. William J. Perry, "Why It's Safe to Scrap America's ICBMs," *New York Times*, September 30, 2016, https://www.nytimes.com/2016/09/30/opinion/why-its-safe-to-scrap-americas-icbms.html.

22. See Herbert Lin, "A Two-Person Rule for Ordering the Use of Nuclear Weapons, Even for POTUS?" *Lawfare* (blog), November 9, 2016, https://www.lawfareblog.com/two-person-rule-ordering-use-nuclear-weapons-even-potus.

23. Richard K. Betts and Matthew Waxman, "Safeguarding Nuclear Launch Procedures: A Proposal," *Lawfare* (blog), November 19, 2017, https://www.lawfareblog.com/safeguarding-nuclear-launch-procedures-proposal.

About the Editors and Contributors

Harold A. Trinkunas

Harold A. Trinkunas is the deputy director of, and a senior research scholar at, the Center for International Security and Cooperation at the Freeman Spogli Institute for International Studies at Stanford University. His research focuses on issues related to foreign policy, governance, and security, particularly in Latin America. Trinkunas has coauthored *Militants, Criminals, and Warlords: The Challenge of Local Governance in an Age of Disorder* (Brookings Institution Press, 2017) and *Aspirational Power: Brazil on the Long Road to Global Influence* (Brookings Institution Press, 2016). He authored *Crafting Civilian Control of the Military in Venezuela* (University of North Carolina Press, 2005). He coedited and contributed to *American Crossings: Border Politics in the Western Hemisphere* (Johns Hopkins University Press, 2015), *Ungoverned Spaces: Alternatives to State Authority in an Era of Softened Sovereignty* (Stanford University Press, 2010), *Global Politics of Defense Reform* (Palgrave MacMillan, 2008), and *Terrorism Financing and State Responses* (Stanford University Press, 2007). He received his doctorate in political science from Stanford University in 1999.

Herbert S. Lin

Herb Lin is a senior research scholar for cyberpolicy and security at the Center for International Security and Cooperation and the Hank J. Holland Fellow in Cyber Policy and Security at the Hoover Institution at Stanford University. His research interests focus on cybersecurity and cyberspace. Lin is particularly interested in the use of offensive operations in cyberspace as instruments of national policy and in the effects of information warfare and influence operations on national security. In addition to his positions at Stanford University, he is chief scientist emeritus for the Computer Science and Telecommunications

Board, National Research Council of the National Academies, where he served from 1990 through 2014 as study director of major projects on public policy and information technology; and is an adjunct senior research scholar and senior fellow in cybersecurity (not in residence) at the Saltzman Institute for War and Peace Studies in the School for International and Public Affairs at Columbia University. Lin is a member of the Science and Security Board of the *Bulletin of the Atomic Scientists*. In 2016, he served on President Obama's Commission on Enhancing National Cybersecurity. He received his doctorate in physics from MIT.

Benjamin Loehrke

Benjamin Loehrke is the program officer for nuclear policy at the Stanley Center for Peace and Security, where he designs, organizes, and implements all aspects of the center's work on solutions to halt the spread and avoid the use of nuclear weapons. He previously worked at Ploughshares Fund, an international security foundation. His areas of interest include nuclear strategy, arms control, nonproliferation, and the implications of emerging technologies for international security. His writing has appeared in the *Bulletin of the Atomic Scientists* and the *Stanford Social Innovation Review*. He holds a master's degree in public policy from the University of Maryland and a bachelor's degree in political science from Indiana University.

Kelly M. Greenhill

Kelly M. Greenhill (PhD, MIT) is associate professor and director of international relations at Tufts University and research fellow at Harvard University's Kennedy School. Greenhill has published four books: *Weapons of Mass Migration: Forced Displacement, Coercion, and Foreign Policy* (winner of the 2011 International Studies Association's Best Book of the Year Award); *Sex, Drugs, and Body Counts: The Politics of Numbers in Global Crime and Conflict*; *The Use of Force: Military Power and International Politics* (8th ed.); and *Coercion: The Power to Hurt in International Politics*. Her fifth book, *Fear and Present Danger: Extra-Factual Sources of Threat Conception and Proliferation*, is currently under review. Her research and political commentary have also appeared in myriad peer-reviewed journals and media outlets and have been cited and employed in legal briefs in cases argued before the US Supreme Court and in policy briefs and planning guidance for other civilian and military organs of the US government.

Danielle Jablanski

Danielle Jablanski is the cyber program manager with the Program on Geopolitics, Technology, and Governance at the Stanford Cyber Policy Center at the Freeman Spogli Institute. She is responsible for delivering multistakeholder boot camps on the fundamental principles of technology and serves as a liaison for the cyberpolicy work being done at Stanford University. She coordinates core research initiatives, student and professional education programs, stakeholder relations, multimedia, and strategic marketing. Prior to her role at Stanford, she was the program associate for nuclear policy at the Stanley Center for Peace and Security, where she tracked policy developments related to emerging technologies, researched their trajectories, and engaged with experts to determine their impacts for nuclear-weapons policy. She earned her bachelor's degree in political science from the University of Missouri–Columbia and her master's degree in international security from the University of Denver Josef Korbel School of International Studies.

Jaclyn Kerr

Jaclyn Kerr is an affiliate at the Center for International Security and Cooperation at Stanford University and a New America Cybersecurity Fellow. Her research examines the politics of cybersecurity, information warfare, internet governance, and the internet policies of nondemocratic regimes. Areas of interest also include risk and governance in relation to emerging technologies, misperception, and crisis stability; and the relationships between security, privacy, and freedom of expression in internet policy. She holds a PhD and MA in government from Georgetown University and an MA in Russian, East European, and Eurasian studies and a BAS in mathematics and Slavic languages and literatures from Stanford University. She has held predoctoral fellowships at Stanford and Harvard Universities and research fellowships in

Russia, Kazakhstan, and Qatar, and has previous professional experience as a software engineer.

Mark Kumleben

Mark Kumleben is a research fellow with the Digital Intelligence Lab (DigIntel) at the Institute for the Future. His research at DigIntel scrutinizes computational propaganda and online disinformation in varied contexts, from election security to public health. He is also an MA candidate in the Department of Politics and Economics at Claremont Graduate University, studying the political philosophy of technology. Academically, his research covers the philosophical and social consequences of modern developments in artificial intelligence and big data. He previously received a BA in philosophy at the University of Chicago. Now based in Washington, DC, he is an advocate for science communication and sound technology policy.

Jeffrey Lewis

Jeffrey Lewis is the director of the East Asia Nonproliferation Program at the James Martin Center for Nonproliferation Studies, Middlebury Institute of International Studies at Monterey, California, and the founding publisher of the *Arms Control Wonk* blog network. He is also a nonresident affiliate at Stanford's Center for Security and International Cooperation and a contributing editor to *Survival*. He is the author of three books, including a novel, *The 2020 Commission Report on the North Korean Nuclear Attacks on the United States*. He holds a PhD in policy studies (international security and economic policy) from the University of Maryland.

Rose McDermott

Rose McDermott is the David and Mariana Fisher University Professor of International Relations at Brown University and a fellow in the American Academy of Arts and Sciences. She has held fellowships at the Radcliffe Institute for Advanced Study, the Olin Institute for Strategic Studies, and the Women and Public Policy Program, all at Harvard University. She has twice been a fellow at the Stanford Center for Advanced Studies in the Behavioral Sciences. She is the author of five books, a coeditor of two additional volumes, and author of more than two hundred academic articles across a wide variety of disciplines, encompassing topics such as experimentation, emotion and decision making, and the biological and genetic bases of political behavior. She received her PhD in political science and MA in experimental social psychology from Stanford University and has taught at Cornell and the University of California–Santa Barbara.

Ben O'Loughlin

Ben O'Loughlin (DPhil Oxon, FRSA) is professor of international relations and director of the New Political Communication Unit at Royal Holloway, University of London. He was specialist adviser to the UK Parliament's Select Committee on Soft Power, producing the report *Power and Persuasion in the Modern World*. He is coeditor of the Sage journal *Media, War & Conflict*. His latest book (coedited with Alister Miskimmon and Laura Roselle) is *Forging the World: Strategic Narratives and International Relations* (Ann Arbor: University of Michigan Press, 2017). He has recently completed several projects on digital engagement with the British Council and the Goethe Institute. In 2016 he and his coauthors won the Walter Lippmann Award for Political Communication at the American Political Science Association. In 2019 he was appointed Thinker in Residence by the Belgian Royal Academy for his research on democracy and disinformation.

Paul Slovic

Paul Slovic is a professor of psychology at the University of Oregon and a founder and president of Decision Research. He studies human judgment, decision making, and the psychology of risk. He and his colleagues worldwide have developed methods to describe risk perceptions and measure their impacts on individuals, industry, and society. His recent research examines "psychic numbing" and the failure to respond to mass human tragedies such as genocide. He is a past president of the Society for Risk Analysis and in 1991 received its Distinguished Contribution Award. In 1993 he received the Distinguished Scientific Contribution Award from the American Psychological Association. He has received honorary doctorates from the Stockholm School of Economics (1996) and the University of East Anglia (2005). He was elected to the American Academy of Arts and Sciences in 2015 and the National Academy of Sciences in 2016.

Kate Starbird

Kate Starbird is an associate professor in the Department of Human Centered Design & Engineering at the University of Washington. Her research is situated within human-computer interaction and the emerging field of crisis informatics—the study of how information communication technologies are used during crisis events. One aspect of her research focuses on how online rumors spread during natural disasters and man-made crisis events. More recently, she has begun to focus on the spread of disinformation and other forms of strategic information operations online. She earned her PhD in technology, media, and society from the University of Colorado at Boulder and holds a BS in computer science from Stanford University.

Kristin Ven Bruusgaard

Kristin Ven Bruusgaard is a postdoctoral fellow and assistant professor in the Department of Political Science, University of Oslo, where she is part of the Oslo Nuclear Project. Her research focuses on Russian nuclear strategy, deterrence, and crisis dynamics. She has previously been a Nuclear Security Postdoctoral Fellow and a Stanton Nuclear Security Predoctoral Fellow at the Center for International Security and Cooperation, Stanford University, a research fellow at the Norwegian Institute for Defense Studies, and a senior security policy analyst in the Norwegian Armed Forces. She holds a PhD in defense studies from King's College London. Her work has been published in the journals *Security Dialogue*, *Survival*, *Texas National Security Review*, *Bulletin of the Atomic Scientists*, *Parameters*, and *National Interest* and the web magazine *War on the Rocks*.

Samuel Woolley

Samuel Woolley is a faculty member at the School of Journalism at the University of Texas at Austin. His work examines computational propaganda—the use of social media in efforts to manipulate public opinion. He is the founding director of the Digital Intelligence Lab at the Institute for the Future and cofounder of the Computational Propaganda Project at the Oxford Internet Institute, University of Oxford. His recent book (coauthored with Phil Howard) is a collection of essays entitled *Computational Propaganda* from Oxford University Press. His forthcoming book, *The Reality Game* (PublicAffairs, 2020), discusses how the next wave of technology might challenge perceptions of truth. He is a fellow at the German Marshall Fund of the United States and a former fellow at the Anti-Defamation League, Google Jigsaw, the Center for Media, Data and Society at Central European University, and the Tech Policy Lab at the University of Washington. He has current and past research affiliations with the Project on Democracy and the Internet at Stanford, the Center for Information Technology Research in the Interest of Society at the University of California–Berkeley, and the Oxford Internet Institute.

Index

bots (*continued*)
  sockpuppet, 66
  spam, 66, 93
  troll, 66
  on Twitter, 7, 65–68, 93
Breitbart News, 155n32, 165
Brexit, 19–20
Brezhnev, Leonid, 163
Britain, Labour Party in, 71–72, 199
Brown, Robin, 185, 189
bum dope, 159, 161, 163, 171
Bush, George H. W., 161
Bush, George W., 32, 128
business model, social media, 34, 209

C3 systems. *See* command, control, and
  communications systems
Cambridge Analytica scandal, 30, 207
Canada, 95, 103n24
casualties, excessive, 49
Catholic Church, 207–8
chain of command. *See* command-and-
  control chain, nuclear
China, 73, 123
  arms-control negotiations rejected by,
    204
  in G2 system, 181
  online censorship of, 144
civil defense, 69–71, 199
climate change debate, 27, 29, 181–82,
  184
Clinton, Bill, 170–71
Clinton, Hillary
  Macedonian-produced fake news on,
    3, 21
  Trump and, voters on, 20
Cohen, Zachary, 94, 103n23
The Colbert Report, 20–21
Cold War
  arms race in, 39–41
  on crisis stability, debate in, 137
  psychic numbing in, 46–47
  public opinion during, 180
  war scare, 1983, in, 162–63
command, control, and communications
  systems (C3 systems), 140, 210
command-and-control chain, nuclear,
  54–57
Committee for Public Information, 19
communication, uncertainty in, 186–87
compassion collapse, 45–46, 45f, 53, 56,
  58
computational propaganda
  bots in, 7, 64–68, 79

civil defense disrupted by, 69–71, 199
Corbyn targeted by, 71–72, 199
in crisis scenarios, 69–70, 73–74, 199
defining, 64–65
in elections, 67
as escalatory, perception of, 69
increase in, 206
journalists targeted by, 66–67
leaders influenced by, 64, 71–74, 199
North Korea and, 71
on social media, 63–64, 67–68
concurrence, nuclear decision-making,
  211
confirmation bias, 24–25
Congregation for the Propagation of the
  Faith (Sacra Congregatio de Propaganda Fides), 207–8
consensus
  manufacturing, 65–66
  perception of, 27, 30
conspiracy theories
  QAnon, 92, 102n19
  Republican, 161
  research on, 160–62, 174n10
  Russian, on US, 11, 164–69, 172
Corbyn, Jeremy, 71–72, 199
Corker, Robert, 161
Creel, George, 19
crisis stability
  adversary manipulation and, 150–52
  bad information undermining, 159–60,
    172–73, 194, 212
  blowback in, 159, 162–63
  Cuban Missile Crisis, 141
  debate on, traditional, 137–42
  deterrence and, 10, 138, 140–41, 146,
    203–4
  emerging technologies undermining,
    204–5
  fast thinking undermining, 195–98,
    201, 210, 212
  first use disrupting, 140
  of information ecosystem, impact on,
    148–53, 157n42
  information operations undermining,
    9–12, 95, 200–201
  nuclear crisis as traditional concern of,
    137–38
  nuclear preemption in traditional, 139
  perfect, absence of, 10, 138
  politicization influencing, 146–47
  principles of, 11–12
  strategic defensive systems disrupting,
    139–40